HANDBOOK OF MANAGEMENT GAMES

Third edition

Handbook of Management Games

Third edition

Chris Elgood

Gower

86776

Published by
Gower Publishing Company Limited,
Gower House,
Croft Road,
Aldershot,
Hants GU11 3HR,
England

and

Gower Publishing Company,
Old Post Road,
Brookfield,
Vermont 05036,
U.S.A.

British Library Cataloguing in Publication Data

Elgood, Chris
    Handbook of management games.—3rd ed.
    1. Management games
    I. Title
    658.4'0353   HD30.26

    ISBN 0-566-02442-X

Typesetting by Graphic Studios (Southern) Limited, 16b High Street, Godalming, Surrey.
Printed and bound in Great Britain
by Billings & Sons Limited, Worcester.

Contents

v

PART TWO   DIRECTORY OF BRITISH MANAGEMENT GAMES

Preface

This is the third edition of *Handbook of Management Games*. Like the first two, it explains what they are, what types there are, how they work, how they can be useful, and how to get the best value from them. Unlike the first two, it deals explicitly with the images – sometimes damaging – that surround the use of the word 'game' and considers similar devices that are described as 'simulations' or 'exercises'. These, though created for a variety of purposes, are seen as sharing a vital characteristic with games in that they contain an action-result cycle which is only partly controllable and which provides an enjoyable learning experience. Since it seems almost impossible to distinguish between the titles, and since all are concerned with learning in some form, the boundaries of the word 'game' have been set very wide. A number of items have therefore been included to which the originators perhaps never attached the word 'game' at all.

Thus the Handbook will interest not only those involved in training, education and staff development. It has value also for those who seek to improve the internal efficiency of their organisations, for it deals with games as methods for promoting interpersonal cooperation, for studying the way an organisation works, for exploring alternatives, and for demonstrating the expected results of some new policy. In addition it has much to offer those interested in planning, for it deals with games as experimental tools which generate previously unforeseen possibilities and create a fuller awareness of what the future may bring.

The early part of the book, being concerned with definition and scope, shows the objectives and traditions associated with the competing words used and thereby emphasises the need for a game-user to be very clear about what he is himself attempting to do. Linked to objectives is the concept of control, and games are considered as

ix

covering a wide spectrum from those carefully constructed to favour a single 'right' policy (full control) to those that are entirely open-ended and from which different people will learn different lessons (no control). Taken with the later analysis of different types of game, this part of the book offers the reader a more complete and satisfactory rationale for management games than has ever been available before. Confronted by a critic who sees games as 'non-serious', 'inappropriate to a work environment' and 'not a legitimate learning device', the game user should now be able to show very clearly why he is using a game, what he expects to achieve, and on what facts he bases these expectations.

The middle chapters of the book deal with the different types of game in existence, and with particular subjects that cut across this classification but are too important to ignore – such as umpiring devices and the impact of the computer. The classification, and the terminology, have been altered slightly for this new edition because the variety of the material is steadily increasing and items appear from time to time that hardly fit into existing categories and demand that these be revised or extended. Widely defined as it has been for this book, the field of management games allows contributions from numerous different disciplines, is highly dynamic, and has no established bureaucracy. If the creator of a game has a problem, he solves it by personal choice from his own stock of expertise – not by reference to any canon of 'approved' methods – so there really is novel material in quite a steady flow.

Some of this new development is mentioned in the context of a particular game or a particular type of game. Other aspects get a general treatment of a paragraph or two included with the type of game to which they are most relevant. A good example is the growing legitimacy of certain 'proper' games (meaning games played for fun) as subjects in which one can study human organisation. Other aspects are so noticeable that they have to be linked to a chapter of general comment rather than to a specific type of game. The most obvious example here is the impact of the micro-computer, which is now put to all sorts of imaginative uses in all sorts of different games. It can only go with the chapter that deals with computer applications in general. The same place is chosen for comments about the breakdown of the barrier between the numerate and the behavioural approaches, for this is well shown by the way both groups employ the micro-computer.

The final chapters are about choosing the right sort of exercise for an objective, and about the problems of using it and administering it well. Then there is the Directory section of the book, which contains more entries than before and includes all those devices which prove – by their variety and imagination – that the previous classification is no longer adequate.

Chris Elgood
July 1984

PART ONE
How to use
management games

1

What is a management game and what is it for?

Two words in this chapter title clearly require definition and elaboration. 'Management' does so because the field of study to which the word is applied seems to enlarge every year, and numerous intellectual disciplines are involved. The word 'game' creates problems because there are alternative titles like 'simulation' and 'exercise' which are often thought to be more suitable. So to say that a management game is 'a game about management' is hardly illuminating.

The role of the contributory disciplines will be mentioned at appropriate points in the text, but the use of the word 'game' must be examined straight away. There are nuances attached to that word, and to 'simulation' and 'exercise' as well, which are fundamental to their use.

A good starting point is to reflect that there are certain situations in which the seriousness of the consequences restricts the way in which one can gain experience. The most obvious of these is warfare, in which the idea of learning by direct practice is potentially self-defeating: the person who is practising (in order to be more skilful in the future) gets killed in practice and thus has no future to practise for! A similar situation often arises in business. There is a risk of financial loss which concentrates attention on a single goal and reduces the extent to which other avenues – such as experiment – can be pursued. Both situations are also continuous and cannot be interrupted for critical examination or the development of new strategies.

Activities of this sort naturally give rise to simulation. It is intended as an intermediate stage between theoretical instruction (which has obvious limitations) and the real thing (which is too costly or too dangerous to be attempted). There are examples – stretching far back into history – of attempts to create battlelike conditions which would

3

prepare individuals or groups for conflict. They sought to show people 'what it was going to be like' and to allow them to practise the skills they had been taught as lessons or learnt as drill. Today, there are engineering simulations that perform a very similar role – those that are used to train the captains of super-tankers and the pilots of spacecraft. These simulations are highly specific to the task being practised, and the more real they seem, the better. In fact, their vital characteristic is being similar to the real world and 'simulation' is an excellent name.

A different situation emerges if a simulation is not designed for the person at 'the sharp end' but for someone in a senior position whose work is to command others. Reality for such a person is more a matter of information and information-based decisions. The senior commander may not have physical sight of the forces on the battlefield: he is usually informed by others about the state of the engagement: where his forces are, in what condition and so on. Similarly, the controller of a space mission is not in the capsule but sitting at a desk in mission control making judgements on the information that reaches him. Simulations for this sort of person can legitimately use symbols instead of real events because they convey the required information in a wholly adequate manner. Maps and charts will be used for the terrain, and models or tokens for units of men or items of equipment. These things are natural features of a genuine command post situation, where they are altered in response to movements in the real world so that they accurately reflect what is happening. To create a simulation it is only necessary that they should move in a realistic manner and reflect a situation which *might* happen. This requires rules, and a set of rules is built up to govern the way an 'umpire' may manipulate enemy forces and how a 'student' may respond. There has now been a break with direct physical involvement because that is not the condition that has to be simulated. It can still quite properly be called a simulation, but is often referred to as a game instead because it is much more obviously a pretence and because it has precise, formal rules. When this development has taken place, two other things have also happened. First, the cost of the simulation has been drastically reduced. In the War Game example all the men have been cut out, and in the Space example all the sophisticated machinery that simulates physical conditions. Secondly, the link with real time has been broken. It may be desirable to exert time pressure on the person who is undergoing the experience, but it is now possible to interrupt events for review and discussion. The cost reduction and the added flexibility are benefits, but they also have the effect of making the experience look more like a game. This is particularly so when it is brought within the range of those who can afford the equipment and enjoy playing with it but have no intention of tangling with reality. A war game, for instance, that is a legitimate simulation and used with great seriousness by the Forces, but which is also played for fun by enthusiastic civilians, will always be seen as game rather than simulation. The nomenclature, therefore, is very imprecise: it often happens that a device is called one thing or the other dependent on who is playing it, and for what purpose.

The use and value of such devices can be considered under three headings.

1 *To prepare*
   By simulating the conditions that will exist in the real state it is possible to acclimatise people so that they will know what to expect and can be physically and psychologically ready. It is also possible to allow them to practise their skills so that they have a greater chance of success. This practice is seen as subsequent to a teaching process in which they have been provided with suitable knowledge and with the theory which underlies the skills.

2 *To examine performance*
   After any 'real' event there is the possibility of examining what was done to see just how good or bad it was and what implications there may be for future policy. But there are things that can be learnt from a simulation that will not readily emerge in real life. In war, for example, the commander may be dead so that there can be no authoritative answers as to why he did one thing rather than another. Further, reality has the disadvantage that there is always an outcome and the activity is judged thereby as a success or a failure. Naturally, this judgement distorts any review and there is a danger that a decision may be seen as 'right' just because the outcome was good. The fact may be that the decision was an extremely poor one and only a miracle saved the day. Conversely, a very good decision may not be recognised for what it was on account of some unforeseeable accident that provoked disaster. Because a simulation can be halted, critical examination can be undertaken whenever it appears profitable to do so, and before events have had time to pass their own, possibly biased judgement.

3 *To experiment*
   Where the situation is real and the consequences serious there is extreme caution about experimenting with alternative strategies and unproven new staff. Every human instinct says 'Stick to the decision

that is most likely to succeed'. That means, of course, that until
some policy or person *has* succeeded, no opportunity is given.
Naturally, that reduces the chance of a demonstration of success. In
a simulation the case is different, and all sorts of strategies can be
tried out by all sorts of people. Further, if the simulation is being
used by a group of people – say the management team of a company
– it is possible to examine the overall performance of the group and
answer questions like 'How are we really doing it at the moment?'
(for there may be several different perceptions) and 'What would
happen if we tried it in such-and-such a way?'

These three purposes can be fulfilled in differing degrees by devices
which may be called either 'simulation', 'exercise' or 'game' depending
on the nature of the device itself, its subject matter, the objective of the
session and the personal bias of the presenter. Whilst these words are
treated as interchangeable, there are still some concepts which relate
more to one word than to the others.

A simulation is more likely than the others to be used for purposes of
prediction. Because it seeks to model a specific situation with
considerable accuracy there is a belief that it can give useful information
about what results would follow if a particular decision was taken. In the
case of, say, an economic simulation assumptions are fed into a
computer model and a prediction is offered about 'How the economy
would behave if decision X were taken and these assumptions held
good'. In the case of a flight training simulation the belief is that
'Performance within this simulation is a reasonable indicator of how
well the person concerned will perform in reality'. The words 'game'
and 'exercise' do not have this connotation so strongly.

A game is distinct from the others in that it clearly implies competition –
the emergence at the end of winners and losers. It also has a connotation
of being 'not serious' and being a leisure activity played for enjoyment.

An exercise is a title suggesting the practice of something that has
recently been taught, and a judgement about how well it has been done.
There is a connotation of control by some teacher or instructor which is
less marked in the ideas of simulation or game. Exercise is a title often
used by people who are offended by the 'fun' connotation of the word
'game', so it has a powerful meaning that could be described as
'not-game' or 'anti-game'.

The management games that were developed in business schools and other institutions between 1945 and 1960 have had a powerful influence on what is expected under the title, but they did not, and do not, fit neatly into any of the categories examined above. They were not simulations in the strict sense because they had little predictive success and because they were obviously different from 'proper' simulations which were flourishing in the world of technology. They were more than exercises because they generated competitive and complex interactive situations that went beyond rigid tutor control. They were games in the sense that they were competitive and a great deal more fun than lectures, but they were not in any way lacking in seriousness. With frequent reservations, 'game' became the accepted word. It still seems marginally the best, though the types of device in use, and the range of subjects handled, have broadened considerably since that time.

The influence of those professionally engaged in business education has in fact attached to management games an assumption that they are mainly an educational tool, employed with an intention to instruct. One thinks of a management game as having been chosen by somebody in authority as a valuable experience which people in his organisation, or attending his course, ought to go through. The direction and control of it will therefore be unilateral. This assumption is often made but is seldom explicitly stated, so there can be confusion when a game has a different purpose and is conducted in quite a different way. The assumption generally holds good when the purpose is *to prepare,* but is less common when *examination* or *experiment* are involved. These purposes have become more common in recent years. Games mounted for such reasons often assume that information, ideas, opinions, direction and even attempts at control are welcome from all those involved. They do not assume an imposed educational objective and sometimes rely wholly on group consensus to decide the course they shall take. The image is no longer an instructional one involving teacher and taught, but rather that of a group of colleagues reviewing policy. Naturally, such activities are discussed in different terms and a description of them sometimes seems out of line with that appropriate to an instructional game. As an attempt to relate current practice to present or future events, the obvious practical bias of such devices makes them look more like simulations than games. Sometimes the two words are coupled together as 'gaming-simulation techniques'. This is done by C. Green in describing his exercises about building development. He writes 'these . . . have been specifically designed to provide a framework for tentative and schematic solutions to be produced and evaluated in a simulated context free of risk or delay'. This surely implies a belief that there are positive advantages in a simulation undertaken for planning purposes. The question might be put 'What can possibly emerge in a simulation that would not do so rather better in the course of the real planning activity?' The answer lies in the concept of risk mentioned by Green – the missing item in reality could be the slightly unusual, innovative solution which draws critical attention to its promoter but often triggers off exciting new developments. To some extent the human desire for conformity and group approval militates against efficiency. In a simulation, where no real-world action is to follow, the climate is favourable to adventurous exploration. This is not to say that any serious planner is opposed to that sort of exploration as a matter of principle, but they do see certain situations as being appropriate for it and others as not so. The formal planning sessions always happen, but sessions devoted to simulation are far less frequent and perhaps useful ideas are lost because of it.

In this book the use of the word 'tutor' or 'instructor' without any subsequent qualification can be taken as implying an educational/instructional context. Where this is not the case, and the person actually running the activity is more in the nature of consultant, administrator, facilitator or even technician, it will be made clear.

Without pretending to perfection, the boundaries of the word game have been set to include any device which satisfies the following characteristics:

1   Has a sufficiently clear framework to ensure that it is recognisably the same exercise whenever it is used.
2   Confronts the players with a changing situation, the changes being wholly or in part a consequence of their own actions.
3   Allows the identification beforehand (if desired) of some criterion by which it can be won or lost.
4   Requires for its operation a certain level of documentation, physical material, computation or administrative/behavioural skill.

Winning and losing is a sensitive subject. Some behavioural games achieve their purpose better if the competitive element is played down and the emphasis directed instead towards the way the experience was handled. This reflective activity can sometimes mean that those who 'lose' gain more from the experience than those who win. However, the competitive instinct is so powerful that if players are able to identify a winner and a loser they will do so. This means in practice that the sort of exercise which players tend to describe as a game, and about which they use game terminology, has been included. A range of behavioural exercises is therefore included because they have a measurable, objective outcome by which in-game success is judged. Sometimes a winning criterion in such exercises is totally obvious – one team builds a higher tower of bricks than another – while at other times it can be much more subtle – the balance of points gained or conceded at a role-playing conference, for instance.

What types of management game are there?

The variety of games available has increased. One cause has been the natural extension of the technique to new backgrounds and another has been the dramatic acceptance of the micro-computer, making it possible to create games that are highly sophisticated, yet easy to play and visually attractive. A third has been the extension of those subject areas that are thought to be a legitimate part of management education. While management was still seen as an intellectual problem concerned with the analysis of economic figures and the manipulation of relatively obedient 'factors of production' the games and exercises produced had a restricted scope. Today there is an emphasis on the social responsibility of management and almost anything likely to increase a man's understanding of his fellow human beings can be considered relevant. A fourth factor in extending the variety of games is the gradual breakdown of the division between work and leisure. People in paid employment have more time off than they used to, and those not in employment have leisure in abundance. An orderly society requires that leisure should be used in a positive way, so leisure activities have become legitimate. They are no longer seen as an irrelevance – something to be contrasted with the 'serious' business of work – but as a potentially valuable form of human activity. This means that a rich field of ideas and images represented by things that are games in the popular sense is now available to the creator of 'serious' games. He can draw upon a 'fun' game that illustrates a point or allows the practice of a skill and will not necessarily be seen as abandoning his serious intent. The increase in variety has made it more difficult to offer a classification of games, for there are numerous hybrids that borrow some features from one type and some from another. It is, however, useful to examine them by reference to the 'model' that in many cases underlies them.

The concept of a model – definitive models

Management games require the players to make decisions, and the word 'model' is used to describe the mechanism whereby these decisions are translated into results. A game is intended to reproduce certain aspects of real life, and through the operation of the decision-result cycle the creator is saying to the players 'if you do *this* in real life then *this* is the sort of thing that is likely to follow'. The mechanism is based, therefore, on the pattern existing in the creators mind about how the real world behaves. A great influence in the development of management games was the scientific management movement with its emphasis on measurement, accurate analysis of data and detailed planning. Another influence was the computer, with its ability to handle extensive mathematical problems rapidly. There followed a generation of management games that were primarily concerned with the manipulation of data and were both complex and highly numerate. The mechanism for translating decisions into results was a computer program and the model of how the world behaved was expressed in mathematical statements. This has meant that the words 'model' and 'model-based' are commonly associated with those games where the mechanism is mathematical and rigid. The same set of decisions submitted to the model in the same circumstances will always evoke the same answer.

The concept of a model – probabilistic models

For some of the other disciplines now contributing heavily to the field the word 'model' means something different. To social scientists, for instance, the word can refer to a pattern of relationships that they see as representing society. It is a generalised pattern and allows them to predict what will happen in a probabilistic way. A game based on such a model might not provide answers from a set of rigid rules but might place players in specific roles and rely upon their own interaction to supply the decision-result sequence. To illustrate, imagine a negotiating exercise in which a group of 'workers' were informed about their existing wage rates and given some cost-of-living data which showed these to be inadequate. Faced with a group of 'managers' who did not have that data, but had instead some performance figures for their company (showing it to be in a desperate financial state) it is highly probable that a demand for a large wage increase would be made and resisted. In this case the model is the belief in the mind of the game creator that in certain conditions human beings are likely to behave in a particular way. He sets out to create the conditions, believing that by this he will probably influence the result. A significant influence in creating the conditions, of course, is the choice of roles that players are asked to assume. There are some roles not well enough known to have a predictable influence on behaviour, but others are tightly defined and almost anybody, when asked to assume them, would act in a broadly similar way. In the latter group 'journalist' and 'shop steward' and 'politician' might be cited. An illuminating description of this idea is the phrase used by Maxim Consultants when describing a game as 'role-bound rather than rule-bound'. The invocation of a role takes the place of what might otherwise be an extensive set of rules. Obviously, this sort of game is not as tightly structured as the other: the consequences of a decision can never be exactly predicted because there will be individual interpretations of what behaviour each role allows. There is less control by the tutor (or administrator or facilitator or consultant) and some-times unexpected things can happen. The approach is not fully satisfac-tory when the game user is trying to say to students 'this is what the world is like and this is how you should handle it'. On the other hand it is highly satisfactory when the objective is to create an awareness of possible alternatives or when it is the interpretation of roles itself which is the main focus of study. This last point touches on a topical use of management games, which is to bring to light the personal attitudes held by members of an organisation and to show how different interpreta-tions of an apparently common concept can create misunderstandings and inefficiencies.

The concept of a model – individual models

The sort of model just described can reasonably be called probabilistic and contrasted with the definitive type that will always give a single answer. It differs also in that, while it operates in the mind of the game creator to determine the exercise he will set up, it does *not* determine what actually happens in the game: that is the outcome of individual models existing in the minds of the players which conform fairly well, the creator hopes, with his own. Where the deviations from a common pattern are greater, one can distinguish a form of game in which 'model' refers more aptly to some general concept of 'rightness' existing in different minds. Here the players are offered a range of facts or ideas and asked to show, in some observable way, the relationship that they believe to exist between them. An example is the game Profile from Northgate House, in which the material is offered by means of cards, each bearing the name of some quality that might be thought desirable in a manager. By sorting these cards into groups the players indicate their own perceptions of how important different qualities are, and how they hang together. Another game called Manco, from G. I. Gibbs, deals with a broad range of managerial activities and, rather than grouping them, provides arrows to make a link between them and so build up a 'conceptual map' of the management task. A further idea is to use the concept of a jigsaw that can be assembled in different ways and can therefore demonstrate the perception each player has of a particular organisation. In this sort of approach there is clearly a model in the mind of each player and the value of the game lies in the comparison between them. There may also be a model in the mind of the game user, and it may be his intention to compare the answers produced by the players with his own 'right' solution. If that is the case, and rightness and wrongness are to be judged against one man's predetermined standpoint, then the model might well be called a definitive one. When the intention is more to compare solutions in a non-judgemental way, exploring the differences and learning from them, then the appellation is wrong. Believing that the latter is the more common use, such games will be described as based on 'individual models' and given the title 'exploratory games'.

In some senses such exploratory games might be considered to fall outside the definition given earlier – mainly because they are single-stage games and do not have a repetitive cycle. Each person or group works independently to prepare an 'answer', there is no interaction between them, and the judgement (if any) terminates the exercise. They conform more nearly to the idea of a competition rather than a game. On the other hand they have, in their use of physical tokens, the appearance of games and they do allow for repeated trials prior to the submission of the chosen answer. They encourage the formulation of alternatives, and the acceptance or rejection of each. For these reasons they have been included.

A classification of games can, then, be based upon this concept of a model and will give three categories. Types of game already in common use can be fitted into them, and novel types examined from this standpoint to see whether the classification must be modified or expanded. A current listing will give:

Games based on a definitive model
1   Traditional model-based games
2   Puzzles
3   In-basket exercises
4   Mazes
5   Programmed simulations
6   Enquiry studies

7   Encounter games
8   Adult role-playing games

Games based on a probabilistic model
1   Structured experiences
2   Organisation games
3   Organisational simulations
4   Practical simulations

Games based on individual models
1   In-basket exercises
2   Exploratory games

The classification puts some order into the field for purposes of study, but it is far from absolute because it takes no account of differences in their method of use. A game user may have some particular objective in mind which will cause him to use a game in one way rather than another and to emphasise on one occasion some feature that he ignored last time. It may even cause him to amend the rules of the game, or not to run it in the full format, thus cutting out some lessons that normally come through at the end. This can mean that the game is, for that event, not the same type of game as it was before. There are also changes of attitude amongst practitioners, and sometimes these are so marked that an exercise generally used for one purpose a few years ago is more often used for a different purpose today. The in-basket exercise is a case in point, this having been previously grouped only with 'games based on a definitive model' and now being shown as well under 'games based on individual models'. The change reflects a decreased interest in emphasising 'right' solutions and an increased desire to recognise and explore a range of alternatives. It is a shift of emphasis, from an attitude that tended to see differences of opinion as things to be ironed-out in the interests of uniformity, to one that sees them as potential sources of strength because they increase the variety of ideas upon which an organisation can draw. Missing from the above list is role-playing. The concept of role-playing is essentially simple but it is employed in many different ways as an ingredient of other methods already mentioned. So while it certainly still exists, it is dealt with in particular contexts rather than on its own.

Classification by scope

Another useful classification is that first set out by C. Loveluck, dealing with the scope that a game covers. He defines a 'functional game' as one 'covering only one (or possibly two or three) functions performed within the simulated company'. A 'company game' is defined as one 'where most of the functions of a company are simulated . . . but the participants are only concerned with the internal operations and consequences of their decisions'. A 'business game' is one that 'involves the simulation of competing and interacting companies'. (Loveluck actually uses the term 'management game' for this type, but in this book it has been considered preferable to use 'management game' as a general term.) To these can be added an 'environment game' which concerns itself with the interaction between an organisation and its socio-economic environment.

How does a management game compare with alternative methods?

This is a question most frequently asked in the context of education and training, and is based on the undisputed fact that games are very time-consuming. The benefit claimed for them in response is that they promote a greater depth of learning than some other methods, and also that they extend the scope of what is learnt.

In terms of the quantity of information offered to the learner in a given period of time, a well-prepared lecture must rate very high. But the offering of information is of no value unless it is understood and accepted by the learner and integrated by him with knowledge that he already possesses. It is here that the game has an advantage, for while it will handle less in terms of sheer quantity than a lecture, it has the benefit of allowing the learner to make personal and immediate use of the information that it does contain. There is a world of difference between knowing that something is true because one has been told it by some authority and knowing that it is true because one has experienced it (albeit in a simulated situation) for oneself. So the depth of learning claimed for management games is linked to the concept of personal involvement: the fact that players must themselves make decisions about the simulated situation and experience the outcome and endure its effects.

Just how does this personal involvement make a difference? Surely a description offered by a lecturer as to what mistakes were made in a certain case, and how they came about, is just as effective as making similar mistakes oneself – and a lot less time-consuming? The difference seems to be that in the descriptive method it is always *somebody else* who is involved, *and at a previous moment in time*, and that the message lacks impact because of it. When a decision taken in a management game turns out to be disastrous, an analytical review may cause players to say 'the information was in front of us, the possibility of disaster could have been foreseen, but we were so blinded by our concentration on another aspect of the problem that we did not look carefully enough at what was happening?' This is the sort of learning that a person retains, and which may later on influence his real-life behaviour.

The depth of learning is increased, then, because one is not just learning from what somebody else has done, but also from what one has experienced. It is further increased because one has a different attitude to the learning environment brought about by the administrative circumstances that surround a game. The traditional forms of education and training tend to emphasise the position of the tutor or teacher (the one who 'knows') and leave the learner in the subordinate position of one who must merely listen and absorb – a person to whom 'something is being done' – whose role is mainly passive. For adults (and possibly for children too) there is something rather unwelcome about this state. Motivation is improved if, rather than just following a course determined by an authority, learners can have a direct influence on what happens. This is just how a management game proceeds. There is an original scenario (which is determined by the tutor) but once the first decision has been made his influence is reduced. The results achieved by the first decision, and the situation that follows, are the consequences of the actions of the players. They have begun to have ownership of the exercise.

This commitment to the experience, and the high motivation that it typically creates, has also a dangerous side. In many cases the tutor will have specific points in mind that he believes the players should learn, and since the experience is less controllable than a lecture he may find that these are getting lost. Players may be so obsessed with strategies for winning the game that they make little effort to relate its lessons to their own world. It is quite easy to see game and reality as separate entities, for as well as the likenesses there are some very obvious discrepancies. The consequences of an action, for instance, are not usually so immediate and obvious as they are made to appear in a game. The atmosphere of real life is far more pedestrian than the competitive excitement of a game. And the people with whom one is supposedly relating (perhaps a production manager or an advertising agent) may in real life be a cold, remote and seldom-heard voice on a telephone. So while the opportunity for increased learning is latent in a game, it requires skill on the part of the tutor to make it real.

The previous paragraphs argue that learning which could well be offered more economically in terms of time is in fact absorbed to a greater depth because of the game format. It can also be claimed that additional learning that would not be offered at all by a lecture does in fact become available. This is because, if the course of a learning activity is completely controlled, then only the subjects chosen by the tutor are going to be covered. The scope of the event will originate from a single source. If the activity is dynamic, influenced by the players, and not wholly predictable, then the situations that have to be considered, and the learning that can be drawn from them, will be wider. It will originate not just in the mind of the tutor but in the interests and biases of the players which caused them to take certain decisions. It will come from the situations that arise when one team decides to do *this* and at the same moment another team decides to do *that*. The experience will therefore be richer and more varied than the lecture.

The concepts that epitomise our traditional view of education are so powerful that when we speak of a learning activity in which there is one large group and one small group we almost inevitably think of the large group as 'students' and the small group as 'staff'. Having done so, we attribute to them the differential status that normally goes with those words and make a further assumption that there is something known to the small group which the large group have still to learn. This tradition sometimes makes it hard to recognise a situation in which the person or group apparently conducting the experience is properly the servant of the 'student' group rather than a figure of authority. The word servant may seem somewhat extreme but it is deliberately chosen because it emphasises the change of role and it could quite well be true. If, for instance, the management team of a company had decided to use a simulation as a means of examining their own pattern of cooperation then it might well ask an expert in simulation to conduct it. In all probability his expertise would make his role more nearly that of a consultant, but according to the balance of personalities his role might become little more than that of a technician – engineering different scenarios as the client group decreed.

The point about role needs to be made because the use of simulation for purposes of examination and experiment is becoming more common and the parties may well come to it with slightly confused expectations. The roles they are to play must be clarified if a simulation is to yield its full benefits. The comparison here is not with a lecture, but with some sort of formal discussion – almost certainly chaired by someone in authority. The advantages of a simulation include the following:

1   Because it is more dynamic than a controlled discussion, and much freer, it will generate a greater variety of events for examination.
2   Being both dynamic and based on reality, it may generate events that are a natural outcome of some combination of circumstances but have not in fact been foreseen by anybody. A formal discussion is limited to the ideas in the minds of the participants, and human beings can only look a certain distance forward before getting lost in the many possible combinations of circumstances. A good simulation can cause these events to happen, perhaps making people aware of some possibilities for the first time.
3   The informal and experimental atmosphere makes it more likely that participants will attempt imaginative and innovative behaviour which would be frowned on in other circumstances.

Simulation is by no means a new technique and it seems logical to ask why its use in the past has been limited. A possible answer is that because of the freedom it generates it can seem damaging to the authority structure of an organisation, and to its unity. The very nature of simulation is to permit the emergence of new strategies, and if one of these prevails against the established wisdom it can be highly embarrassing. Organisations reach a point where firm commitment to one definite policy is better than endless debating, so there is a natural and partly justifiable tendency to bolster existing beliefs rather than to challenge them.

Examination and experiment as described here are themselves a form of research, but games are also used for research in the academic sense. There is some very interesting material of this type from J. H. Klein of The Polytechnic of the South Bank and D. F. Cooper of the University of Southampton. ('Cognitive Maps of Decision-makers in a Complex Game', *Journal of The Operations Research Society*, 1982.) They used a research war game known as The Organisational Control Game, recording the comments made by players about the situations they faced at different times. Analysing these, they identified the mental concepts that each player seemed to be using and constructed for him what they call a cognitive map. Discussing their results, they write 'The use of cognitive maps to facilitate communication can also be envisaged in the teaching of decision-making skills and for assessing the way in which decision-makers acquire problem-solving strategies as they learn about a new problem and its environment'. This is clearly of interest in the management education field.

2

Types of definitive model

The traditional type

This title is chosen to distinguish the oldest and best known type of management game. The creator of the game decides upon certain causative links between decisions to be taken by the players and results to be returned to them once they have committed themselves. He builds for himself a 'model' which will allow him, once a decision has been made, to say 'the result is so-and-so'. The players do not know the nature of this model. They know that they have to make decisions about particular subjects, they have some data to help them make a reasonable attempt, and they know what areas of interest the results will cover. They do not know which decisions affect which results, nor the strength of any such relationship. Their task is to form hypotheses about 'what might be' and enter experimental decisions to test out 'what is'. Their objective is to gain an understanding of the model so that they can obtain the results they want by entering those decisions that will get them.

Figure 2:1 is a 'model' of how one particular market is believed to behave. Even a model as simple as this contains a significant amount of information: it shows that sales are expected to be greatest if the article is sold at £3, and will fall off if it is more expensive or less expensive. The idea of lower sales at a higher price is an obvious one, but lower sales for a lower price is a slightly more sophisticated concept, suggesting a feeling among customers that a particularly cheap variety of this product is hardly credible. The model also shows that sales first decline gradually as the price moves away from the ideal level, and then at a faster rate. It shows this happening more quickly as the price falls and more slowly as it rises, meaning that some people, at least, are prepared

18

Price asked £	Number of units that would be sold at this price
1	80
2	100
3	110
4	100
5	90
6	80
7	60
8	40

Figure 2:1   Price/demand relationship

to pay high prices.

In a game based on this model the players would be asked to decide upon a price to be charged for the product during one 'time period', which might simulate a week or a month or a year. Once the decision had been made, they would be told the number of sales achieved during that time period. In effect, they would have been given one piece of information about the model. To make clear some of the terminology:

1   The thing that players are asked to decide on is called a 'decision variable'
2   The fact that they are told after they have made a decision is called a 'result'
3   The relationship that determines what result should follow any given value of the decision variable is called the 'model'. (The result is sometimes referred to as the 'output' of the model.)
4   The person who administers the decision/result process is usually called the 'umpire'

It is fairly obvious that there are other aspects of the game which take place before this interface between the players and the model. For instance, the players must be given some indication of the range of decisions worth choosing. This information is often called 'starting data' (being part of the overall description of a management situation, which is sometimes called the 'scenario'). Once a result has been given out by the umpire it has to be translated into business terms and in the example in Figure 2:1 it is necessary to multiply 'number sold' by 'price asked' to get 'revenue received'. It would be necessary to subtract the purchase price, or production cost, of the number sold in order to arrive at a profit or loss figure. If, in the example, the purchase price was £1, the maximum profit would be achieved if the article was sold at £6 a unit. Note that this is not the price at which the actual number sold is the greatest, emphasising that the player's task is not just to get the largest number sold: it is rather to use the relationship built into the model to achieve some other objective. There is, therefore, a phase in the game that can usefully be described as 'interpretation of results' and there is obviously an 'objective' for which the players are aiming.

One other term that needs to be made clear is 'convention'. It is already obvious that rules play a major part in this sort of game, and sometimes they enter a grey area in which they are unable to make much of a show of simulating reality. In the example used, it will have been noticed that price is given only in units of £1. This would never be the case in reality and a player might well ask: What is the point of having such an unrealistic rule? It is there as a concomitant of the extremely simple model and has become a convention. A convention found in many management games is that sales only become known at discrete intervals, usually the end of the time period. In real life a business obviously keeps a cumulative record and would be able to say what sales had been achieved up to a particular date and, hence, what the total for the month (or whatever time period) was likely to be. If a thing is described as a convention it suggests that there is a degree of unreality present, and that it is attributable to the mechanical limitations of the game.

The universal availability of the micro-computer has reduced the area in which a game designer is compelled, for technical reasons, to fall back upon the use of conventions. Even a small machine can handle quite complex models and there is a temptation to go for increased reality in the simulation just because it is technically possible. This desire can be re-inforced by the belief that the exercise must be seen as 'credible' by the players or they will not commit themselves seriously. These are arguments that must not be taken too far, because no simulation can ever be real in all respects – if so it would cease to be a simulation. In the present context a game is being used for educational purposes, and education naturally selects certain features from the environment for special study. The designer of a game must ask 'What is it that I am now seeking to simulate?' The subjects that fall outside his intention are better handled by simple conventions than by any attempt to make them real – for reality usually means extra complexity and this will probably make the game less 'playable'. The obsession with 'reality' is partly a relic of the early days when something that seemed real to the players was such a great novelty. The difference it created between games and lectures overshadowed any differences between individual games. The emphasis is now on using the right game for the right situation, and reality is only critically important within the chosen area of study.

Since traditional model-based games are still very common they are described in detail in Chapter 3, and Chapter 4 is devoted to the umpiring devices associated with them.

Puzzles

A puzzle does nothing more than is done by a good examination question. It offers a problem to which there is a definite solution and which students should have sufficient knowledge to solve. By way of illustration Figure 2:2 shows three production shops, each containing a small number of machines. Each shop is controlled by a foreman, and the three foremen report to a production superintendent. The numbers in the boxes each indicate the presence of one machine and its production capacity over a given period. The article being made in the factory has to be processed in each shop by any one of the machines (within a shop they all do the same job) and it passes from shop A to shop B to shop C. The student is asked to assume the role of the production superintendent and to judge a request from the foreman of shop B for the purchase of a new machine to replace No. 2, the oldest one in his shop. The foreman is quoted as saying, 'The maintenance

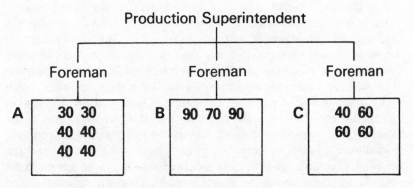

Figure 2:2   Production capacities of machines in three shops

staff give me little service and always seem to be busy elsewhere. I get about half the possible output from the thing and nobody seems to care.' The student is also told, 'A replacement will cost £6000, will have a 35 per cent higher output and excellent reliability. The foreman is a recent appointment, young and very keen. In your time £8000 has been the highest capital expenditure approved for your area in any one year. Most years it has been well below this figure. Are you going to recommend the scheme to the production manager or not?'

This is a problem in logical thinking, which requires the consideration of alternative objectives and the association of different items of information. Addition of the capacities of the machines in each shop gives the following:

Present (theoretical)	A	30 + 30 + 40 + 40 + 40 + 40=	220
	B	90 + 70 + 90 =	250
	C	40 + 60 + 60 + 60 =	220
Present (actual)	A	30 + 30 + 40 + 40 + 40 + 40=	220
	B	90 + 35 + 90 =	215
	C	40 + 60 + 60 + 60 =	220
Proposed	A	30 + 30 + 40 + 40 + 40 + 40=	220
	B	90 + 95 + 90 =	275
	C	40 + 60 + 60 + 60 =	220

Once that sum has been worked out it is obvious that the output of the three shops is reasonably in balance as things are at the moment and that, if made in isolation, the change will only create a gross imbalance in capacity. If a student is in doubt about the answer there is supporting evidence in the current attitude of the maintenance people (who probably know quite well what maintenance is *needed*) and the remarks about the new foreman, who is doubtless keen to make an impression.

There is nothing complicated about the problem, and every time it is used with a group of people there will be one or more who come up with the right answer very quickly, but there will be others who miss the point completely because they have not considered the overall purpose of the little production line, nor made good use of the other 'clue' which is the obvious one of figures – they must be included for some good reason. So the student is offered information which is known to be sufficient for an answer but which requires him to examine the problem from different points of view until he finds one for which the data have meaning. It could be described as a challenge to the imagination: What possible solutions could the writer intend? Since the context of the problem is known, this question is quickly transformed into: What are the conceivable consequences of each possible decision? Examination of each of them in relation to the sufficiency or otherwise of the data should lead students to the right answer. If they do not reach it, the outcome of the exercise, for them, is failure: either because they are insufficiently aware of the possible consequences of the two alternative decisions or else because they have not worked hard enough on the figures. Either way some inadequacy is displayed.

The process is very similar to that undergone with great frequency by those who complete crossword puzzles: a searching of one's mind for possible answers, continual reconsideration of the clues, failure, and then a 'kicking oneself' reaction when the answer is revealed – for one knew all the facts but was just not mentally agile enough.

A puzzle, having a single inflexible answer, could be seen as quite irrelevant to those practitioners in management education who concentrate on the 'people' side of the subject. Yet that is not the case, and a puzzle like the one described can show the fascinating manner in which the boundaries between the 'numbers people' and the 'people people' are beginning to crumble. If the tutor uses the discussion phase following the exercise to explore the mental standpoints from which different students approached the problem, he will probably find that some fairly obvious clues were missed not because a person was incapable of seeing them but because his attention was directed elsewhere as a result of his own interests. It is possible, for instance, for somebody to have suffered so much from lack of capital investment that he will encourage any major spending on plant just in the hope that it will lead to a serious change of attitude. His viewpoint may be 'If I go against this now, after campaigning for new plant for so long, they will never listen to me again'. Other students may be found who have erected a mental block against anything that even looks mathematical and have just refused to work out the figures! So a discussion that seems to have an entirely logical problem as its focal point may quite rapidly move into an examination of personal conditioning and perception.

In-basket exercises

An in-basket exercise presents students with a number of written communications said to be the contents of the in-basket on his desk (the player occupying some stated role – for instance traffic manager of a distributive company) at a particular moment. The papers range from detailed reports of no great urgency to cryptic messages describing some immediate crisis. The task of the player is to decide the order in which he will tackle the problems facing him and the action that he will take on each. The action is usually expressed by writing on the papers themselves or in some sort of diary. If the papers are all concerned with the same project, then the problem is to attach the right meaning to each item of information and fit them together in such a manner as to reach a solution. It is predominantly a problem in logical analysis. If they are concerned with different problems then the obvious point of presenting them at the same moment in time is to force a choice between different courses of action.

To illustrate, a manager might be given three pieces of data. The first would be a telephone call from the factory to say that an industrial-relations problem had arisen and that his personal presence was urgently needed. The second would be an invitation to tender for a valuable job with the current day's date shown as the last on which tenders would be accepted and a note on it from a clerk, 'I found this in Mr Bertram's in-tray. As you know he has been sick for a week.' The third would be a message from his secretary saying, 'Your 7 p.m. flight to Paris for the vital meeting with M. Hericot has been cancelled. If you are to get to Paris on time you must catch the 4.30 p.m. flight, which means leaving in half an hour.' The constraints in this situation could be that the only member of the senior staff available is the recently appointed sales manager.

Such an exercise obviously has merits in that it calls for decision-making in conditions of uncertainty and under some degree of pressure. On the other hand the choices that can be made by the players are not defined so it is not possible to prescribe in advance all the consequences that might follow from them. There is always the possibility that a player will conceive of some totally novel solution, and the tutor is then left to make an immediate and subjective judgement about what the outcome is to be. At times he will make a poor decision, the players will disagree violently, and the exercise will lose credibility. This illustrates one of the inherent problems of model-based games: they have to have rules in order to provide a result, and the freedom of action permitted to the player is therefore limited. The creative, original strategy that starts a commercial revolution in real life can not be allowed in a game because it cannot be 'scored' without depending on personal opinion. This does not, of course, render a game unplayable and there have been many exercises – including numerous war games – that relied upon an umpires ruling. This is clearly unsatisfactory if the umpire is believed to be biased, or even if he is believed to be psychologically committed to one point of view rather than another. Against this it can fairly be argued that a written model can be just as biased as an instant, personal judgement: but the inference seems to be made by players that something which has been considered beforehand, and to which the author has committed himself by writing it down, provides a more acceptable method of assessment.

The in-basket exercise is being considered here as a game with a definitive model. It has such a thing in that the tutor using it has presumably a 'right' solution in mind, but it cannot – at least when first created – have a definitive model in the sense of an assessment mechanism. One way of providing it with that model is just to let experience accumulate with use so that a great variety of actions has been proposed, and consequences for them devised. Another way is to limit the actions allowed to the players, specifying a list of permitted actions and so preventing anything unforeseen.

If the limited choice method is adopted, it becomes possible to provide answers for all the allowed choices for all the items in the in-tray, and all possible interactions between them. From such an analysis, 'windows' can be prepared which represent the accumulated consequences of the decisions that have been made when reviewed at various times in the future. That is to say, the original material for the in-basket can be represented as 'how it looks first thing in the morning' and once the decisions have been made there can be windows showing 'how things look at 11.30 a.m.' and 'how things look at 3.00 p.m.' and so on. There can even be opportunities to take corrective action. For this sort of development the micro-computer has good potential: it can process the decisions very rapidly, and it possesses its own timing mechanism which allows the revelation of new data at scaled intervals. Supposing that an exercise had called for decisions as at 9.00 a.m. in the simulated day, and the next scheduled decision-making 'window' was at 12.00 noon, then the three hours in between could be telescoped to cover 15 minutes and 'events' could be flashed on the screen during that period to simulate in-coming data. Present technology would even allow choices to be linked to an interactive video system so that alternative film sequences added dramatic value to the consequences.

Mazes

A maze, as its name implies, is entirely based on the concept of limited choice that was mentioned above as an option when dealing with in-basket exercises. The maze has till recently been a manually operated exercise and the description and example assume that background. However, it is well adapted to expansion by use of the micro-computer and that development must also be discussed. An exercise starts by describing a particular situation and requiring the player to examine a limited number of possible actions before committing himself to just one of them. Depending upon the choice made a new situation is described of the sort that could reasonably be expected to follow. Obviously, this could generate a very large number of possible states, but a maze is carefully designed so that all the 'lines' that could be followed lead back to a limited number of critical points. These can be experienced two or three times and a player is naturally going to choose an action different from his previous choice – just as a person does when working out a conventional maze. Sensible decisions allow a player to find a satisfactory solution – to get out of the maze – in a small number of moves. Errors of judgement make the sequence much longer or, in some cases, lead to some disastrous results such as a strike, resignation of a trusted employee or bankruptcy. The information is usually conveyed to the player on separate cards or papers. He is directed to the one that is appropriate in the light of each decision.

There are two differences in the challenge offered by a maze from that offered by a puzzle. First, it compels the choice of one or other of the options described and there is no opportunity for 'giving up', because the problem appears too difficult. It is seductive, leading a player on to a new decision and possibly into greater difficulties. Second, since the courses of action are stated, the student does not have to formulate them for himself. It requires imagination to foresee the possible outcomes of each action but the starting point is provided.

The following extract is printed by permission of Supervisory Management Training Limited and describes seven courses of action open to the Service Manager of a company called Excelsior Machines Limited when faced with poor performance by one of his engineers. (The exercise is called The Old Soldier.) A page of text describes the situation, and then the choices are listed, each choice referring the user to a new, but different page of the exercise. On that page will be found the new situation considered to exist because of the particular choice made.

A   Transfer Jack to the totally internal job of Workshop Engineer
     where you could keep an eye on him.   Go to Page 58
B   Call Jack in; let him know that his performance is less than

expected; and warn him that he will be dismissed if it does not improve. Go to Page 15

C Consult your Personnel Department. Go to Page 21

D Keep a closer watch on Jack's work, give him fewer opportunities to be outside unsupervised, move key jobs to other engineers and generally ensure Jack has plenty of work but not tell him about his poor performance – after all, he's only 10 years from retirement. Go to Page 39

E Refer the whole problem to your boss. Go to Page 45

F Send Jack a written warning on his poor performance and tell him he will be dismissed unless his performance improves in the next 3 months. Go to Page 76

G Consult the Union Shop Steward. Go to Page 63

This type of simulation asks players to cope with conditions of uncertainty. Whatever actions a player takes may, it seems to him, easily turn out to be wrong. Therefore his task is to look at the available data, interpret them in the light of his experience, and decide on the course which seems most likely to be successful. It exercises not so much his intellect and his imagination, as his experience and judgement. It confronts him with a result of his decisions that he may not have foreseen at all, and obviously he learns something because of it. There is less risk of frustration with a maze than with a puzzle, because one can always *do* something, even though it turns out to be wrong. Also, to have made a wrong choice is less of a failure than the failure to solve a puzzle because there is nothing absolute about the answer given in the exercise, it is only one person's opinions about the likely result of a course of action. As such it may be disputed, and such disputation is often welcomed as a useful adjunct to the exercise.

The manual form has obvious limitations on its complexity because of the need for every result to be available in writing – whether it is needed by a particular player or not. If each result is to be a page in a book, then an elaborate maze will mean a very thick volume. If the pages are set out individually on tables (which is a common way of running such exercises) then a vast amount of table space will be needed. The micro-computer solves this problem totally, for the text that makes up each page is stored in the program and only the desired page is displayed at any given moment. There can be more 'routes' through the maze and each individual route can be longer. Another advantage is that while written pages take time to alter, the text carried in a program can be changed fairly easily. It thus becomes possible to enter amendments that will make the exercise more convincing to some particular audience because it uses the terminology of their world. Before and after the exercise there can be test questions built into the program to provide an indication of what has been learnt. Besides these advantages there is the fact that for many people the computer is still not a familiar object, and is even rather frightening. Just the simple experience of entering responses to questions is a psychological help in this regard: the person concerned can say, for the first time, that he has used a computer.

Programmed simulations

This device is similar to the maze but more authoritarian in its approach. It starts in the same way by describing a situation and offering a choice of possible actions, but instead of each choice leading to its own sub-set of further actions it leads to a short comment upon the action chosen and a revelation of the official right answer. Alternatively, it may lead to such comment plus some variation on 'return to the previous page and try one of the other options' – thus allowing the player a second chance to get the answer right on his own. All players are brought back to the preferred path at each stage, so the distance they can vary from it is strictly limited. The advantages are very obvious when there is in real life a right way to handle a problem and this can be learnt and applied. It is also very convenient for the tutor because a brief can be provided which speaks authoritatively about every situation that can arise. For instance, a six-stage programmed simulation with five choices at each point allows a total of 30 situations: not an impossible number for which to provide comment. A maze could quite easily have three times that number.

The fact is that the two methods take different approaches and are both completely valid in the right context. The message of the maze is 'Here are some of the things that might happen. Think them through so that when you are faced with a similar problem you will be better able to make your own judgement.' The message of the programmed simulation is 'There is a right way and a wrong way to do this. Learn the right one and apply it.'

A scoring mechanism is easily attached to a programmed simulation by grading the allowed responses at each stage. A player thus builds up his score as he moves through the exercise. Included with the range of programmed simulations offered by Management Games Limited is a standardised score sheet on which a player marks first his own choice of solution and then the choice of solution resulting from discussion among a group. All players then turn to the appropriate pages and can write down an individual score and a group score. Another format is that offered by Chris Elgood Associates Limited on behalf of Sigma Consultants. Here the text is very short and the answers are hidden under shutters on a playing board. The number of shutters removed gives an immediate check on performance and the instant nature of the feedback increases the feeling of drama. It has advantages in terms of simplicity, flexibility and speed: programmes are interchangeable because the text appears through windows in the playing board and a new text can be inserted without delay.

Both maze and programmed simulation, since their medium is words rather than numbers, are well adapted for emphasising the human aspects of management. Choices can be offered that are entirely in quotation marks, representing what the player might actually choose to say to another person in a face-to-face interview. This can be used to show how powerfully we are all influenced by our perception of the meaning of words rather than by the real attitude of the speaker, at which we can only guess.

Enquiry studies

An enquiry study is a variation of the case study, in which only a part of the necessary data is provided initially. The students are given instead the identity of one or more sources of knowledge from which further information can be gained. The sources are often role-played by the instructor. He commonly omits to give the essential data unless the right question is put to him – the question that implies a definite line of investigation. Thus, if he was asked, 'Do you know anything about our production efficiency?' he would give a vague and fairly useless answer. If asked 'What is our throughput per month in the finishing section?' then he would say, 'Two thousand and ninety-eight.' The failing most frequently exhibited by players is inability to think beyond the limits of the situation as it appears on paper and to visualise instead the context within which it would exist in reality. They are, in fact, weak on imagination.

An enquiry study, like an in-basket exercise, has a potential weakness due to subjective judgements by the tutor, for he must make a decision about the quality of the question put to him. Does it or does it not show sufficient awareness of what might be learnt from the answer? Is it specific, or is it just an optimistic probe put out 'to see if there is anything there'? There is obviously room for variable judgement by the tutor, and also for variable ability in the player when forming his questions. He may have a very clear idea what he wants to know, and why, but not be able to articulate this in an impressive way. There is also the danger that until an enquiry study is fully mature there may be unforeseen gaps in the data available which the tutor has to fill up in a hurry when he is asked a surprise question.

The situation alters as an enquiry study becomes well-established, for the facts will be sufficiently extensive to warrant being described as a Data Bank and to have some sort of index. It will be a substantial task for a tutor to answer all the queries himself, so the logical step is to make the index available for direct use by the players. The question must then be asked 'Since they have an index which tells them what data is available, is there any longer a need for them to decide what they ought to look for? They have got a very obvious clue to the boundaries of the exercise and all they need do is look down the headings of the index to see if there is anything shown that might be relevant. If they look up some item and find it is useful, then they have won a benefit: if they look it up and find it useless, they have lost nothing.' Viewed in this light, the provision of an index can be said to have negated the purpose of using an enquiry study rather than another method – it is no longer necessary to think of an option *without any prompting at all*.

The evidence suggests that this is only a minor disadvantage. The titles and sub-titles of an index are apt to be single 'omnibus' words and they do not give too much away about the detailed content of the pages they refer to. Also, their very number can be a distraction, sparking off new ideas in the minds of the players so that they are diverted from their original line of enquiry. This is allied to the common human character-istic of fixating upon an item because some past experience seems to link it to the present problem, though in fact it is hardly relevant at all. When this sort of fixation happens it is likely that material of high current relevance will be overlooked and wrong conclusions drawn. So being allowed to scan a descriptive list of available data – as opposed to having to identify each wanted item – does not make things substantially easier. Any benefit that would appear to exist from a technical point of view is outweighed by the ability of a human being to confuse himself and his colleagues!

This is another area in which the computer can contribute. Even small micro-computers can store a great deal of data, and an enquiry study linked to a major organisational data base can be very complex indeed.

It can get to the point where different players or teams come up with quite different answers to the same problem because of differences in the data they have looked for and found, and differences in the way they have interpreted it. All of these are differences originating in the individual rather than in the material, and the idea can be linked back to the use of games for examining different perceptions as mentioned in Chapter 1. From this viewpoint an excellent game could be prepared that drew only upon existing organisational data but used as its objective, say, 'The preparation of a detailed plan for entering such-and-such a market'. There might or might not be a model against which different plans were judged, but the chief purpose of the exercise would be to reveal the attitudes and assumptions that members of the organisation brought to the task and how these influenced their approach. The inference for future organisational efficiency is that these attitudes and assumptions are – as long as the staff remain unchanged – a permanent feature of the way the organisation works. They ought to be understood by everybody – possibly modified in some cases – but certainly recognised and understood. That way the cooperation between individual members will be more effective.

There is a further value to enquiry studies in that, developed in the way described, they can make players more familiar with the current explosion in information technology and the ready availability of data of all kinds. It would be quite easy, for instance, to create an enquiry study that caused players to make extensive use of CEEFAX, thus learning about the service and its capability as well as learning whatever the subject matter of the exercise itself was.

Encounter games

The essence of this sort of game is that it simulates the details of the future. In general terms this can always be foreseen: there *will* be some sort of industrial-relations problem, there *will* be some difficulty over supplies, there *will* be new products launched by competitors. The *exact* nature of each problem cannot be predicted and there is a tendency to sit back and await events. An encounter game gives students experience of this dynamic and unstable situation. It prepares them for reality in one of three ways. It offers a sample of the incidents that may occur, thus ensuring that some at least of them have been handled in practice sessions. It makes people aware of the wide range of problems likely to be encountered and of the effect that these will have upon the business, thus encouraging them to develop contingency plans so that when events do come upon them they are partially prepared. In its more sophisticated versions it also demonstrates the use of specialised management techniques that will enable one to avoid the catastrophes that are avoidable and minimise the effects of those that are not.

There is a very wide range in encounter games, for the simpler sort require only a large number of different problems and a random method of deciding which one a player or team is to encounter. This can be done by choosing a card from a pack, or moving a token on a board a certain number of squares depending on the throw of a dice. At the other end of the scale are some very complex devices which invite players to make statements about the policies they would like to follow and then show how things would actually work out if they did so. They can be powerful exercises for showing the complexity of the real world and the need for comprehensive scientific study of a situation if unforeseen and undesirable results are not to appear. In the way they work these are identical with the facilities sometimes offered in traditional model-based games that allow a team to 'probe' the environment and ask questions of a 'what if' nature without actually committing themselves. A similar effect is produced by the game called VISA (Variable Incident Simulation Apparatus) which consists of 'a number of simulator units capable of representing any type of situation where work is being done and delays occur'. It is possible to establish a plan and then use the simulator to discover how it will work out in practice. A later stage is the development of a policy that optimises work output under the conditions shown.

Encounter games of the simpler sort have a clear identity of their own, but the complex ones have much in common with the conventional model-based game and are hard to distinguish from that type. This is particularly true where the consequence of a decision is determined by a computer model. Nevertheless a distinction needs to be made because the administrative processes of the exercises differ. The conventional model-based games normally require an umpire or tutor to operate the computer, waiting till he has received the decisions from all his teams. In an encounter game the teams may themselves be allowed to use the computer, making experiments with different policies in order to test the outcomes and identify the best results. In such cases they have direct access to the model and are, amongst other things, learning how valuable a good model can be for making predictions. Games of this sort may either be won by comparing the 'best' results from the experiments of the individual teams or by entering the decisions that produced them into an additional, interactive model.

Adult role-playing games

These are a new resource in the management education field and one of the ways in which the work/fun division can be seen to be breaking down as ideas and images are borrowed and adapted. An alternative title is 'fantasy games', as they allow players to live through a series of fictional and fantastic adventures, making choices at various points about what they will do when confronted by some fearsome danger. A series marketed by TSR Hobbies (UK) Limited has the general title Dungeons and Dragons, which transmits the flavour of the games quite well. They are of interest in management education because of the current concern with individual personality as an influential factor in group cooperation. It is felt that a team will work better together if the members have a deeper understanding of each other, and exercises are commonly set up to encourage a revelation of what people are really like inside. The belief, of course, is that people become conditioned by their experiences in life and may present an image that is *not* what they are really like but is, on the contrary, *what they think their colleagues think they ought to be like*. The bad effect seen as likely to follow is that individual A presents himself as 'the sort of man likely to do X' while he is in reality more likely to do Y. When some crunch point arises, his colleagues assume that he has done X (and act accordingly themselves) only to find that he has reverted to his real self and done Y. The result is probably confusion and failure for the group. If it is thought better for people to be known for what they really are, on the basis that we are all inadequate in various ways and can make allowances for each other without taking advantage, then anything that will encourage the lowering of the outward facade is good. The fantasy game allows players to do the things they would really like to do rather than the things that they know themselves able to do or the things they believe to be acceptable.

Although the use that can be made of the method in management education is primarily concerned with human behaviour, the method itself is model-based in a fairly extreme form, drawing upon some of the ideas for simulating conflict that can be found in war games. The adventure is run by a 'Dungeon Master' who takes players through the scenario stage by stage and has an elaborate set of rules to enable him to establish, for instance, the outcome of a fight between a one-eyed dwarf with an axe and an agile young man with a pen-knife, given that the man has the initiative but is already suffering from a wound in his left forearm. The outcome includes a chance element also and can prescribe differing degrees of damage to one or both parties.

The value of these games is readily apparent to the specialist concerned with individual and group behaviour, but since they are designed as leisure activities they do not necessarily fit within the time scale of a training course. Indeed, some devotees of Dungeons and Dragons are reputed to play all night. It was therefore only a matter of time before an adaptation of the idea appeared, and 'Temple', offered by Oldfield Payne Management Associates is designed to run for about two hours and needs six players and three observers. The six characters start off inside a temple (represented by a board) and have to escape from it, despite the fact that the exit is not shown. On their search for the exit, 'they encounter a wide variety of situations/creatures with which they have to deal/fight. Par for this game is that one or two characters survive and escape: the other four or five characters expire along the way (or are just left).'

3

The traditional type of model

The traditional type of model-based game is still the most common. It sets out to simulate the real business world, and for this purpose the very simple model discussed in Chapter 2 is not going to be convincing. It must be expanded and developed and given a logical framework of rules.

Several variables, one result

One common development is to have more than one decision variable contributing to a result. It is, for instance, unlikely that an article would depend solely on price for variations in the number of units sold. Quality must often have just as much importance, a better type of product being able to command a higher price without losing sales in the manner of something less well made. Advertising is relevant, and a whole range of other factors such as the nature of the competition, how long the product has been in the market, how much money potential customers have to spend, the channels through which the product is distributed, the competence of the salesmen, the discount structure, the credit structure, fashion and chance. A list of all the considerations that can affect sales volume would be a long one, but the writer of a game usually has a clear picture of the situation that he wants to model and is able to pick out the most significant factors to use as decision variables. As soon as there is more than one such variable to be altered, the game offers new scope for the exercise of skill.

The model described in Figure 2:1 would be totally explored by eight different decisions: once a team had tried all the different prices they would know for certain which one was the best. In a game they would

35

probably not take as many as eight decisions to get to the right answer. They would very soon fix on the critical formula for maximising profit, 'number sold times price asked, less cost of number sold', and they would be trying to identify the point at which this was highest. Supposing that they had made decisions of £7 and £4, they would know that the profit figures achieved were £360 and £300 respectively. They would deduce that though the maximum could still be at £8, £6 or £5, it was most unlikely to be below the £4 mark since it was already falling off when £4 was used. Now suppose that sales volume is also going to be affected by advertising expenditure and that this is determined by another model (unknown to the players) as shown in Figure 3:1.

Amount of money spent on advertising £	Additional number of sales achieved
50	30
100	50
150	80
200	140
250	215
300	290
350	320
400	325

Figure 3:1   Relationship between sales and advertising

The situation now becomes markedly different, for instead of there being just eight different policies that can be attempted there are 64: each of the eight advertising options matched with each of the eight sales prices. If the result given back to the players is just a single figure of 'sales' then they will face a major problem in deciding which of the two decision variables should be changed. This begins to demonstrate the value of a management game as an educational exercise, for the problem has this in common with real life: reliable data cannot be obtained without actually making a decision, and every possible decision carries a degree of risk. The players can tackle it purely by trial and error, or on their knowledge of some similar situation, or on the evidence about the behaviour of the model that is inherent in the results given back to them, or in a manner that makes use of all these approaches blended together.

The pure trial-and-error strategy is not likely to pay off, but the actions of some teams in management games suggest that they come pretty close to using it.

The strategy based on knowledge of a similar situation is a logical one to adopt, and needs discussion in detail. Obviously, players who are entering a game situation need to have some 'clues' about what they should do: to offer them none at all is just to encourage the trial-and-error approach, but the clues must not identify the game with an exact management situation so that a player feels that he knows beyond doubt how the model should behave. Provision of that sort of clue just leads him to feel, at the end of the game, that he has been misled or cheated. The object must be to show the *type* of situation being simulated and to suggest 'strategies worth trying out' rather than strategies that are certainly applicable. In the enlarged example, the advertising model shows that the benefit attributable to advertising ceases to grow significantly above a certain expenditure level, and the price/sales model shows that, without advertising, sales are not going to rise above 110. Therefore the description given to the players must suggest a product for which the market is quite definitely limited in size. It must fit the general characteristics that have been built into the model so that the players can make sensible deductions from what they have been told without feeling that their assumptions are necessarily right. This will not be too difficult, for in setting the values in the first place the game writer is bound to have had a certain product in mind, and he must just search for a general description covering that one and others. Players then have a basis on which to make their first decision and against which to compare the result. There is, therefore, a continual process of adjustment to be undertaken: a continual revision of the players' thoughts in the light of new experience. One effect very often seen is that the original theory has a strong hold on the mind and the evidence gathered from the decision/result sequence is misread, disregarded, misinterpreted or just ignored if it does not conform to that idea. Such mistakes are all too common in real business activity, when a strong-minded character is unwilling to revise his ideas or unwilling to accept that conditions have changed.

There is, of course, a logical way of analysing a model such as this, which is to hold one variable steady and alter the other one. If the results for successive periods are different, then the difference has to be attributed to the variable altered, for there is no other possible cause. However, this is a difficult policy to carry through in a game situation because it means that some decisions are going to be made for the purpose of gathering information without regard for the effect of the result upon the fortunes of the team. This dilemma is a fair simulation of the problem that faces many businessmen who would like, for instance, to know what their sales would be if they increased their price by 50 per cent but cannot afford to take the risk of trying it. This policy of exploration might also be abandoned because of doubts about its validity, for it rests upon the assumption that the two effects are independent of each other. Much of the value of a management game lies in the discussion that takes place between the players as they debate possible courses of action. The analytical approach might provoke the following discussion:

> *Player A*   We have now made eight decisions in which we sold our product at £3 and steadily increased our advertising from £50 to £400. The results prove that the effect of advertising increases steadily and that the steps are 20 additional sales, then 30, 60, 75, 75, 30 and 15. All we now have to do is to hold advertising steady while we find the optimum price. Then we can work out the most advantageous combination of price and advertising.
>
> *Player B*   Is that quite true? All we have really done is to prove that advertising gives certain benefits for each level of expenditure *while the price is held at £3*. The benefit does not have to be the same for an article sold at £8. I, personally, would be more susceptible to advertising when applied to a lower priced product because the sum involved is one that I am happy to take risks with. I would be more careful in the case of a product that cost £8.

Knowing what relationships have been set down in this case, it can be seen that player A happens to be right and that there are in fact two independent models, each having its own effect upon the result. However, this does not have to be the case since the two factors can be included in the same model. The umpiring table would then look like Figure 3:2 and then player B would be right while the policy advocated by player A would prove misleading. The players are uncertain about the nature of the relationships existing in the model. A good management game demands a mind-searching and experience-searching activity. It is an exercise in the imagination of *what might be* and the analysis of *what is*.

				Advertising				
Price	£50	£100	£150	£200	£250	£300	£350	£400
£1	90	100	110	130	155	180	200	215
£2	130	140	150	200	250	300	320	335
£3	140	160	190	250	325	400	430	445
£4	120	140	160	200	250	300	325	335
£5	110	125	150	185	220	255	280	290
£6	95	110	125	155	190	225	245	255
£7	75	100	125	150	175	200	225	250
£8	50	65	80	95	110	125	150	175

Figure 3:2   Sales achieved at varying levels of sales price and advertising

Interacting results

The game has been described so far as if it was noninteracting. That is to say, the improvement of its policy by one team did not adversely affect the results of a team which left its policy unchanged. This does not have to be the case.

Consider a very simple game that calls for decisions on price and advertising expenditure and gives back sales demand as a result. Suppose four teams give in the decisions shown in Figure 3:3.

Team	Price	Advertising
A	£4.00	£3000
B	£7.00	£5000
C	£5.00	£2000
D	£3.00	£7000

Figure 3:3   Decisions of four teams

If the umpire's 'model' was the formula:
thousands (advertising) − 100 × sales price = sales demand
then the application of this formula to the above decisions would give the following results:

Team A: 3000 − 400 = 2600
Team B: 5000 − 700 = 4300
Team C: 2000 − 500 = 1500
Team D: 5000 − 300 = 4700

The actions of the teams would be independent, a better strategy by one team not acting to the detriment of the others. The results would be different if the figures of 2600, 4300, 1500 and 4700 were treated as an index and the teams were allocated a percentage share of some market depending on the percentage their own index represented out of the total index figure. In the illustration the percentages work out roughly at 20, 33, 11 and 36. Should team D achieve a higher index in the next playing period, the other teams remaining the same, then team D would get an increased share of the market and the others would get a reduced one. This would occur without any apparent mistake on their part but would be due to a better strategy by an opponent. In short, the game would have become interacting.

There are several other forms of interaction. The one adopted by Chris Elgood Associates in Lawn Trimmers relies on the concept of a market segmented by price. There are five price bands, in each of which there is a known market size and a known number of 'non-playing teams' which compete for the available sales. The playing teams must choose which segment to enter. If only one team enters a segment it will fare reasonably well: if a large number enter it there will be fierce competition and inadequate sales for all. Each team's strategy is assessed independently and the first calculation gives the sales that it would have achieved if it were the only team entering the segment. If more than one team has entered it, the figure is then reduced by an appropriate fraction. Under this arrangement, a better strategy *would* get a better result (despite another team making an even greater improvement) *provided the number of teams in the segment was the same*. If the number of teams had increased, then the advantage might be out-weighed by the increased effects of competition.

Another method is to employ the concept of 'average price'. This means adding all the prices charged by the playing teams in one round and using it as a 'marker' for the next. A team with an above average price is then at a disadvantage, and a team with a lower one gets a benefit. It is a very simple method, but has some advantages when there is a need for rapid umpiring. Both the methods previously described need decisions from all the teams before the results can be calculated. The average price method does not, the marker having been established before the playing period commences.

There are other forms of interaction in use as well, and all of them will reflect the writers beliefs about the behaviour of the market he is trying to simulate. They all make the same essential point that a business seldom operates in controllable conditions. Apart from market variations, there are competing firms whose decisions are not predictable in advance and these can defeat what seemed beforehand to be completely reasonable plans.

One model, several results

Another growth stage in a game is the provision of more than one result from a model. Continuing to look at the original example, it might be argued that two consequences of a high price and extensive advertising would be likely to appear: there would be an increase in the number of articles returned to the manufacturers as faulty, and a percentage of the sales would only be paid for after a delay. The first of these would be based on the argument that people are more demanding in respect of something for which they have paid a high price than they are in regard to something known to be cheap. The second feature would assume that advertising is, generally, an attempt to persuade people to buy something that they would otherwise pass over. If this is the case there will be a percentage of those persuaded to buy who are not really able to afford the expense and who purchase it on credit, paying only after a delay.

One excellent background from which to demonstrate this multi-output feature of a model is a game that requires players to assume a supervisory or management position and to allocate their own working hours between activities characteristic of their position. If, for instance, these activities include training, technical and administration the model can assign consequences for the inadequate allocation of time to each one of them. If training is disregarded, the obvious consequence is lower output from the player's staff, either in quantity or quality or both. Insufficient time on technical matters will cause the breakdown of machinery (for the production man) or failure to interpret customer requirements correctly (for the salesman). Lack of time spent on administration will mean discontented staff, failure to have adequate supplies on hand, delay in getting payment for work done, and so on. The provision of multiple results from a model creates an interesting problem for the players, because they must decide the importance of each result and assign a cause for it, and speculate about the best method of putting it right.

To be specific, such a model in the production area might throw up productive hours achieved during a period of time (the actual number of hours that all the resources of production were available and working), the production rate (the number of units per production hour that were made) and the scrap rate (the number of units that, having been made, were found to be faulty). It is then for the players to decide which of these is likely to yield the greatest benefit in relation to the cost. (The cost being probably some degree of falling-off in the others.) Will it be better to increase the number of hours worked, or to accept the present level of hours worked and ensure that they are made more productive? Will it be better still to concentrate on getting the scrap rate down and so making sure that all the articles that are produced are good, saleable ones? This, like the analysis of different decision variables, can be attempted in a logical manner. It is possible to work out theoretical results, keeping two of the variables exactly as they were for the last playing period and assuming that the third has somehow been pushed up to the maximum level. This gives a reasonable idea of the extent to which that particular factor leaves scope for improvement. Like the other analytical exercise, it is a useful guide rather than an absolute test, for it ignores at least one thing: the *cost* of pushing the chosen variable up to its maximum value, which has still to be discovered. This sort of situation demands what is sometimes described as a 'heuristic' approach: the use of logical analysis pushed as far as one's mind can take it as the basis for empirical testing. This can be restated as 'more intelligent guessing'!

Constraints on decisions

The discussion of decision variables and results has so far been conducted as if the decisions could be altered with complete freedom. This is clearly unrealistic, and another step in game construction is to place restrictions on the way these things can be manipulated. This can be done by arbitrary limitation, or by a time qualification, or by a cost constraint, or by a mixture of these three. An arbitrary limitation is far the easiest, players being told, for instance, that a price is not allowed to change by more than 10 per cent each time period. This means that any major change has to be planned some time in advance. A similar effect is created by ruling that some development, say the expansion of production capacity by recruiting extra labour, requires so many periods of notice to be given to the umpire. Such a rule frequently makes things difficult for the umpire, who has to count the passage of time periods in addition to his other duties, but it introduces a new and very useful element from the players' point of view because it is comparatively innocuous (it does not cost money) but is terribly easily overlooked. Moreover, such a rule can be applied to a great many different areas: the ordering of raw materials, advertising for staff, purchase of new machinery, renewal of leases, construction of new branches, negotiation of new capital issues, and so on.

The cost restriction is the most common means of regulating changes, and the majority of decision variables have a cost attached to them. Frequently these costs are the central factor in a management game, for business success is judged in terms of profit and loss and the size of the costs incurred by each team is a very important factor in deciding their results. In fact, no decision is without its cost, though it may not be spelt out immediately in cash. There is a cost attached to raising a product's sales price – the cost of the sales that will *not* be made because of the new, higher price – and there is a cost attached to lowering such a price – the revenue lost on each item that could still be sold at the higher price. It is simply a matter of balancing the expected cost against the expected benefit and hoping that the overall effect is good.

The element of cost is a critical one, for by this means a player's success in understanding the model, and using it, can be measured. It is also a restriction upon his freedom to make decisions, for a game can imitate the real-life situation in which a person may believe that a certain policy is correct but nevertheless be unable to put it into practice because he cannot find the money to do so. Making this situation clear to the players demands additions to the structure of rules. There must, for instance, be some means of deciding how much money is available at the start of the game, how revenue and expenditure are to be balanced, what facilities are available for borrowing in the event of a player making a loss (or for investment if he makes a profit) and so on. These rules tend to multiply for a reason not directly connected with the model or with the lessons to be learnt from it. They grow because of the need for a game to have credibility in the eyes of those asked to play it. The demand for credibility may seem strange in something known to be a game and bound to fall short of reality in many directions, but the players are asked to make a considerable investment in terms of time and effort and they are reluctant to do this if the game seems to them ill-prepared. Hence there is an emphasis on inserting rules that show an awareness of business reality.

One of these is some sort of 'overhead' cost: a figure that varies little or not at all from month to month and represents the unavoidable costs of being in business at all, whatever the actual scale of the month's operations. It would represent such things as rents, managerial and staff wages, power costs, licences, depreciation of plant, maintenance costs, and similar items. As well as being necessary from the point of view of increasing the credibility of a game, it also adds another problem to the decision-making because it decreases the range of outputs from the model which will yield a profit. Reverting again to the first example used (see Figure 2:1), to state that the company concerned had to carry an overhead cost of £250 each time period would make the £2 and £3 selling prices unprofitable. Generally, the inclusion of an overhead factor encourages players to attempt greater production and greater sales, so as to spread this cost more thinly over a larger number of items. Another very important subject is the amount of capital originally invested in the company, for in business almost all conventional sources of money require to be given some return on their investment. It is therefore unrealistic to ask players just to 'make a profit' without giving them some standard by which to judge what that profit ought to be. The simplest way is to fix the size of the investment, thus allowing the players to work out what profit figures would give them, say, a 15 per cent return per year.

Simulating the passage of time

Closely related to the accounting aspect of the game is the need to simulate the passage of time, for when dealing with the payment of money and the resulting bank balance of a company, it is essential to know just when a transaction takes place. For instance, the work involved in manufacturing an article has largely to be paid for before the revenue is received. Raw material has to be purchased, and probably a large element of the labour cost has to be paid out weekly. Therefore, if a company in a game is incurring costs in manufacture and in sales administration, and gaining revenue from sales, can that sales revenue be held to be used for the costs of that month, or must the company have sufficient working capital before the month starts? This sort of thing has to be spelt out in the rules: it need not always be true to life, for some of these things can be handled by conventions, but it must be apparent that the instructor is aware of the point.

The interaction of money and time is apparent again over the payment of credit accounts. If a company is selling goods on credit, at just what point in the game are they to credit themselves with the receipt of cash in respect of previous sales? Such rules form another benefit of a business game, for they highlight the difference between profit and loss and cash flow. If a business is attempting to discover whether its current operations are profitable it will count up all the revenue attributable to a chosen time period, whether or not this has actually been received, and subtract from it the costs incurred in earning it. To do so gives a clear picture of whether or not the business is on the right lines, but it says nothing at all about whether there is actually enough cash in the bank at some given moment to pay the bills. It shows how much money the company is entitled to but not whether the company has got its hands on that money. The money/time rules show up this difference clearly, and in doing so encourage managers to be conscious of one more aspect of business activity.

Rules and forms as a representation of reality

To those with no experience of management games it may now appear that the players are going to be faced by an extremely complex task. They have not only to read and understand the rules that will regulate all the points but they must also apply them conscientiously whenever it is appropriate. Most model-based games do in fact have quite extensive instructions for players, but these are greatly helped by the provision of certain specially prepared forms that must be completed every playing period by every team. One of these will be designated the decision form and on this a team indicates the value it wishes to set for each decision variable in the game. The form is given to the umpire, who carries out his assessment procedures and enters the results upon the same form before returning it to the team concerned. It is conventional to show a great deal of additional data on the form as well, so that it can be used as a reminder to the players of all the different things that need their attention and as a means of helping them to work out their results correctly.

The form illustrated in Figure 3:4 is taken from Exercise Lemming used by Slough College of Higher Education. All the boxes on the form are identified by the titles or by numbers and there are references to them in the players' instructions so that they can be correctly completed. The bottom right-hand corner is used to show the coding of certain boxes: those that have to be completed by the umpire and those that cannot be completed at all until he has done his job. Thus in section C, line 1 the centre box (the top one of those headed 'Prices') is clearly a decision variable to be set by the team, and the box to the left of it is shaded, indicating that this will be filled in by an umpire. The box to the right of it (the top one of those headed 'Receipts') has an asterisk, and

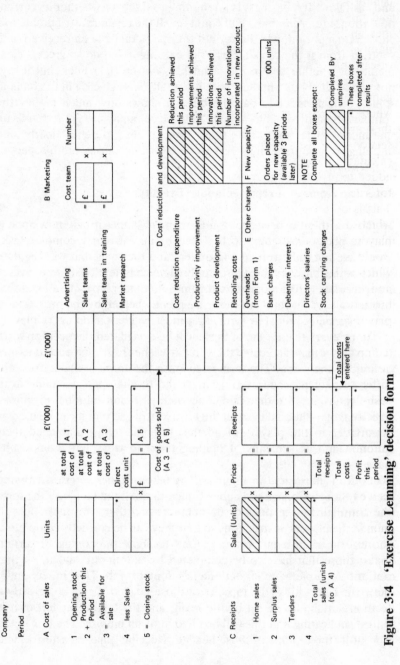

Figure 3:4 'Exercise Lemming' decision form

cannot be completed until after the umpiring. Between the centre box and the left-hand one is a multiplication sign, and the overall logic is inescapable: the team decides selling price, the umpire tells them the number sold and the team multiply these two together to get the amount of cash received.

A form such as this is not intended simply to help students play the game correctly: the whole intention is to simulate reality, and except where the relationship is obscured by some convention the calculations they are asked to perform will be the same as apply in real life. In section A of the Lemming form, the logic by which the stock level is calculated is both clearly set out and entirely realistic. Opening stock is added to production achieved this period to give the quantity available for sale, and then the number sold is subtracted to give closing stock. This is an obvious piece of logic, but symptomatic of the manner in which the rules of a game follow normal business practice and cause players to carry out in an off-the-job situation the same tasks that they would have to do in real life. This is one answer to the school of thought which argues that players spend too much time learning to play a game and insufficient time learning lessons that will be of direct value in business. If the game and its forms are well designed then learning to play the game can be the same thing as learning for life.

To reinforce this point, Figure 3:5 is the form handled by the 'company accountant' in the game called Function. This requires the accountant to collect relevant information from his colleagues in different departments and create a profit and loss account and a cash-flow statement. The collecting task is highly realistic, for this is exactly what accountants have to do, usually setting up some sort of reporting procedure which causes the data to be sent to them automatically. Then the different boxes in the two columns sometimes have different headings. For instance, boxes 4 and 13 both deal with the cost of raw materials, but box 4 contains the cost of only such materials as went into the goods sold in the current month while box 13 contains the total sum paid out for the purchase of materials in the current month. These two figures are relevant to different calculations: the former will help to establish whether the company is or is not currently making a profit while the latter will help to show whether it has or has not got adequate cash available. There is a similar sort of difference between boxes 8 and 14. Obviously, a person learning to handle the form is going to learn at the same time an important principle about the difference between profit and loss and cash flow.

Figure 3:6 is again from Function and shows in the revenue and

Team	Company accountant	Month

Monthly profit loss

Operating cost [____]1

Monthly cash flow

[____]1

Number of units made this month	average material cost per unit	cost of materials used	cost of materials purchased this month
[____]2 X	[____]3 =	[____]4	[____]13

Stock cost: materials [____]5   [____]5

Stock cost: finished goods [____]6   [____]6

Overhead costs [____]7   [____]7   cash received this month

Expected revenue from this month's sales 8[____]   14[____]

	Profit or loss	net cash inflow this month	net cash outflow this month
	[__]9 [__]10	[__]15	or [__]16
Totals	[__]11 [__]12	[__]17	[__]18

Cumulative profit or loss

Previous cumulative profit/loss [____]19   [____]22

+ or −

This month's profit/loss
= [____]20   [____]23

Profit/loss carried forward [____]21   [____]24

Cumulative cash flow

Previous cash position

+ or −

This month's figure
=

New cash position

Return on assets

Fixed assets [£250,000]25

Raw-material stock at month end (£1 per unit) [____]26

Finished-goods stock at month end
......units at £3.50 each [____]27

Debtors [____]28

Total assets [____]29

Return-on-assets ratio = $\dfrac{\text{Profit} \times 100}{\text{Assets}}$ [____ %]30

Figure 3:5 Form used by the 'company accountant' in 'Function'

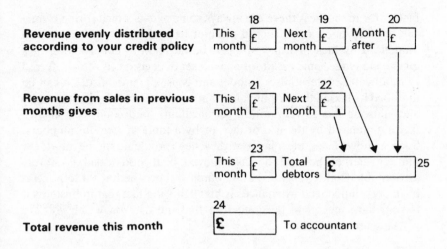

Figure 3:6 'Function': revenue and debtors calculation

debtors calculation how a game can simulate real circumstances. The expected revenue from one month's sales is entered into one box if no credit is to be given (indicating that the income will all be received in the current month) or split between two or three boxes if one or two months' credit are to be allowed (indicating that part of it will not be received until a future date). The form allows for cash payments attributable to previous months' sales to be added on to cash received for the current month's sales, and all cash due in the future to be added together as debtors.

One of the 'only learning a game' criticisms sometimes levelled at management games is that these forms are not set out in the manner to which a particular company is accustomed. This is an intensely company-oriented viewpoint that has no real value. It implies that training should be related to the understanding and pursuit of particular routine procedures, whereas the real need is to get students to understand the principles involved in a task. Once those have been grasped – once a person understands *why* a certain thing must be done – the particular procedures of a company are not hard to figure out.

Simulation of chance effects

There is much to be gained from the inclusion in a game of a chance factor, for in business there are always some events which spring from a cause which one can or should attempt to control but which are also influenced by luck. To have a game based upon a model that *always* gives exactly the same result for a given set of decisions is often referred to as a 'wholly deterministic' model and is usually unrealistic. It can be modified by taking the output value that would be given by such a model and allowing this to vary within certain limits on account of a chance factor simulated by the use of dice or by a table of random numbers. Such a move faces the player with a new problem, for he must ask himself whether the result he has achieved, be it good or bad, is entirely attributable to the policies that he employed or whether these policies have been influenced by chance. It highlights the fact that in business it is very hard indeed to be quite sure that the data on which you are working are truly reliable.

Allocation of roles

One of the most severe hindrances to business efficiency is that the complex nature of business makes it essential to divide the decision-making authority. This, whatever benefits it brings, makes possible an extensive range of disagreements, misunderstandings, partial understandings, personality conflicts and outright communication failures, all of which are damaging to a business. Some management games allow functional divisions within the team, and conflict arises between the immediate goals of one or more departments and the overall objectives. Nor is this just selfish disagreement, for all members may accept the need for an agreed team policy but believe that they can, if given adequate resources, prove their own case about what it should be. Consider the position of a team's marketing executive who firmly believes that a large advertising appropriation will more than pay for itself in improved sales. His claim may be resisted by the team's accountant who argues first that the money for such a policy is just not available and, second, that if it was available it would be better spent in improving the quality of the company's product. In this way the two protagonists not only experience the argument in business terms but must also cope with the personal problem of trying to get somebody else to listen sympathetically to their views when their immediate interests are admittedly in opposition. This is an exercise in interpersonal behaviour which can either be amicably resolved or else disrupt the whole team.

Management games as simulations of real life

It has been said that one can learn to do something by imitation, by following a set of rules, or by understanding and applying a principle. Of these methods, the last puts the student in a very much better position, assuming always that there is time for him to understand and he has the ability to do so. One can legitimately contrast the algorithm and the management game as educational tools. The algorithm is an excellent device for helping people to achieve a desired effect without necessarily understanding the process they are operating; management games are an attempt to demonstrate the principle involved so the students will be able to form judgements for themselves. In doing so, they naturally simplify the real world and select from it specific items that are to be studied.

The facts of simplification and selection need to be faced because some very exaggerated claims have been put forward, and this is most true in the area of traditional model-based games. They have been around the longest and have had more time for development and improvement, so there are some now in existence that are extremely complex and handle numerous aspects of reality very well. They are sometimes regarded as broadly similar to the engineering simulations that are used for skill development purposes, such as the training of aircraft pilots, oil-tanker captains and spacecraft crews. These, like management games, imitate a situation, call for decisions, and throw up a consequential result. They, too, offer an inexpensive likeness of something that would be too expensive or too dangerous to practise on in reality.

The critical difference here is that an engineering simulation attempts to produce an exact model of conditions likely to occur, and the hope of the trainer is that the student will both learn the correct response to a set of conditions and reproduce that response in real life. The assumption is that the circumstances of reality are sufficiently constant to allow this reproductive approach and that there will be no gross change in the environment between the time of training and the time of application. This is broadly true: the range of wind speeds likely to be encountered does not grow or shrink, and air traffic regulations are well documented and stable. It is legitimate to argue that – till further notice – the types of condition simulated are those that will actually be encountered.

A management game does not enjoy quite the same advantages, for the things that it models (such as buying patterns, production capabilities, responses to advertising, etc.) are ultimately determined by human behaviour which is not fully predictable. The things that people are willing to buy are influenced by their personal value systems: the amount of work they are willing to do is influenced by their current ideas about what is 'fair' or what constitutes 'exploitation': their willingness to be persuaded is influenced by their beliefs about the person who seeks to persuade them. What people believe in these areas does change, is sometimes changed by chance events, sometimes changes without people really noticing, and always influences their behaviour. This is a much more fluid situation than is handled by the engineering simulations: the captain of an aircraft does not have to worry about a new machine produced by a competitor that will actually change the meteorological conditions in which he is flying! The captain of industry does. In fact it would be a great disservice to a manager to encourage him in the belief that he lived in a stable, predictable world.

Having said that, it is still necessary to have controlled conditions if a situation is to be useful for practice. It is a need that the model-based games supply very well, provided there are no misconceptions about the boundaries of the model and the things that have to be left out. Assuming them to be based on the most informed current beliefs about how the economic and social world behaves, they give the player a deeper understanding of those beliefs and an increased ability to use them. If these games were for a time excessively praised, it was probably because people did not then recognise the importance of many other aspects of reality which are now seen as vital factors in the equation. A person with his roots in Operational Research, looking at a world in which many managers were economically and financially ignorant, can well be forgiven for thinking that in a well-researched model-based game he was offering a total simulation. A much broader view is taken today, implicit within the paper by Klein and Cooper already quoted about Cognitive Mapping. Quoting from it, 'However, human decision processes never take place in this objective world. All that can be observed are some of their effects. Human decision processes always take place within the subjective world of the individual decision-maker.' That is a very clear recognition that facts and figures – the traditional currency of the model-based game – cannot by themselves simulate reality. The way in which they are perceived and weighed by the individual is a major variable. The broader attitude must be partly due to the activities of the social scientists who have made real progress in showing why people behave in particular ways. The importance of the human element was always obvious, but for a long time nobody saw anything very constructive that they could do about it. Therefore it received inadequate attention. Now that there is a credible area of study, most model-based games show an awareness of it. Some games accept the limitations of the numerate approach and define the human element as beyond their scope. Some incorporate rules that reflect the restrictions which it places on managers. Some make a point of studying the personal behaviour exhibited by the players and drawing from it lessons of general applicability.

Some of these developments are discussed in greater detail in Chapter 6. The overall effect is that while no management game can be regarded as a totally adequate simulation of real life, the range of real life features that can be modelled is steadily increasing. A game that combines many different aspects can thus be a few steps more realistic than before. However, it still has to be accepted that a simulation is useful precisely because it is in some respects *not* like real life. It is not physically or financially dangerous and it does not occupy so much time. These and other aspects of reality are deliberately excluded and it follows that total realism is an unattainable objective. The search for reality reaches its logical end when one considers war games: the final step towards making a war game real is to go to war – and when you have done that it is not a game any more. Rather than to pursue realism as an end in itself, the correct technique is to ask oneself repeatedly 'What am I trying to simulate? Why am I trying to do so? What are the aspects of reality that I must strive for and which are, for the moment, unimportant?'

4

Umpiring devices

The umpiring device is the means by which players are given feedback on the consequences of their actions. In this sense it is always present, even when there are no calculations to be carried out by the instructor or by a computer. In a puzzle or an in-basket exercise the feedback is simply the revelation of the 'right' answer. In an enquiry study it is provided by the answers which the instructor gives to questions. In a maze it is inherent in the act of reading the information on the chosen result sheet. In behavioural games it is shown by the reaction of one player to another. In a practical simulation it lies in the visible degree of success or failure of the given task. In the simpler type of encounter game it is merely the evaluation of a player's action by the umpire, while in the complex type it is the result of his detailed plans being submitted to the 'rules' in whatever form they exist. An umpiring device only becomes a major feature in a model-based game where the rules determining what the feedback should be are complex.

Variables independent of each other

The very simplest umpiring device is just a table, showing the value of the result that is appropriate to each value of the decision variable (see example in Chapter 2). This has a great advantage in that it is easy to use and the players' forms can be judged and handed back in a very short time. On the other hand it has a disadvantage: it gives only a fixed number of values, and for any figure in between two marks the umpire has to interpolate. This will either take him longer or, if he refuses to do it, will make the device insensitive to small changes. An alternative is to express such a relationship as a graph, which will have the opposite effect, allowing the umpire to find a result that is exactly appropriate to any variable, but often taking longer to read off. An additional advantage of a graph is that one can cope fairly easily with values which are off the end of the curve. One can see the direction in which the curve is moving and extend it.

Both graph and table relate one variable to one product, but very often the thinking behind a game calls for a result to be affected by a number of different variables, some having more influence than others. This can be handled by making a separate graph or table for each variable and allowing the output of each to be combined in one overall result. As an example, consider a game about recruitment. Potential employees might be reached by the following means:

1　Newspaper advertising
2　Cinema advertising
3　Leaflets delivered to homes
4　Loudspeaker vans in the streets

Players would be asked to determine their spending on these methods. Let us assume that the writer of the game has decided that newspaper advertising is going to be the variable that has the greatest effect in getting recruits, followed by leaflets and cinema advertising, with loudspeaker vans as the least effective. Four graphs can be drawn relating effectiveness and expenditure for each type of advertising as in Figure 4:1.

Each of these graphs relates a certain expenditure to a certain effectiveness and each shows that there is a point at which maximum effectiveness has been reached and no improvement will be gained by spending more money. The scope for sensible investment in any recruitment method can be fixed by putting figures against the horizontal scale, and these need not be the same figures on each of the four graphs. Newspaper advertising is thought to go on giving extra benefit till quite a lot of money has been spent, and so the horizontal scale runs from £0 to £10,000. Advertising in local cinemas can be done to saturation point on a much lower budget and so the scale on that graph runs from £0 to £4000. In the first case money spent in excess of £10,000 would be wasted, in the second the limit would be £4000.

The remaining question is how much 'effectiveness' is to be contributed by each method. A simple way of tackling this is to decide beforehand what the maximum is to be and to break this down between the four methods. If the writer of the game decides that it is possible to recruit 500 people and newspaper advertising is the most important

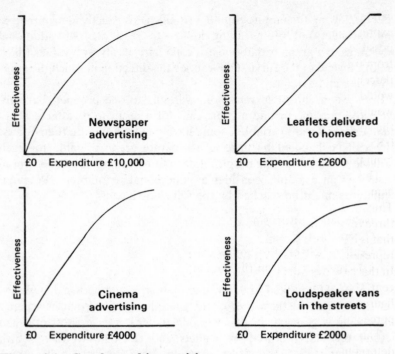

Figure 4:1   Graphs used in umpiring

method, he would make the vertical scale on that graph run from zero to, say 250. This means that maximum spending on the newspaper advertising would get 250 recruits even if the other methods produced nothing at all. Conversely, he might decide that loudspeaker vans in the streets would never get more than 50 recruits, so the vertical scale on that graph would be from 0 to 50. In this way limits are set to the useful expenditure on each method and also to the degree of influence which each has.

It is also possible to vary the nature of the curve drawn on the graphs, for the writer of a game may believe that effectiveness relates to expenditure in different ways. In the case of leaflets delivered to homes it might be argued that the graph should show a straight line rather than a curve, because the number of homes in the area is finite and identifiable, and the last leaflet delivered has as much chance of getting a response as the first.

This way of working out the contribution made by each variable depends upon a 'potential' result that is known beforehand and remains stable. If that is not going to be the case, then a variation is needed. This can take the form of an index, the vertical scale of each graph not being expressed in units but in a proportion or percentage of the total that is possible. In such a case the graph for newspaper advertising would read from 0 to 0.5 or 0 to 50 per cent depending on whether proportion or percentage was being used, and the graph for the loudspeaker vans would run from 0 to 0.1 or 0 to 10 per cent. The output of the graphs would then be added together to get a total and this total used to reduce the 'potential' figure. Thus, if the outputs of the graphs should total 0.85, or 85 per cent, and the potential available be 600 recruits, then the team making these decisions would be told that it had gained 510 men.

This method will also cope with the requirements of an interactive game, for the total output of the graphs will be different for each team. Thus if the total labour market is said to be 1200 men, and there are three teams with outputs from the graphs totalling 1,8, 0.69 and 0.91, all that is necessary is to add them together, find the percentage of the total represented by each one, and apply this percentage to the total market. In this case the total of the figures given is 3.4, and 1.8 represents 53 per cent, 0.69 represents 20 per cent, and 0.91 represents 27 per cent. The figures are rounded off. Applied to a total market of 1200 the percentages give 636 recruits, 340 recruits and 324 recruits respectively.

The figure to be shared out among the competing teams may be one determined beforehand by the umpire or it may itself be the product of the teams' past or present decisions acting upon a preset figure. Thus the 1200 mentioned might be related, *before* being broken down into percentages to, say, average newspaper advertising (of all teams added together) in the preceding six months. This would mean that if that average figure was below a certain level then the potential labour market would be reduced to 1150, 1100 or some other figure. The argument here would be that the low advertising level in times past caused fewer people to look for work in the local papers and more to look elsewhere.

These suggestions about how the umpiring device is built up make it more obvious than ever what 'model' really means, for every relationship that a writer builds into the device reflects his belief about the environment simulated in the game. It becomes his own model of that environment. It is common to hear arguments about the extent to which any such model is realistic and about how desirable a 'true-to-life' model really is. Two things have to be said. The first is that no model is anything but a poor substitute for reality and the second is that models are built for different purposes. This second point is particularly relevant in regard to management games, for there are writers in the

Hours training	Sales index	Number of salesmen	Sales index
1	3	1	10
2	6	2	15
3	9	3	20
4	11	4	20
5	13	5	18
6	15	6	16
7	16	7	14
8	17		
9	18		
10	18		
11	18		
13	18		
14-20	18		

Figure 4:2   Table used in umpiring, relating a sales index to number of salesmen and hours of training

field who have their background in computer science and there are others who have their background in education. Those from the former background are influenced by the fact that sophisticated models, run through a computer, are frequently used for predictive purposes – to answer the question: What would happen if we did . . .? For this sort of task it is clearly important that the model should ·reflect life just as accurately as that can be done. On the other hand a person with his roots in education wants to emphasise a limited number of points that are appropriate to the student's current state of development and is not desperately worried that the details extraneous to his purpose should be perfect. He is quite willing to sacrifice some aspects of reality in order to make his point.

Variables which modify each other

The description of umpiring devices so far has dealt with one or more variables that each contribute to a result in an independent manner. That is to say, variable A set at a value of 15 has X units of influence, whatever the state of variables B and C and so on. That situation does not always apply, as has been shown in Chapter 3. The state of one variable may condition another, making it more or less powerful. To take an extreme case, let us consider a game about retail selling which called for decisions on 'numbers of staff to be employed' and 'hours of training per month'. The writer of the game might compile a table like Figure 4:2 giving a 'sales index' related to various decisions.

Sales effectiveness

Number of hours training per man	1	2	3	4	5	6
	1.0	2.0	4.0	3.6	2.6	4.25
24	1.4	2.8	4.6	4.0	3.2	4.25
23	1.8	3.4	5.2	4.6	3.6	4.25
22	2.0	4.2	6.0	5.2	3.8	4.0
21	2.2	4.8	6.5	6.0	4.0	4.0
20	2.8	5.3	7.0	6.4	4.6	3.75
19	3.2	6.0	7.6	7.0	5.0	3.75
18	3.7	6.5	8.4	7.5	5.4	3.5
17	4.2	7.2	9.0	8.0	5.8	3.5
16	4.8	8.0	9.5	8.5	6.0	3.5
15	5.2	8.8	10.0	8.8	6.6	3.25
14	5.4	9.2	10.5	8.8	6.8	3.25
13	5.5	9.4	11.0	9.0	7.0	3.0
12	5.6	9.2	11.0	9.0	7.0	3.0
11	5.7	8.9	10.6	9.0	6.8	3.0
10	5.8	8.4	10.0	8.6	6.6	3.0
9	5.9	7.6	9.0	7.8	6.0	3.0
8	6.0	6.8	8.0	6.8	5.4	3.0
7	5.0	5.8	6.5	5.6	4.6	3.0
6	4.5	5.0	5.0	4.2	4.0	2.75
5	3.0	4.2	3.8	3.4	3.0	2.5

Number of salesmen

Figure 4:3 Sales effectiveness index, as a function of 'number of salesmen employed' and 'hours training per salesman per month'

The idea would be to add together the two sales indices, so that to employ five salesmen giving them six hours training a month, would produce an overall sales efficiency index of 18 + 15 or 33, which would then be equated with a certain level of sales. The problem is that the hours training feature ought logically to be different depending on the number of salesmen employed. If five men are employed then it seems very possible that the optimum of ten hours training each is sensible, for it will always be possible to spare one man of the five, but if there is only one salesman, such a policy will result in the shop being shut for 10 hours and no business being done. As the model stands, this will still be the best policy, despite the fact that most managers would disagree with it. They might feel that if there really was only one man then the best figures to be achieved ought to occur when he received, say, four hours training a month. They would not expect the one man *ever* to get the results that two or more could get, but if there was only one then his optimum training time would be different. The 'number of salesmen' variable should condition the behaviour of the 'hours training' variable, so that properly there should be a different 'hours training' table for every possible value of 'number of salesmen'.

This situation can be handled by a table like the one in Figure 4:3 which gives 'hours training' along one side and 'number of salesmen' along the bottom and contains just one space that belongs to each combination of the two variables. This sort of umpiring device can be extended to include another variable if necessary. Suppose that sales efficiency in the shop in the example determines its ability to cope with a wide variety of items. Thus, if the sales efficiency index is 20 then stocking the greatest possible variety, which can be arbitrarily set at 50 items, will give far more benefit in overall sales than it would if the sales efficiency index is only 8. This could be set out as another table using the output of one as the input of another. Such a table would show sales efficiency along the bottom and variety stocked down the side, with value of sales in the squares.

Nomographs

This sort of information can also be presented by means of a nomograph. This is a specially prepared graphical representation of the model. The one illustrated in Figure 4:4 shows a similar interplay of relationships to that just described, but draws upon a different background. The article being sold is some sort of major consumer durable, and the company selling it may have a number of different locations where it can be seen and examined. It may also have a larger

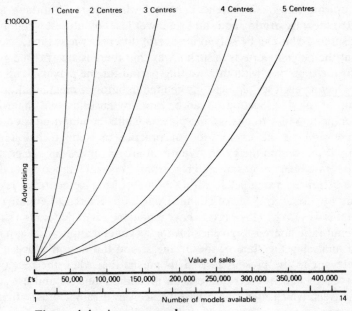

Figure 4:4   A nomograph

or smaller range of models to offer, and is accustomed to advertise in the national press. On the nomograph, a separate curve has been drawn for the situation existing when the company operates one, two, three, four or five centres. The method of use is to identify the point on the vertical scale that corresponds to the amount the company has decided to spend on advertising, and place a ruler horizontally across the nomograph at that level so that it cuts all the five curves. Note the point where it crosses the curve appropriate to the number of centres which the company has decided to maintain. Then place a ruler from this point down to the mark on the bottom scale which corresponds to the number of different models which the company is offering. At some point this is bound to cut the intermediate scale headed 'Value of sales', and all that is necessary to read off the figure. The logic behind the five curves is simple. Advertising will not be very effective if it is not possible for a potential purchaser to view the article reasonably close to his home.

Time required for umpiring

There is quite frequently a problem over the amount of time that umpiring takes. An extended period when there is nothing to do is extremely frustrating and causes a lower level of interest when the game resumes. This can be solved in several different ways. First, by spacing out the playing periods in such a way that there is always time available for the umpiring without a waiting period for the players. This is done by having each set of decisions handed in before a meal break, or at the end of the day. Second, it can be done by ensuring that there is some demanding task to engage the players while the umpiring is done. This may well be the exploration or practice of some technique that is applicable within the game. Where an instructor is using the game as an integrated part of a training programme this will happen naturally, and be extremely valuable. In the Diploma of Management Studies course run by Slough College of Higher Education, Exercise Lemming is used in this way. When the players have made one set of decisions a short talk about ratio analysis is given, showing its general application as a method of analysing the state of the business, and the way in which it can be relevant to the present task. This means that when the results of the decisions are provided there is an immediate and helpful use for ratio analysis, which might otherwise be seen as a rather dreary theoretical subject.

Another satisfactory way of making use of umpiring time is to ask teams to concern themselves with their own efficiency as an operating unit. This can either be done in terms of a formal look at their organisation and its procedures or else from the behavioural angle: what roles do members see themselves and their colleagues as fulfilling? By what means are they really reaching their decisions? To what extent are they using the resources of skill and knowledge that they, collectively, represent? To what extent is each member finding satisfaction within the team?

The umpiring itself can be made quicker. One way is to set out the decision form in such a manner that one particular bit of information must always be shown in the same place so that it can be linked to an umpiring procedure. To illustrate, in a game about retail training called Outlet, the decision form is planned so that the 'catalogue number' of an item of merchandise has to be entered in a space on the form that is related to its chosen display position in the shop. The catalogue numbers are a code, including in each of them one digit that represents 'propensity to impulse buying'. The umpire has a transparent overlay that covers the decision form and assigns to each position in the shop a 'multiplier'. When the overlay is in position the two figures appear next to each other and are easily multiplied together to give 'extra sales'. The effect is that an item with a high susceptibility to impulse buying will get a large number of extra sales (because of its own high code number multiplied by the position figure) *if* it is placed in the right sort of position, but an item with a low susceptibility will not be much affected by where it is displayed because its own code number minimises the effect of the position figure. Devices like this are useful in producing quick results despite complex data.

Variations can be made which cause the players to do some of the work of umpiring, but for calculations they must carry out themselves they must be provided with the necessary information. This means that less information is hidden away in the model and obtainable only by deduction. This may be a good or a bad thing.

To illustrate, it might reasonably be argued that a team's success in selling something was determined by the quality of their sales force and the quality of their product, a separate index being calculated for each. The extreme form of 'hidden' umpiring would mean the calculation and multiplication of these two by the umpire himself to give an overall sales index, the addition of the sales indices for all the teams and the determination of the percentage of the total represented by each, the calculation of the total market by some other means and the breaking down of the market between the teams according to the percentages given by their sales indices. Then the figures given back to each team would be just 'possible sales', leaving them to calculate whether they could meet the demand and so determine 'actual sales'.

Now it can very well be argued that in real life some of the data would be unpleasantly obvious. If a firm is attempting to sell a lousy product at an unrealistic price, the first people who will tell them are their salesmen. Likewise, any reasonable sales manager has a pretty clear understanding of how good or bad his salesmen are. So, in a realistic exercise, there are good reasons for revealing many of what might be called the 'intermediate results' to the players. In the case now being discussed this would mean that the umpire need only calculate total market, and the two indices applicable to each team. If the former were displayed openly, the teams could be left to do the other calculations for themselves.

The question that the instructor, or writer, ought to ask himself in regard to this decision is: For what purpose is the game being used? The particular lesson that it is hoped to teach probably ought to be concealed, for in discovering it for themselves the players will grasp its implications more thoroughly. But is there any point in concealing other relationships which are not closely connected with the objectives? If the objective is to put over the concept (in competitive marketing) that a strategy good in itself can still be defeated by a better one, and the concept is new to the students, then it is reasonable to conceal the interactive mechanism (the comparison of indices and determination of percentages) so that they are left in doubt about the reasons for, say, declining sales of their high-quality, well advertised product. On the other hand, if the students are very familiar with this feature and may be expected to direct their attention immediately to ways of increasing their sales indices, then the methods of so doing represent the chosen area of learning and only the model that determines these must be concealed. The rest can be disclosed. Quite often, a game is used with the objective of 'releasing knowledge'. In such cases the attempt to conceal specific pieces of knowledge is made purely in order to create a situation which is realistic, enjoyable, and which will get people involved. This reinforces the point made earlier that the purpose with which the game is being used has a lot to do with the attitude that should be taken towards the umpiring.

Time-lags in games

One excellent way of solving the problem of umpiring is to introduce, as part of the game, a time-lag between making a decision and the release of the results. In real life a manager is often ignorant of the up-to-date position. This is true of the senior management running several factories, who cannot hope to be instantaneously informed of developments and, when problems arise, must wait patiently to see whether the staff are able to sort them out or not. It is also true of the marketing manager, who has sales staff scattered over the country and would not even know the true picture if they rang up each day – for they are themselves waiting patiently to see whether some customer will or will not sign an order. There is, therefore, good reason for requiring a team to make decisions for, say February, and giving them, in return for those decisions, the results that relate to January.

In this situation every month is seen as an entity for which plans have been made – and are being worked out at a lower level of the organisation – but of which the outcome is not known. Therefore, a team is required to plan for the future in conditions of uncertainty: they know what the position was at the end of the previous month, they know what they *hope* it will be at the end of the current month, and upon this 'assumed' data the decisions must be made. This arrangement makes a great difference to the task of umpiring, for the umpires have exactly the same time available to them as the players have for their decision-making. It enables quite sophisticated procedures to be carried out with nothing more elaborate than a few calculating machines.

This time-lag is also of value when a game calls for notice in advance if certain decisions are to be put into effect. A common feature to which this applies is the introduction of new manufacturing capacity. In real life this takes time to install, and many games require that a team should formally give notice of such an intention several periods in advance. This they sometimes fail to do. Arguments arise about what period constitutes a certain number of months' notice, and different interpretations by different players may mean that some vital piece of equipment is unavailable when required. This is a very convincing piece of simulation, for its causes are exactly the same as those which cause similar failings in the real world: preoccupation with other matters, misunderstanding and forgetfulness.

The use of the computer

The most dramatic way of reducing umpiring time is, of course, the computer. It has very great advantages, but some of these also contain dangers. It can do so much, and so quickly, that it is tempting in the cause of economy and neatness to have it performing functions that would offer valuable learning if they were done by the players. For instance, a computer will readily eliminate any 'interpretation of results' phase by providing the playing teams with profit/loss account, cash-flow statement and balance sheet, when they might gain more from the experience of preparing these documents for themselves. From the umpire's point of view, the computer relieves him of some very tedious calculations but may leave him in the position of not knowing why some particular result has happened. Not having done the work himself, he cannot give informative answers to the students. When running a game manually, he will not only have done it, but will have immediately available records to refer back to. The manual records are an advantage in other respects, too, for they provide a history of each play of a game and if there are any errors it is possible to trace them to their source – even if it lies some periods back in time from the moment of discovery. Many computer programs would merely up-date the position each month and retain no record of previous states. So there may be sound educational reasons for preferring the muddle and stress of manual operation to the slickness and efficiency of the computer.

5

The place of the computer

Computers had a powerful influence upon the earlier management games because they permitted the application of complex rules with great rapidity. It was possible to write a game that had an impressive amount of detail – giving it high credibility – but still returned the results of the decisions without significant delay. By contrast, some of the manually operated games took a very long time to umpire or else used only a few variables, thus appearing simplistic and unreal. They did not cover sufficient subject matter to convey the feeling that one was running a business. Another factor favouring computer-based games was the desire to demonstrate the capability of the machine itself, using a manager's interest in business generally to involve him with this new technology. The more one could demonstrate the cleverness of the computer, the better this seemed from the viewpoint of those promoting it: so in some cases a game grew in complexity as much in order to utilise the computer as for genuine educational reasons. In fact the words 'complex' and 'good' were almost seen as synonymous. To a lesser extent this is being repeated with the advent of the micro-computer and the simplicity of modern computer languages. People without an extended background in computers can now learn the skills that are necessary, and there is a whole new generation growing up to whom the computer was literally child's play. So the old temptation to be complex for complexity's own sake is still there. The good and the bad of that issue has to be debated before examining some of the other opportunities that computers provide.

The question of complexity

If one asks what virtue there is in complexity, the first answer likely to be given is that it will make a game more real. The business world is certainly complex and confusing, it is not fully controllable and there is a good deal of pressure. To offer a simulation that has only a small number of variables, excludes all the irrelevant 'noise' of the real world, and allows students generous time to ponder their policies is, one can argue, a poor preparation. That argument has to be related to the state of development of the student and the intentions of those who are offering him a learning opportunity. Obviously, preparation should be graded into steps of increased difficulty, and a simulation is no exception to the rule. If the students know little and are to be given a chance to manipulate the basic concepts of business management, then the correct technique is to isolate these from their background and present an exercise in which the student has a reasonable chance of success. Having 'got it right' in a fairly simple situation he can then proceed to a more difficult one. The basis of education and training at this factual and authoritative level is the success experience – the opportunity for the student to recognise and practise the right way of doing something so that he can employ that ability in the future. The experience of failure is of lesser value because it leaves him feeling 'I know how difficult it is' without the other essential feelings that 'I know how I ought to tackle it' and 'I have got it right before, so perhaps I can get it right again'. Games of great complexity have sometimes been used with the apparent object of causing failure: so that the game writer has made his point about the difficulty of the real world but has not increased the ability of the students to cope with it.

The other side of that argument, of course, is that for the advanced student a game of great complexity may be exactly what is required: he has the knowledge and experience to tackle it with a reasonable chance of success. If he is offered something less sophisticated then he may feel insulted by it, and refuse to take it seriously.

In both cases the assumption is that the simulation is being used for a particular purpose – to increase the students chance of being successful in some future situation. But other objectives are also possible, and for some of these complexity has special benefits.

One such objective might broadly be described as 'demonstration' – the exercise being used to increase awareness of what the real situation is going to be like, what the dangers are, and what consequences will follow from certain forms of failure. The intention is, perhaps, that a student who regarded some activity as fairly undemanding will be led to think, 'If it is really going to be like that, then I had better prepare for some hard work – I obviously don't know as much as I thought I did'.

Alternatively, the manager who is uncritically accepting traditional standards of performance may be shocked into thinking that, 'If we go on as we are without changes, we will be bankrupt in two years'. The assumption behind these objectives is that the student does not yet have a clear perception of the ultimate state – the objective of the training, why it is necessary, and what conditions it is supposed to prepare him for. Without a clear perception, he may approach his training with a poor attitude or even get himself involved with something that turns out to be 'not what I bargained for'. The assumption behind all these ideas is that the training will go on to provide him with the necessary skills. The fact that he is at first unable to succeed is not a problem. In such circumstances, the earlier arguments against complexity have little value and the fact that it makes a game seem real is a point in its favour.

Another objective might be to practise business management in a situation which is not fully understandable and has no predetermined 'right' answers. The learning looked for here is of a different order from that which emerges from simple games. In the latter there may be 'good' strategies that, if followed, will effectively ensure a successful result. In the more complex sort of game even a theoretically excellent policy may fail: possibly due to some unusual and quite unforeseeable action taken by another team. It is therefore impossible for the tutor to argue 'If you had adopted such-and-such a policy, *which I could have described to you beforehand*, you would have been alright'. The approach has to be more generalised, asking questions of the teams like 'Was your decision a sensible one in the light of the information you had available? Was that information the most that you could obtain, or did you ignore some of the sources? Was your evaluation of competitors' likely strategies a bit superficial?' For although the complex situation precludes a single correct answer, it remains capable of analysis in terms of probability. It is usually possible to make statements like 'If such-and-such is true (as I believe to be the case) then X is a policy more likely to succeed than Y'. In a sense one is still teaching, but it is now the teaching of skill and intellectual behaviour rather than of knowledge. The complexity is necessary to call out a high level of skill.

Computer-based material for creating opportunities

When the decision-making of a team is to be examined in this way, the exercise has clearly become more than the exploration of a mathematical model – for the way a team behaves is going to be determined by the individual personalities of its members. Each of them will bring to the game his own tendencies to notice one thing rather than another, to pay attention to this rather than that, to evaluate certain risks as serious, and others as less so. Success or failure will therefore become dependent upon perception and behaviour as much as upon knowledge. The complex game is valuable in this respect for it naturally provides more opportunity for the exposition of alternative views. In the simpler games there is a possibility of one person 'knowing' and another being ignorant: in the complex ones it is often a matter of nobody 'knowing' and several attitudes all being equally reasonable. So the objective of practising in an unpredictable situation is closely allied to another objective of studying managerial behaviour.

One exploration of this area has been made by Henley – The Management College, who use a psychological approach to develop theories about what constitutes an effective management team and to consider the ways in which people manage situations of which they have incomplete understanding. An interesting comment on the results is that 'good control need not be associated with the ability to give a coherent description of the system of which the control activity is a part'. Here is a valuable lesson for those studying the interpersonal side of management, and it emerges from the background of a complex, computer-controlled game: that there are some highly competent managers in the sense of 'being able to get things right' who nevertheless are not able to explain themselves fully to others.

It can be argued that the broad scope of some computer-based exercises was an invitation to other disciplines to invade the field. There was obviously a great deal involved that was not just a matter of numbers. There were things going on as part of the game playing which were clearly within the province of the social scientists. Also, the general familiarity with computers was growing and there were an increasing number of social scientists to whom the technology was an everyday affair. So the computer deserves at least some of the credit for building a bridge between the numerate sciences and the social sciences, and there are a number of games available that show the cross-fertilisation quite clearly.

This is well illustrated by two games created by M. A. P. Willmer of Manchester Business School. One of these – Crimos – deals with pilfering. The model employs a number of assumptions which are listed as:

1   Those who are searched will become more 'honest'
2   Those who are not searched will become more 'dishonest'

3   The more lenient the sentencing policy the lower the level of
    honesty, and vice-versa

These assumptions are the means by which an attitude of mind –
imputed to imaginary people in the organisation being simulated – has
been turned into a statistical result that can be printed out by the
computer in terms of 'value of goods lost', 'thefts detected' and so on.
They are no less valid than the assumptions about customer behaviour
which are a standard feature of marketing-oriented games, indeed they
might well secure a higher measure of general agreement. The other
game is called So You Think You Would Make A Managing Director?
The subject matter is the establishment of criteria for a subordinate
manager to work to, the degree of obedience with which he observes
any restrictions imposed and the degree of honesty with which he
reports any deviations. The computer allows a person role-playing the
manager to make a range of production decisions. Some of these are
'against the rules' as defined by the person role-playing the managing
director, though all are operationally possible. The computer prints out
the production achieved and the manager must then tell the managing
director what he has been able to do and how many rules he has broken.
He is not obliged to tell the truth, and one of the lessons emerging from
the simulation is that it can at times be very difficult for a managing
director to know what is really happening in the organisation of which
he is the ultimate boss. The game is essentially about human behaviour
in an organisation, and the computer is employed to help create a
credible background. The trend can be seen in other games and
simulations also: there is less concern to demonstrate the cleverness of
the computer and more concern to make good use of its capabilities
within the overall design.

The game just described emphasises the fact that a managing director
is not necessarily making his decisions on the basis of facts. In one sense
this argument could be challenged, for today's information handling
techniques make it obvious that he can, if he wishes, have facts in the
form of printed data spread out on his desk very quickly and in great
abundance. But are these facts going to be useful in his decision-
making? He clearly cannot review them all, for there are far too many of
them. Somebody has to select what he will have, and attach explana-
tions and suggestions. That means that there will be a subjective filtering
process going on (probably at many levels within the organisation) and
the best that the managing director can ever hope to do is base his
decisions on 'facts' that have been modified by the perceptions and

interpretations and biases of others. So there is good reason to focus attention on the mental attitudes of managers and on communication between them. The computer can be useful here, too, and some interesting techniques are described by P. J. Boxer under the title 'Reflective Analysis'. An individual using his computer program Nipper is asked to define the criteria by which he intends to judge a particular group of comparable items and then to apply those criteria, using a numerical scale, to specific items from that group. The computer makes calculations and comparisons based on these figures and feeds back data that cause the user to think more deeply about what he has done and why. An example given by Boxer concerns criteria for choosing a car, in which criteria identified as 'good value' and 'flexible' were found to give very similar results. Reflecting on this data, the user felt that both criteria were a manifestation of a deeply held value attaching to 'soundness' – the extent to which the car was tried and tested in use. A point of great interest here is that a manager's behaviour is the outcome of a set of personal values *not known to others*. It is only deduced by them as they take back-bearings from his observed behaviour. Is that observed behaviour – which is often a matter of the spoken word – a true guide to the ideas and beliefs and values operating in the mind? The Reflective Analysis technique implies that the accuracy with which one puts words to one's beliefs can be improved – and if it can be improved then it follows that the previous performance was imperfect. So the communication gap is not just caused by one person misinterpreting the words of another: there can also be weaknesses in the way those words reflect their parent ideas. And the speaker may not be fully aware of those weaknesses, because he has never before examined his own mental habits. The experience of formulating criteria, applying them, and finding clear scope for improvement must be salutary and helpful. It must make a person think more deeply about his attitudes and express them more clearly because they are clearer in his own mind. This in turn must make him easier to understand correctly, marginally more predictable, and more comfortable to work with. The concept of Reflective Analysis extends into the use of games and simulations, and Boxer's paper 'Designing Simulators for Strategic Managers' explains how he uses such devices to help managers reflect upon the actions they have taken and the concepts that influenced them in doing so.

Information – retrieval and presentation

It has already been mentioned (when dealing with 'Enquiry studies') that the storage capacity of the computer is valuable: an exercise can be made to depend for its outcome on how thoroughly a team explores and analyses the available data. It is also possible that the same data will be perceived in different ways by different teams, and different conclusions drawn from it. The first of these uses assumes that there is some 'right' answer, and the interest of the tutor is to see whether it was discovered or not. The second takes quite a different attitude, seeking to explore the ways in which personality and conditioning modifies the way in which information is seen. Where the second objective is pursued, there could be different data banks available to the playing teams: this would highlight the tendency for people to use their own data and to distrust that provided by others. It would simulate a common problem confronting different departments within an organisation, where each is able to prove a different case to its own complete satisfaction.

The information offered by a computer no longer has to be in the form of written text. It can be in graphs or tables, or even in brightly coloured pictures and cartoon lay-outs. This last idea is in direct contrast to traditional attitudes that see it as 'improper' to infiltrate into the educational field anything that seems to be lacking in seriousness. The prohibition seems somewhat ridiculous when one reflects that the basic concept of a game is to exploit an apparently universal human liking for the experimental 'try it and see' approach to a problem. There is something inherently attractive in committing oneself to a course of action and then waiting in hope to find out whether one has done well. It does not affect the inherent quality of the knowledge that is being offered by the experience, but it does very powerfully affect the motivation of the student and his propensity to involve himself with what is going on. It may possibly be argued that excessive involvement can lead to an obsession with the game itself and a failure to perceive the general relevance of its lessons. If this be so, the correct strategy is surely to find means of redirecting the student's interest rather than to make the game itself less interesting. And a degree of involvement is obviously necessary because the student who is not involved at all is going to learn nothing.

If it is recognised that interest, excitement and enjoyment are emotions naturally associated with the game format, and that the user of games is doing so partly because of this characteristic, then it is quite logical to seek ways of enhancing it. Generally speaking, people do get pleasure from variety, from novelty, from colour, from humour and from the unexpected, so forms of presentation that offer serious information but do so in an interesting way are quite legitimate. They also have certain advantages over the more traditional ways, because they emphasise more limited features but emphasise these more powerfully. For instance, a detailed table of performances may never get read by some team members because they find it difficult to distinguish the vital points from a mass of detail. They may gain more from a succession, say, of pie-charts that shows a company getting a greater or lesser share of the market as the years pass. It is also arguable that traditional methods of presentation commonly offer too much data, and that while analysts spend hours studying detailed figures, the real decision-makers form their judgements on the basis of broad trends that are quite rapidly identified.

The idea of using the computer to offer information in an enjoyable form is not restricted to the use of pictures and colour. Microcomputers have an internal time-keeping facility so that a history of past developments can be re-lived on the screen. Thus, a measure of market share can be offered, showing a column of a certain size for one company at a point five years in the past. At a little distance along the screen appears another column for a competing team, and so on. Once there is a column for all the teams concerned for Year Minus Five, the computer can then place beside them the appropriate column for Year Minus Four. The visual simulation of the changing fortunes of the companies adds interest value to the data.

The 'what if' model

Every decision-maker carries in his mind some image of the world in which he works. It may be extremely vague, or quite well-defined, but he uses it to answer the question 'What is likely to happen if I do so-and-so'. It can be visualised as a causative chain with connections like 'If I do *this,* then *such-and-such* will happen to that part of my business because *that* sort of relationship exists between the two'. There are numerous similar chains, frequently interlinked, and quite soon the possible combinations become so numerous that the mind baulks at the complexity. So before the advent of computers attempts at prediction were sketchy affairs making a few basic assumptions and dealing in a limited number of alternatives. The computer makes it possible to write sophisticated models in which all the known relationships are specified and the total impact of changing an input variable can be seen. The model will not just show the change that is envisaged: it will show all the side effects which are inherent in the specified relationships but which the human mind can seldom work out for itself. A good model can therefore be a most valuable decision-making tool, but 'good' implies that all the relationships are true, which is often difficult to achieve and sometimes impossible. Within the framework of a complex management game there may now be several computer terminals or micro-computers available, and the concept of using models as an aid to decision-making can be fully explored. They can help playing teams to do well within the terms of the game, and they can also demonstrate the value of the technique for real life applications.

One approach is to model just the internal workings of a business, so that the model gives back to the enquirer, say, the profit and loss account that would follow *if* the firm sold its goods at a particular price, won a percentage of a market of a certain size, had no increases in relative costs of its purchases and did not increase its stocks. This sort of model has a fairly high reliability because the conditions are unlikely to vary beyond reasonable limits. It still includes several vital assumptions: for instance there must be an estimate of the promotional effort needed to generate the given market share if the given price is to be charged. This may turn out to be wrong, but generally a model that is good enough to be useful can be produced – and it must be remembered that anything is useful if it brings to light considerations that would have been overlooked without it. A thing does not have to be perfect to be useful: it just has to be an improvement. Within a game, teams can be encouraged to build and use their own such model, or they can be provided with one, or they can be given one of the existing software packages (like VISICALC) which starts them off with an existing framework and allows them to fill in the details.

Another approach is to provide players with a model of a particular market and encourage them to make repeated experiments, comparing one set of decisions with another and eventually identifying the best policy for their company. This sort of experiment is going to be phrased in terms like 'Supposing that we charge £90 and have a promotional budget of £500,000 and keep our quality as high as any of our competitors, what market demand can we expect and what will our financial performance be like over the next few years?' Games like Stella from D. J. Woolliams and J. Cooper, and Plasticity Plight from D. J. Management Consultants, take this approach. Another is The Airways Challenge from M. A. P. Willmer, which encourages teams to enter not only their own strategy, but what they believe to be the likely strategies of their competitors. In this way they are able to study the interaction of strategies and see that they all have strengths and weaknesses if one can only recognise them.

6

Games and human behaviour

Behavioural games is used as a general term to cover games that are concerned with the relationships established between individuals and between groups by the manner in which they behave towards each other and the manner in which this behaviour is interpreted. In this there is an element that has always existed and which is broadly described as 'communication': the question of whether a person does or does not understand the message given, and whether he understands it well enough to carry out the desired action effectively. This is a matter of the meaning assigned to words by each party, the mental image they have of the situation in which action must be taken, and the extent to which the instructions are comprehensive. Behavioural games explore the area of genuine misunderstanding between people over what is meant, or what is intended, or the purpose with which the intention is formed.

Authority and communication

An important feature of life at work in recent times has been a need for consent on the part of those receiving instructions. The classic superior/subordinate relationship took no account of the feelings of the subordinate and relied wholly on the authority concept to ensure that instructions were, if understood correctly, carried out quickly and efficiently. 'Theirs not to reason why . . .' The authority concept today has been greatly weakened, and there is a need for good personal relationships between manager and managed if the instructions, however fully understood, are to be well executed. This relationship is extremely difficult to achieve because of the circumstances in which it must exist. Outside the world of employment, interpersonal understanding is a thing that grows slowly out of common interests and is voluntary on both sides. Inside employment some semblance of it must be achieved without a great investment of time and between people who may well be quite different in character and interests.

These two features interact upon each other, for good personal relationships can triumph over poor instructions and really good instructions can improve personal relations because they inspire respect for the person giving them. It is, therefore, impossible to distinguish accurately between what might be called a communication exercise and a behavioural game, though the former is more often concerned with the factual content of communication and the latter with the manner and circumstances in which it is made. One way of looking at it is to define behaviour as the part of communication which supplements the spoken or written word. This lets in the things that are pointedly *not* said, the tone of communication, the facial expression, the circumstances, the implication, the comparable things that have been said to other people, and so on. Everybody is aware that one can communicate to a person most dramatically by saying no word and writing no letters to him, but doing so to all the rest of the group.

When people communicate in this way it can be done intentionally or unintentionally, but it always reflects their beliefs, attitudes and feelings. When it is done deliberately it means that to display one's attitude openly by saying what one really thinks and feels would be socially unacceptable or would damage one's cause. Often it is linked to a knowledge that the attitude is unjustified. Therefore, although one's feelings demand some sort of expression, one is restricted to showing them in an ambiguous way so that one cannot be convicted of harbouring them. A typical case is that of the formal leader of a group having to accept that his recommended course of action is less sensible than one put forward by a subordinate. He will feel, very naturally, that his position as leader, and his prestige, is undermined by this development and he is likely to speak and act towards his subordinate in a way that is distinctly ungracious. In doing so he is responding to his own attitudes and beliefs about leadership. These identify it to a greater or lesser extent with unilateral decision-making, which demands that the leader be fairly constantly right. A leader whose plan is clearly inferior to that of one of his subordinates has, from this point of view, failed: he will naturally be upset.

When a person's behaviour is unintentionally annoying to others it implies genuine ignorance on his part: ignorance of the extent to which his attitudes are wrong or of the extent to which they are different from those held by other people. The person who behaves in a mildly offensive way because he dare not speak openly knows very well what he is doing: his behaviour is calculated to give maximum annoyance without causing an open row. The case of a person who is genuinely insensitive is quite different: he simply does not know how his behaviour affects other people and his ignorance is due to the unconscious assumption that all reasonable people possess his own attitudes and beliefs. There is, therefore, a wide field of interpersonal behaviour that has to be understood if real cooperation between different people is not to require an extended period of trial and error. The lessons to be learnt concern:

1   The extent to which values, attitudes and beliefs differ between different people
2   The extent to which they are reflected in one's behaviour
3   The extent to which one reacts to the perceived attitudes of another person rather than to his spoken or written words
4   The extent to which one can misread a person's attitudes by interpreting his behaviour in terms of one's own.

Structured experiences

The simpler behavioural games could really be called experiments or demonstrations. The title 'structured experience' has come into use, suggesting that because a device has been designed in a certain way, certain lessons are likely to emerge. They rely upon provoking behaviour that is entirely natural, but also unsuitable for the purpose in hand. An excellent example is the task that can be given to five people requiring them each to arrange cardboard shapes into a simple square. At the start each person has certain pieces before him. It is necessary for pieces to pass from one player to another, usually with certain rules to govern the transactions, such as that no person may actually ask for a piece. The pieces are so designed that many dispositions of them between the players will allow more than one player to complete a square but only one disposition will allow all the players to do so. The effect of this is likely to be that some player who has assembled a square, and thus feels that he has done his part in fulfilling the group task, must in fact break it up and offer some of the pieces to other players in order that a new disposition may be tried. Typically, a person who has made a square of his own is reluctant to break it up and a skilful analysis will eventually show that his reason was a belief in his own correctness, a lower opinion of his colleagues, and a failure to grasp the fact that his personal success was not identical with the desired achievement of the group. It is very easy to take the attitude, 'I have done my bit; the others are just not quite as intelligent as I am,' and fail to realise that one's own apparent success is in fact preventing the group as a whole from succeeding.

Another well-known game requires a group of students to select one candidate to fill a particular job from a short-list they have been given. Often the students are asked to assume a particular role (marketing manager, personnel manager, etc.) but in every case they are each given a slightly different stock of information about the job requirements, the conditions, and the implications of the various qualifications offered by the candidate. The effect is that if all the available information is pooled and correctly assessed then it can be seen that there is only one candidate who is fully qualified. The usual result is that students assume the information given to them is identical, and waste some ten minutes of exercise time before they realise the truth. Even then they may take insufficient notice of the data available to some of their number who happen, outside the exercise, to be of lesser status. The lesson brought out is that problem-solving knowledge is normally dispersed around a group and must be diligently sought out. Too often, members of the group assume that knowledge is held only by the obvious people and make insufficient effort to find it – showing clearly by the people who are or are not asked for help which of them are considered able to contribute. In real life this is the situation of the investigator who puts erudite questions about a job to the manager and to the chief engineer but never thinks to seek the opinion of the workman who actually carries out the job, day in, day out.

A third example is that in which teams are 'paired' with each other and asked to choose between 'strategies A and B'. There is a scoring mechanism attached stating that if both choose A then each team scores 2 points, if both choose B then each scores 1 point, but if one team chooses B and one chooses A then the first team scores 3 and the second 0. There are several variations on this mechanism, but the rules frequently played are that teams may confer with each other at intervals, but must then write A or B on a piece of paper and exchange it with their 'pair'. The normal result is that they agree that both should play A and then one or both does in fact play B. Round succeeds round with the degree of trust between the two being steadily eroded until each is determined to mislead and cheat the other. At the end the instructor, who has been careful to avoid the suggestion of competition and to use neutral words like 'paired', reveals that all teams are in fact members of the same 'group of companies' and that this internecine conflict has in fact greatly reduced the total score of the group. The lesson brought out is how readily people assume a competitive stance, whether or not it is appropriate.

These are games of extreme simplicity, and they all depend for success on a slight element of dishonesty in the instructor, for they 'invite' a certain form of behaviour which they then condemn as being imperfect. The justification is the vital importance of the lessons and the fact that just telling people frequently proves inadequate.

There is, of course, a potential problem in that the behaviour suggested as emerging in each game is only likely rather than certain. If something different happens, the tutor may find himself at a loss to know what to say. His belief about his own position and responsibility may demand that he offer some authoritative 'summing up', but the lessons he was prepared to underline do not match up with the experience the students have had. This raises again the educational assumption – that the overall purpose of the event is for somebody who *does* know to inform somebody who *does not*. Such a purpose implies a degree of authority and control in the tutor, and this is not enhanced if he is obviously at a loss. There are two solutions. The tutor who wishes to maintain an authoritative position can increase his experience of each game to the point that he can comment helpfully on whatever actually did happen: in the simpler games there are only a limited number of possibilities. Using this approach he may still be in the position of having chosen to use a particular game with the hope of getting a particular result, and getting another one instead which does not suit his purpose so well. This is an inherent risk of the method and the best tactic then is to explain to the students just what happened: that is to say, tell the truth. There will probably be a lively discussion, and the desired point may even get made by the students. There is also the option of going on to a different exercise which offers an extra chance of success. But no tutor should deny the fact that human behaviour is predictable in probabilistic terms only. It is not possible to mount a demonstration in the scientific or mathematical sense that, say, 'pouring the white liquid onto the yellow powder *will* produce a smell like rotting cabbages'. The psychological position of the tutor should be that he is taking a justifiable risk in running this exercise: it has often been successful in promoting valuable learning and is worth preferring to some method that is safer but has less impact. The alternative solution is for the tutor to alter his own position so that he acts as facilitator rather than as teacher – encouraging each student to reveal what the experience meant to him personally and trusting that they will be helpful to each other. His control of the exercise will have been reduced, but there may be a new range of benefits to be gained.

Organisation games

There are other games, and other uses of games, that further alter the role of the 'staff member'. But before considering them it is necessary to look at those games that seek to bridge the gap from the 'structured experience' to the work situation. The structured experience is often abstract in nature, illustrating a principle in an effective and elegant way so that students can understand more about the influences that are active in any cooperative effort. The more elaborate type of exercise is similar in that it shares the same energy source – normal human motivation – but different in that it seeks to set its message within a working context. Such games exist, and work successfully, because they exploit certain aspects of behaviour that are in no way new but have not previously been used in this way. One of these – man's deep-seated need to feel secure – is already apparent in the three simple games mentioned. In the broken shapes game it explains the concern of the player who feels that he has not yet got his bit done and the seeming complacency of the one who feels that he has. In the information-sharing game it explains the annoyance of the group when they find that they do not have common data after all – they had made the comfortable assumption that the situation was just like any other one involving the handing out of a set of papers. In the A and B game it explains the common decision to double-cross 'them' before 'they' double-cross 'us' – and therefore have the security of being one jump ahead.

Mental security is a state that most people seek to achieve and are reluctant to abandon. It underlies the numerous cases where people and organisations have refused to change their actions until it was almost too late to do so; and the change, when attempted, has proved extremely painful. The circumstances that show the need for change are ignored or misinterpreted for psychological reasons: people just do not like their implications. Other characteristics can also be employed to make simulations work. One is the need for an individual to maintain a respectable self-image: to feel that he has contributed positively to whatever group he has been working with, has discharged some responsibility well or has sustained a role in the appropriate manner. Every contributor to an enterprise has several motives, including the desire to help in achieving corporate goals and the desire to maintain or improve his own status. The game creator can use this by writing a scenario that has biased role content. That is to say, one or two individuals have a lot to contribute and a greater number have each a small, but possibly vital amount. It is likely that the two main characters will be so excited by their position that they will fail to consider the ego needs of their colleagues. The latter will be demotivated by such behaviour and become careless with regard to the limited contribution they are able to make. The group as a whole will be ineffective and the tutor will probably be able to prove the point that he intended.

Related to the need for a good self-image is the characteristic habit of stereo-typing. This means our tendency to hold firm ideas about how the incumbent of a certain role ought to behave. The logic behind this is very simple: we want to look good, but our idea of what constitutes looking good has to originate somewhere. In fact it originates in the climate that has surrounded us in the past: behaviour that was generally approved becomes identified in our minds as the 'right' behaviour for a friend or a salesman or a clergyman or a policeman or any other person in a clearly identified role. Given some understanding of the stereo-types held by his students, a game writer can evoke certain forms of behaviour by casting people into those roles for which they will see these forms as 'natural'. It is possible, for instance, to set up groups of workers, supervisors and managers and to distribute among them the details of some task the workers are to carry out, plus the necessary materials. All parties are told some of the information they need, and they know of the existence of the other parties, but they are not told that the information they appear to be missing is in fact known to another group. The situation is such that if the parties talked freely and openly to each other, seeking to transcend the boundaries of rank, they would discover what they needed to know and all would be well. Given knowledge of the organisation in which the exercise is to be used it can be predicted whether this will or will not happen. In a strongly hierarchical organisation the top management will probably issue instructions at an early stage, and reveal by the unsatisfactory nature of such instructions that they do not properly understand the situation of the other groups. They do this not from malice but because their concept of the behaviour appropriate to a top manager is inextricably linked to the exercise of authority and the giving of orders. It simply does not occur to them, when cast in the role of top management, to ask rather than tell. The behaviour provoked from the other groups will be resentful and uncooperative: they will themselves speedily adopt the stereo-typed behaviour that they associate with aggrieved supervisors and unwilling workers. In an organisation with a different culture there will be a different result.

In this area commercial and industrial training has been influenced by the social scientists, the social services and the caring professions generally. These have long been aware that by placing people in clearly defined roles and establishing powers and restrictions appropriate to those roles you can provoke the behaviour characteristic of reality. For example, the exercise known as BAFA BAFA establishes two groups that have well-defined cultures within which 'transactions' are simulated by an exchange of cards, each having a numerical value. One culture is competitive and one is friendly. When players are familiar with their own set of rules and observances, visitors move from one culture to the other and have the experience of entering a strange environment in which they do not know how to behave. The experience can demonstrate, amongst other things, the situation encountered by immigrants and minority groups. Such games have an obvious relevance to relations between managerial staff and the shop floor and between different cultural groups of workers in the same factory.

In an industrial setting such games often acquire an objective measure of success or failure. This is seldom as rigid as in a model-based game, but even a single group tackling a non-competitive task will want to know 'How well did we do in comparison with others?' It can mean that an action phase gets added on to the end of an understand-each-other type of game, the industrial attitude being that sympathy and comprehension are not ends in themselves. If they are to merit serious attention it must be shown that the more they exist between individuals and groups the better those individuals and groups can do a job of work. The action phase may well involve some physical task of construction, assembly or drafting, or the provision of some piece of data that is clearly right or wrong: anything that will provide objective, measurable evidence of how well a group has been able to work. In some cases there seems little difference from the form described elsewhere as a practical simulation. In both there is a period of planning and a period of action and an observable result. One distinction in fact relates to purpose: in the Practical Simulation there is a desire to model realistic features of the organisation. In the organisation game this is less important and the work goes not into achieving outward reality but into creating an interpersonal atmosphere in which certain things are likely to happen.

The hope is that in-game behaviour will result from the individual reading into his instructions, or into the situation, concepts that really exist in his own mind only. The more detailed and realistic the structure of the game, the more excuse a person has for believing that the behaviour he exhibited was explicitly prescribed for him and was not, therefore, personal.

An illustration of the different approach can be found in those games which set up a hierarchy, where it is common to have restrictions on the movement of the different groups. The workers may not leave their work place, except to send one representative to see their supervisor or the top manager. The supervisors may move around amongst the workers but must always leave one of their number in the office. The top managers are only allowed a limited number of visits to the work place. The intention is to ensure a degree of separation between the parties, leading to ignorance about each other and the suspicious mistrust and enmity that naturally follow from such ignorance. The person setting up an organisation game has to concern himself with such matters because they increase the probability of the behaviour he wants to study. He is not able, and does not want, to simulate all the circumstances that in real life account for these divisions, so he just prescribes a rule. This is normally accepted because people know quite well that this is the practical effect manifest in reality. They know the rule to be a legitimate short cut. In a practical simulation the objective is to minimise the artificial nature of the task and if there was a desire to reduce communication it would be done by increasing the work load so that the parties were reluctant to give time to it – which is one of the excuses commonly given anyway for failing to communicate properly!

Student ownership of the game situation

The exercises just described all imply a desire in the tutor to make some point through the medium of the experience. He may even intervene to make it 'go well' from his point of view. There is much less tutor control when the emphasis is intended to be on the study by the players of their own behaviour. This goes a step beyond the examination of general human characteristics and recognises that in matters of detail every person and every group is different. The members of a group will now be seeking to examine how they, as a particular combination, function. Each one is also looking for feedback about the effect that his behaviour has on others. Behaviour is different in different situations, and the principal duty of the tutor may be to create situations to order by choosing exercises which he knows are likely to produce them. The definition of what the group wants will probably not be precise, but experience shows a frequent requirement for situations (inter alia) that:

1   Cause success or failure to depend upon total understanding of the task by all group members, and/or:
2   Demand prompt and complete sharing of information, that information being derived from several different people, and/or:
3   Require some of the group to be active while others (though remaining members of the group) are rather bored, and/or:
4   Will evoke contributions based upon personal values, so that these can be brought into the open and discussed in depth.

It may well be that some of the material used is identical with that which the tutor might choose when offering knowledge from his position as a teacher. What has happened is a change of emphasis, the initiative now coming from the students who wish to explore a particular subject area and are presumably committed to making the best possible use of the opportunity. Since the tutor is no longer seeking to make predetermined points of his own, he is not prohibited from taking part in the experience himself. This, of course, will depend on the attitude of students towards him and their own normal relationship to each other. It might be, for instance, that they are the management team of a company seeking to study their own interrelationships. To include an outsider as an integral part of an activity would distort the relationships and would therefore be undesirable.

Exploratory games

Discussing one's personal behaviour within a group involves some degree of self-revelation. There are bound to be statements about one's personal feelings, and questions and answers that review why one behaves in a particular way or reacts to the behaviour of others in a particular way. This is currently seen as a good development, reflecting the belief that if people are to work together effectively on a common task they will do so better if they have a full understanding of each other: not the superficial one that has often been seen as adequate in the past. The sort of discussion required does not happen automatically, one reason being comparative ignorance about the extent and the depth of human differences. The use of a common language, and our collective ability to keep society operational without too many crises, tend to obscure the fact that individual viewpoints differ enormously and that two people rarely see the same situation in quite the same light. So there can be a reluctance to look at personalities and attitudes and values, on the basis that 'there is nothing here to study'. Exploratory games can be helpful, for they offer a means of unveiling some of the mental concepts that influence a person's actions – sometimes without his being fully aware of it. An example is the exercise MANCO (MANagement COncepts). It consists of fourteen concept cards with words like 'authority' and 'delegation'. It is for two players, who are dealt four concept cards each and replace them from the undealt stock as they are used. They also have a stock of cards printed with direction arrows. The dealer having led with a concept card, his opponent must place an arrow going to or from it, hoping that in his next turn he will be able to add to the other end of that arrow (or the end of another one) a concept card of his own. The idea is a little like dominoes, but the object is to build up on the table an acceptable conceptual map of the management task. It causes people to reveal the views they hold about the management task and demonstrates that their views are not necessarily the same as those of others.

A different approach involves the use of two separate professional groups (e.g. bank managers and dentists). Each group has to produce three lists, showing:

1   What we think about ourselves
2   What we think about them
3   What we think that they think about us

Comparison of the lists brings to light a variety of preconceived ideas, and the presentation of each contrary view sparks off a useful debate.

Some exercises seek to encourage the disclosure of beliefs and values in a very direct and forceful way, such as by offering students a list of personal questions, some of them highly embarrassing. The exercise splits the group into pairs, and the rules are such that a person is allowed to ask his partner any question on the list to which he would himself be prepared to give an answer, if asked.

Possibly a more enjoyable way of encouraging self-revelation is through the adult role-playing games described earlier. Because these are fantasy, the players are able to make risk-free choices that may reflect what one part of them would really like to do if it were not over-ruled by another part. Such games can reveal individuals to their colleagues in a different light from the normal one, thus making some of their attitudes more understandable and, quite often, increasing the respect and liking felt for them. They can break up the rather limited picture that one forms about a colleague from seeing him only in the one environment, and from seeing him behave in that environment only in a way that long experience of it has led him to perceive as 'safe' and 'prudent'. If an explanation is needed as to why greater knowledge of one's colleagues is valuable, this can be found in the fact that it usually increases respect and liking rather than the reverse. There is much in human experience that is common to all, and knowing what a person thinks and feels about a subject – and what has caused him to think and feel that way – tends to emphasise human similarities. A person is likely to reflect 'If I had had the same experiences as he has had, then it is quite likely I would react in a very similar way'. The other party thus becomes a more reasonable and understandable person. This broadens the subject areas about which the two parties are prepared to converse. There is no point in the work environment being complicated by personal disagreements, so the normal human tactic is to discuss only 'safe' subjects or 'necessary' subjects, steering clear of anything that may create discord. When a colleague is perceived as sensible and reasonable it follows that discussion at a deeper level, even if there is no agreement, will not create that discord and may therefore be attempted. It becomes possible to express opinions about what one is doing, and ask questions and make suggestions without the fear of a sharp answer or of just being ignored. An example of the disadvantages of not knowing one's colleagues might be the continuation by three men of a routine practice that has become obsolete and useless: all three believe that it should be dropped, but all three also believe that it is important to the other two. They are not accustomed to talking to each other except in an official way. They do not have any special sympathy for each other, but they do not want discord. So none of them raises the matter and the obsolete practice continues.

Organisational simulation

This more weighty title describes material sufficiently detailed and specific to be used for the examination of a particular organisation or system. It is often custom built, for existing material inevitably has a structure, and that structure will incorporate objectives and conditions and rules that do not fit the case. So an organisation may find that before such a game can be played it has to be created. The construction process is a most interesting one, for while there is doubtless an 'official' description of 'what this organisation is like and how it works' such descriptions can be a poor reflection of what actually happens on the ground. And if one is going to use a model to generate material for examination, the model must relate to what really does happen and not to what is supposed to happen. Otherwise it will be recognised as futile by the people asked to play it. So whoever creates the model will have to gather numerous opinions about the reality, and remember as he does so that each member of the organisation has his own perception of the truth depending on his status, his role in the organisation and his own personal convictions. The point can be illustrated by considering the idea of success. The managing director might say that success is measured by the production of a high rate of return on the capital employed, and that if a simulation is to be made then the result of any 'run' must be judged by that criterion. The marketing department might argue 'It is impossible to say that we are doing well unless we have a reasonably broad customer base'. The trade unions might claim 'If financial success was the only goal, and other benefits were sacrificed for it, then you might well find you had no labour force and everything else fell apart'. These are all quite reasonable statements, and they reflect the fact that different parts of an organisation are in fact pursuing different goals, relying upon people at board level to reconcile conflicts of interest in such a way that the ever-changing demands of the environment are met. So a simulation could not just give a blanket instruction to the players 'The objective is to make money'. There would have to be objectives set for each part of the organisation, and a power structure established so that decisions could be made, and a dynamic environment created so that the needs of the moment were changing. In this way the interest groups within the organisation would have greater or lesser influence as their skills appeared more or less relevant to the immediate problems.

Building such a simulation can be specially difficult when it comes to the subject of communication. All organisations have prescribed systems to ensure that information gets to the right people through the right channels, but at times this serves only to regularise deals that have already been put through on a personal and unofficial basis. 'Who speaks to whom' is not in fact a thing that can easily be regulated, and frequently the grape-vine is faster and more accurate than the official channels. To build a simulation that reflects only the formality of an organisation is to build a bad one, but the reality is hard to uncover because there are many different perceptions of it and people are not necessarily going to tell the truth. When asked by a stranger how one handles a certain matter, one does not know what use is going to be made of the answer and it is probably wisest to describe what one is supposed to do even if in fact one never does it. Therefore, the construction of this sort of game or simulation is best done by an experienced consultant. He can have interviews with organisation members separately, in non-threatening conditions, and gradually build up his picture of how they see their own roles and the roles of others. Then he can produce his own model of how the organisation works in order to get their comments and criticisms. The research can also be done through more general meetings, but it is not an approach that will succeed unless the organisation has a tradition of honesty and openness extending across boundaries of rank and status.

The benefits of this sort of game commence when the interviews first start, because members have commonly not thought about the subject at all. The experience of analysing their own role and their own actions can by itself give them a better understanding of how they fit in. Then, when a model is produced and run through, there will be many cases where unrealities are perceived. Members will find themselves saying 'it is not quite like that'. This happens because of the inherent difficulty of describing formally something that is going on around one almost below the level of consciousness. There is so much which one takes for granted and does not think to include in the first attempt at explanation. So the description given earlier will be found to be inaccurate. There will also be conflicts between descriptions, and a reconciliation must be made. In the course of this, members will further refine their understanding of their positions, and learn more about their colleagues and the organisa-tion. When an agreed model exists there follows the stage of experi-ment. The normal mode of operation can be tried out under various sets of conditions, and new modes of operating can be attempted to see what happens.

Similar games, different uses

A simulation built up to model an organisation in this way could become very complex. In real life a person has arguments and data to support the case that he is promoting, and it would be quite reasonable for that facility to be imported. There might be groups drawing facts from different sources, analysing them by different computer programs, emphasising and ignoring different points. In the end, the overall appearance might be similar to a group playing one of the traditional model-based management games – for these also are used to study behaviour. They are complex enough to allow for role differentiation, they permit several different opinions to be legitimately held, and, because they are interesting and demanding, they generate full commitment from the players. It is quite common for the more complex games to be run not for their 'knowledge' value but just for the opportunity to observe the behaviour of the players and to offer comments upon it. Students can be assigned as observers (taking no direct part in the game themselves) or the entire action can be videorecorded for later review. So, starting from different points and with different objectives, games and simulations can emerge that have much in common with each other. This is an understandable result, for the truth is that in the real world it is not possible to separate the knowledge element and the personal element. So the simulator starting from the knowledge end of the spectrum reaches a point where he knows that his work is inadequate without the inclusion of personality and behaviour. The simulator starting from the behavioural end is forced to accept that behaviour is heavily influenced by knowledge – even the simpler exercises illustrate basic points such as the fact that positive behaviour is greatly influenced by feelings of confidence or of doubt. So he finds himself building in a knowledge element.

Getting good value from a behavioural game

Getting maximum value from a behavioural game depends heavily on the skill of the tutor, particularly on his ability to stimulate a positive attitude in the players. The lessons each individual can learn are apt to be highly personal and can also be unwelcome, for they can suggest that his current way of behaving could be improved. He, therefore, has the opportunity to deny the validity of any suggestions made to him (for no third party can possibly know *why* he behaved in a certain way or what he meant by it) and he may very well have a psychological desire to deny it, too. Lessons that are unpleasant do very often get acknowledged over a long period of time, but if the tutor wants any short term acceptance of the value of the exercise his only hope is to create a climate in which the players positively want to get new insights. He must also face the fact that the game can develop in various different ways and that there can conceivably be an outcome that he has never encountered before. There is no substitute for extensive experience of this type of work, but a few general comments can helpfully be made.

1   Students need to be familiar with the concept of 'perception'. That is to say, they must be aware how the mind interprets data seen or heard by relating it to previous experience, which naturally differs between individuals. It is therefore possible for two observers to see and hear the same thing and to come to different conclusions about it – not because either is incompetent or careless or dishonest but just because they have a different life experience. If it is clearly understood that, in discussing a group member's behaviour, another member (or the tutor himself) is offering only his own perception and not trying to make a factual statement, much of the defensiveness common to such situations will be avoided.

2   Observations about behaviour are more helpful and less likely to arouse resentment if they are specific. References to particular words or actions leave the character and motives of the person commented upon inviolate. Even if the comment is unfavourable, he need only conclude that he made an unfortunate choice of outward behaviour. Generalised comments that make assumptions about his motives and attitudes are far more damaging and far more difficult to absorb without anger.

3   The human mind is immensely sophisticated, picking up and interpreting (or misinterpreting) the most rapid signals. This can at times take place below the level of consciousness so that two people go away from an encounter with an unfavourable impression of each other but without really knowing why. It can be just a single word. Individual A describes some action of Individual B and chooses, without any critical intention, a word that carries, in the mind of B, a critical overtone. It is not actually an attacking word, just one that B would not normally expect to hear used about his actions by a friend. His next response to B is therefore marginally less friendly than it would otherwise have been. Individual A notices the change, can see no good reason for it, and concludes that B is moving psychologically away from him. His next response is therefore itself a bit less friendly and the relationship goes slowly sour. Nor is this subtlety of language a danger only in personal relationships. It can affect what happens in a cooperative effort because of purely conceptual misunderstandings. An illustration of this can be drawn from one well known structured experience in which players are asked to 'make' words from a number of letters given to them. Each

letter is written on a separate piece of cardboard but they are enclosed in an envelope that may not be opened till after a theoretical plan of action has been made. It is quite common for a group to be unconsciously confused over the meaning of 'make', which can be interpreted as simply writing down words or as placing the pieces of cardboard in position on the table so as *physically* to make each word. The people holding each view are not aware that those with the other view have in fact got a different concept in their minds. Each is so convinced that his view is natural and right that the alternative concept does not enter his thinking. The group is then using very similar vocabulary but is discussing two different ideas and the words somehow do not mean anything. This is an aspect of communication that a tutor should be aware of – for the most common assumption of all within organisations is that 'we all know what we are talking about'. Quite often we all 'know' differently!

4   There is a wealth of material now available on observing, describing and classifying behaviour, including at least three formalised systems that give names to particular forms of behaviour and spell out in detail what is meant by them. It is a valuable approach, because students who are working in this area for the first time do not naturally have a language with which to handle it. The tutor should be familiar with some of these systems and should ensure that his students are adequately equipped with the jargon of the behavioural world.

5   There is also much to be gained from what are often called 'instruments', meaning lists of questions that students are asked to complete after an exercise in order to help them reflect upon the event, the interaction of group members and their own feelings. One typical questionnaire is shown in Figure 6:1. If all group members complete one and the results are then collated, the spread of answers can be seen and interesting patterns shown up. It is often best if these are completed anonymously, so that individuals retain the right to speak up in any discussion or maintain their own privacy.

A particular comment is needed with regard to the use of the word 'interactive' in behavioural games. It may still mean, as it does with model-based games, that a decision taken by one group affects the results achieved by another group – but it may also mean personal interaction between individuals. The difference is very apparent when the word is used in the Directory section.

1 Did the group maintain high standards of work or was it easily satisfied?

1_____2_____3_____4_____5_____6_____7

2 To what extent did group members really listen to each other?

1_____2_____3_____4_____5_____6_____7

3 Did attempts to influence the group come mainly from one, or a few people (score towards the LH end of the scale) or did they come from all quarters (score towards the RH end of the scale)?

1_____2_____3_____4_____5_____6_____7

4 Was I able to contribute to the group without having to fight for noise space?

1_____2_____3_____4_____5_____6_____7

5 Was disagreement within the group more often expressed and resolved (score towards the RH end of the scale) or was the tendency to sweep it quietly under the carpet (score towards the LH end of the scale)?

1_____2_____3_____4_____5_____6_____7

6 To what extent was work with this group enjoyable?

1_____2_____3_____4_____5_____6_____7

7 To what extent did you feel it was proper to express your feelings in this group?

1_____2_____3_____4_____5_____6_____7

8 To what extent did the group members exhibit concern for the group as an entity rather than concern for themselves as individuals?

1   2   3   4   5   6   7

9 Did you feel that the group was working as a team and trusted one another?

1   2   3   4   5   6   7

Figure 6:1   A typical questionnaire

7

Practical simulations

A practical simulation involves some task whose outcome can be judged by obvious criteria and which demands the organisation of a group of people in a manner characteristic of business. It is so planned that success cannot be reached without the application of business knowledge nor without great skill in personal relationships. Therefore it tests both the mental and the behavioural abilities of those who play. The best way to examine it is to consider one typical exercise and trace the problems that it raises for the players. The exercise is one in which all teams are asked to assume the role of the management of a factory and to plan the production of a number of articles. After a considerable period of preparation each team has a chance to try out its ideas, using one of the others as a labour force to manufacture its goods. There is thus a planning period in which the teams work in parallel, and a succession of activity periods in which one team works under another's direction.

Clearly, the type of product to be manufactured has to be defined beforehand, for materials and tools have to be available in adequate quantities. A good basic material is the type of plastic foam sold in all do-it-yourself shops and widely used as padding and as insulation. This can be bought in large sheets and in several different thicknesses. It can be cut, with scissors or a model-maker's knife, and it can be stuck together with glue. Altogether it is an excellent material for the manufacture of novelties such as are sold to children at Christmas, and a competent team of players is well able to make articles that could later be sold at bazaars, jumble sales, village fêtes, etc.

Product planning, costing and pricing

The first action is for team members to consider what should be made. Discussions naturally centre on the cost of manufacture and the selling price that can be achieved. This leads at once into a serious consideration of business problems, for the instructor will have decreed that each thickness of material costs so much a sheet, each item of equipment costs so much to buy, or hire, that labour costs so much an hour and that factory overheads are running at such and such a rate. It will, therefore, be necessary to examine each suggested product and see what costs it would mean in terms of material, how much labour it would need, and how much machine time. Effectively a standard cost for the product has to be worked out and if this is to be done accurately it needs some quite sophisticated thinking. What, for instance, is to be done with waste material? Can it be resold? If not, is the design of the product such as to make the best use of material? What production method is to be used? Will it be more economical to cut it with scissors or with a model-maker's knife? Which method will be quicker? Which will be the most accurate? Exactly how much time is each likely to take in production conditions? If the design calls for some particular shape, should this be achieved by cutting the product from a single piece or by cutting two or more pieces separately and sticking them together? These considerations will give players some idea of the costs involved, and almost simultaneously they will be thinking of the price to be asked.

The umpire must act as a prospective purchaser, being extremely vague in his replies when approached with a mere idea, a bit more specific when shown a drawing and pretty definite when offered a prototype. It is up to the team to ask for a particular price, and there is often a conflict between two schools of thought. The more traditional people will use costs as a basis of calculation and ask a price that will give them a reasonable margin on what they expect to pay out. Others will base their first price on what they believe the market will bear, and here some genuine marketing skill comes in. A good team will have elaborate ideas about the benefits their product might bring to the purchaser. A spider can be bounced up and down on a string, or hung from the ceiling of one's bedroom, or used to frighten adults: a toy fort can be used for playing soldiers: a bear or elephant can be taken to bed: a complete set of farm animals can be sold as a zoo – possibly at a grossly inflated price.

There is great scope for producing an article that will, by the sheer imagination of its design, command a price wildly in excess of its intrinsic value. The reactions of the instructor will, of course, be subjective, but if he is normal they will be similar to the reactions of a reasonable cross-section of parents.

When agreeing to the price of a product, the instructor must specify clearly that the price is dependent on a particular number of items, for one purpose of the exercise is to determine whether the team can arrange efficient manufacture in factory conditions. Too often the players are absorbed in the problems of the present, and when assessing the costs of a design they assume both that it is capable of mass production and that the labour force they are going to employ will make it. This may prove untrue.

It is also open to the instructor to specify the quality level that he will accept. Prototypes are often put forward with little thought on this matter, yet it is up to the supplier to make sure that there is agreement between him and his customer on the exact terms of the order. If this is not mentioned, then the instructor has the opportunity, when the goods are finally presented, to reject them as being 'not the same as the product originally offered'.

Setting up the factory

When a team has determined on one or more products, and won an order for them, they need to purchase both material and equipment. Here an instructor may, if he wishes, ask them with what currency they intend to pay for it. This will certainly be a shock, for it will not yet have struck them that this is a total simulation and no factory is permitted to start operations without first raising money. Typically a team meeting with this response will retire into conference to estimate the amount they require. Then, confronting the instructor in his role as bank manager, they can be questioned about the rate of return they feel able to offer. In this way the constraints imposed upon business by the need for operating capital become apparent. Profit no longer appears as something theoretical that one may or may not make, but something that is essential if one is to survive. Players come to see that money lost in trading means more money needed if one is to keep going, yet money lost once makes new money more difficult to obtain because of reduced confidence in the borrower.

The game will already, therefore, have provoked a consideration of investment, design, costing and marketing. Now it enters the area of human organisation, because a team has to ensure that its workers will produce the goods required in the time and to the standard expected. Many teams discover at this point that they have created for themselves one almost insoluble problem, for they have made unilateral assumptions about cost: that is to say, they have not consulted their labour force. This dilemma is intensely realistic, for negotiations have to start from some basis and to have worker representation at the first, conceptual stage would slow things down dramatically. Yet the workforce assigned to a team in an exercise is perfectly at liberty to reject the rates offered and stand out for a wage that will make nonsense of the agreed price. This part of the exercise is particularly revealing to the more traditionally minded student who relies on the adage 'management has the right to manage' for he very soon finds that management today is a matter of winning the consent of those managed, not of just issuing orders.

There is a need to win cooperation by interpersonal skills and most of the problems arising can in fact be dealt with, for people do not shed their own personalities when they enter an exercise and a good argument put forward by a pleasant manager in an acceptable way will have the same result in a game as on the shopfloor. In a similar way, an argument put forward in an abrupt, aggressive manner with no consideration for the other person's feelings will get both of them locked into a win/lose situation and frequently ends in a strike.

Running the factory

If a management team is successful in reaching a broad agreement with its workforce about how much money is to be paid for how much output, there are still details to be considered like the method of organisation, the method of manufacture and the standard that is acceptable. The most frequent cause of trouble is again an assumption that is made almost instinctively by the management: this time that money is the only really important thing and that once this has been agreed the workforce will be happy. It may turn out that the management has planned a traditional sort of conveyor-belt factory in which one man marks out the pieces of foam, another one cuts them and a third sticks different pieces together. Whether this classic production technique proves efficient will depend on how accurately the management have done their planning. It will be affected by such things as whether the number of workers and the work to be done are evenly balanced between the sections, whether there are any bottlenecks or any shortages, and whether time is lost in movement of goods from one location to another. Even if all this is perfect, there may well be failure due to the unwillingness of the workers to accept the degree of specialisation, and the boredom that goes with it. A forward-looking management team may well prefer to have some more rewarding system whereby a group of workers has total responsibility for a product and can switch jobs between themselves as they wish. Another alternative would be a craft approach in which each worker sees one product through from beginning to end. This rather extreme method would soon show up the need for an excessive quantity of equipment so that each worker had it available at the moment he needed it. Quite obviously this would be expensive, but players would then be considering the very basic question of the relative costs of the different factors in the production process. If ten machines and 20 men produce more goods for the same amount of money than five machines and 20 men – because in the latter case the men are on strike half of the time – there is no point in worrying because the ten machines are not always in use. It is a simple matter of which alternative is most damaging, idle machines or idle men. The organisation problem is one quite often overlooked in this exercise, and a management team may find its workforce throwing down its tools with some such remark as, 'This is not work for human beings. What about some job enrichment?'

Training is another area in which the management team can fall down. When one has the concept of a product fully developed in one's own mind it becomes difficult to tell another person clearly what he is required to do, and why. This is another area in which one tends to make assumptions about people based on the function currently being asked of them. In fact, this has been a characteristic of industry since the industrial revolution. It does not really want to employ the whole man: it only wants to employ that part of him which enables him to carry out a specific function quickly and accurately. The rest of him is often an embarrassment. However, this cannot be done: asked to use a pair of scissors to cut a certain shape out of plastic foam in a certain way, a human being will sooner or later start doing it in a slightly different way, either in an honest attempt to do a better job or else simply to avoid boredom. As he goes ahead with his work the human part of him comes to dominate the automaton part of him and he explores his environment in a manner that is not expected. In a way he is just as much to blame as the manager, for he is making assumptions of his own: he is assuming that there is no good reason why he is required to do something in one particular way and one only. He is assuming that the manager has not done his own very thorough planning of the work. When players encounter this sort of reaction from their labour force they are only seeing in microcosm a persistent and almost universal characteristic of industrial organisation. There is not a great deal that can be done to avoid it, for the reason underlying it is two different attitudes to the same problem. The worker, when first accepting a job, is not interested in the details of it except in so far as they answer his current problem: Will I be able to do it to the required standard? Until that question is answered, he is not really interested in all the logic and planning behind it. Therefore, the manager, be he never so eager to impart full understanding, is wasting his time if he seeks to do so at the wrong moment. Later on, when the workman is assured of his own competence and is beginning to take an intelligent interest, the manager has forgotten him. So there is no short answer to this problem of fully communicating the 'how' and 'why' of a manual job to the person engaged to do it. Nevertheless it helps to be aware of the misunderstandings that are going to arise.

Related to this problem is the one of suggestions. From time to time a member of the workforce is going to come up with a really good idea about the manner in which the work should be done: an idea that has so far escaped the minds of management. In a practical simulation, what will the management do? Frequently there is an adverse reaction, mainly due to the preoccupation of management with a range of other problems and a slight resentment at being offered advice from an unsuspected quarter.

The quality problem

In this factory, as in many real ones, there will be a conflict between the need to get production at a reasonable cost yet without sacrificing quality. Theoretically the time allowed to a worker for performing his particular operation is sufficient for him to do it carefully and accurately. In fact this is rarely achieved because the initial timings made by the management make insufficient allowance for contingencies and for production-line conditions. There is certain to be a percentage of substandard goods made. It is doubtful whether the management team will notice the low quality, or if they do, whether they will take any action before offering the goods to the instructor. If they have sufficient foresight to realise that there is going to be a problem, and come along with a sample of the 'production model', then it is wise for the instructor to be comparatively lenient and lay down acceptance criteria that are achievable without too much distress. If, on the other hand, they fail to notice the difficulty and then try to pass off on him a large quantity of shoddy goods, it is better for him to reject them out of hand and observe the chaos within the team that results. The difficulties are an accurate reflection of what really happens, because the achievement of quality always involves potential conflict between the person who does the work and the person who inspects it. The latter has to endure considerable pressure. There is also the problem of the point of manufacture at which a thing is to be inspected. If, after operation A, it has some minor fault, is it worth allowing it to continue down the line in the belief that good work at operation B will put right the defect? Is it, on the other hand, better to scrap it straight away rather than take the risk of still having to scrap it later on when operations B, C, and D have been carried out and will represent additional waste? Of course, bad workmanship is not the only cause of an unsatisfactory product: poor-quality material and faulty tools can have the same effect. The instructor may, if he wishes, put a certain amount of substandard material in with the stuff that he issues, or include blunt or loose scissors among the available plant. Quite likely the management will not notice the danger and will, when their goods are rejected, instinctively blame the workers.

It may be argued that the instructor is in this case asking far too much of the trainees. In the circumstances of the exercise, they can hardly be expected to foresee all the possible dangers. This is true, but it is also true of real life and it is towards real life that training is directed. The experience of being caught out in a simulated situation makes people aware that the danger exists and therefore a bit more likely to guard against it at work. Connected to the problem of quality is the problem of achieving the correct batch size. If it has been agreed that the factory shall produce, say, 50 rabbits in pink foam one does not want to produce 55 or 45. How much allowance is to be made for scrap and how is the management to know just how much has actually been made? Supposing that sufficient material was issued to make 55, which allowed for an estimated five to be scrapped, how is management informed that after operation B seven have already been ruined? And when they do know, what action will they take?

This is one illustration of the need for an information system in a factory: some procedure that will reliably inform the management about what has happened, and do so just as soon as possible. An obvious case in point is the extension of the time needed to complete an operation. If management only learns after the goods have been completed that they did in fact take half as long again to make as was expected (and therefore should have been priced differently) this will be too late to save them from a similar mistake on the next contract: the times will have already been estimated and a price quoted. When something deviates from the plan, when there is any sort of variance, management need to know as soon as possible.

Supervision

When the factory is running, most teams feel it necessary to have a foreman. He finds himself in the traditional situation of facing demands from the management that seem grossly excessive, and at the same time having to cope with the problems raised by his men. It becomes obvious very soon how much supporting effort is needed to keep a factory running smoothly and how closely interrelated the various parts are. If, for instance, the person doing operation A encounters a problem, this will mean that the workers on operations B and C run out of work to do and are left idle. Apparent chaos on the shopfloor leads the management team to intervene personally, which gives offence to the foreman. It illustrates the need for real understanding and respect between the various parties.

8

Choosing a game for an objective

To choose one thing rather than another implies a purpose – that there is an objective for which the thing chosen is to be used, and that competing items will be judged by the apparent likelihood of their achieving it. What sort of objectives might influence the choice of a management game?

The need which most commonly sparks an interest in management games is a need for variety. The existing training material is found to be sensible and useful but a little uninspiring and not permitting very much student involvement. So the person responsible sets out to find something that is active and enjoyable but yet obviously justifiable within the programme he is supposed to run. No management game is going to achieve all possible objectives, so the vital ones must be identified and the less important ones ignored. If the need is to experiment in search of variety, then there is no harm in saying so: it then becomes possible to ask 'Are there any other conditions that must be satisfied?' The answer to that one is always in the affirmative, because the person making an experiment is taking a risk and will want to minimise the dangers so far as possible. The danger in general terms is that his experiment will not 'go well' from the viewpoint of the students: that it will be judged a failure. What normally causes that sort of reaction? Strong possibilities are a feeling that the material is not relevant, not comprehensible, or poorly administered. So the tutor making an experiment is going to start by having regard to the stated subject matter of his course. He will want a game that is manifestly 'about our sort of work'. His next concern will be with the level of difficulty that it represents – for it would be dangerous to have something that the students cannot cope with, and just as bad to have something that they saw as beneath them. Then he wants something that he will himself be able to understand fully, so that he can run it competently and make changes if necessary. This personal understanding is a most important point, and suggests that it is better on the whole to err on the side of too simple a game rather than one that is too complex: the man who is lost can take no sensible remedial action, while the man who is on top of the material often can. So the best advice to the experimenter, is go for relevant subject matter, and go for the simplest game that has a reasonable chance of success. (It is also true that students who have found something a bit too easy will delight in suggesting complications with which to confound those who come after them.)

It is frequently this need to experiment that creates an interest in games, and the people who become interested are usually those who have an educational or training role. So what more specific objectives are there in that field that they might wish to pursue? A possible list is:

1 *To demonstrate,* meaning to create a situation in which students watch something happen, or cause something to happen, and thus gain a deeper understanding than they would by just being told. It is a process similar to teaching and makes the assumption that there is something that the students 'don't know' or 'don't sufficiently appreciate'.

2 *To distribute,* meaning to promote an exchange of knowledge within the student group so that things known to one may become common to all. The underlying assumption is that most of the desired knowledge is possessed not only by the tutor but by somebody else as well – possibly by several.

3 *To examine,* meaning to examine the behaviour of students within the exercise so that it can be related to knowledge about human behaviour in general.

4 *To stimulate thought,* meaning to use a game as an intellectual exercise in the hope of increasing the reasoning ability of students.

5 *To assess* some of the skills and abilities of the students.

6 *To practise skills:* either those related to facts, figures and business relationships or those related to personal behaviour.

In addition to the above, there are specific objectives which would probably not originate from a training specialist but more probably from a chief executive or some other senior official:

7 *To preview,* meaning to indicate an expected sequence of events.

8 *To build a team,* meaning to increase the cooperative effectiveness of a group.

Other classifications are doubtless possible, but the essential point is that any clear statement of objectives will give clues to the sort of game or exercise needed.

To demonstrate

If the intention is to demonstrate, then the point to be made must be made clearly. It is no good having open-ended material which leaves the answer still very much a matter of opinion. The game has got to be won or lost by getting the central feature right or wrong.

Demonstrations to promote business knowledge

One way in which a lesson can be presented is through the relationship existing between the decision variables and the results. If, for instance, players are asked to decide on the price to be charged for a product, the amount of advertising to be spent on promoting it, and the extent of credit to be allowed to customers, and are given back as a result the number of units of this product sold, then it is a clear indication that the writer of the game believes these three things each have some degree of influence on sales volume. As players explore the game they come to form an estimate of the relative importance that the writer has attached to them. Presuming the writer to have some reasonable degree of business knowledge, there is an obvious lesson to the effect that in some situations these values are realistic. A further lesson can be built into the way in which each variable behaves. Supposing the effect of a lower price is, through most of the price range, set to produce an increase in sales (the other variables being untouched), it is possible to build in a reverse effect once a certain level is reached. This will mean that if the price asked becomes too low, the sales will not go up as a result but will instead go down. When the game is played by an unsophisticated player this effect may well come as something of a shock – but the explanation (that if a thing is too cheap customers lose faith in it altogether) will soon be accepted as reasonable, and an important lesson will have been learnt. Conversely, it can be shown that there are always a few customers for even the most expensive things in the market, and that provided the scale of operation is right it is possible to make money at the high-priced luxury end.

Another way in which learning can be presented is through the accounting calculations which players must use to make sense of the results given back to them. To illustrate this, let us assume that a game causes players to make decisions about the production and marketing of two different articles, and states that certain overhead costs are present as well. The decision variables provide the basis upon which the umpiring device calculates 'number made' of each item and 'number sold'. They also determine the cost of producing each item and the revenue achieved by its sale. The game can either lump the two products together and cause the players to work out 'total costs' and balance this against 'total revenue' or else it can be rather more sophisticated and call for the calculation of 'costs of manufacturing product A' and also 'costs of manufacturing product B' (defining these so that they are direct costs only). Players are then able to compare these costs with the revenue from each product and determine the 'contribution' each makes to 'overheads'. By this means players have been led through the concept of marginal costing.

The examples given would be suitable in one case or another depending on the lessons that the tutor intended to demonstrate. A game that concentrated entirely on customer behaviour would be of no value if the intention was to study production economics, and a game with sophisticated costing problems would hardly contribute to an examination of personnel planning. A common objective under the 'demonstrate' heading is 'to show how the different activities within a firm fit together': for this purpose it is clearly pointless to choose a game that models one industrial function only. All the main functions must be there, or the interrelationship cannot be perceived. So the best approach here is for the prospective user of a game to identify the subjects on which it calls for decisions. Are those subjects in accord with his objectives? If players spend time debating alternative actions within these subject areas, and the reasons for them, and experiencing the consequences of their choice, will they be doing what he believes they need to do?

The need for a positive lesson to emerge from the experience probably means that one should look towards model-based games. Lessons about facts and figures and economic relationships will abound in traditional model-based games and in puzzles. Lessons about staff matters will be more frequent in programmed simulations and in mazes.

Demonstrations about human behaviour

Where the intention is to demonstrate some point about human behaviour, the simpler sort of behavioural game, or structured experience, is the best bet. Because they are not totally predictable it is wise to consider the objective in general terms rather than to plan on obtaining an exact result. For instance, in the 'broken shapes' exercise described in Chapter 6 there may or may not be a moment when one member of the group has a complete but incorrect square and sits back in a self-satisfied way. So the tutor can not rely on being able to point out this rather dramatic instance of concern-for-self surpassing the concern-for-the-group. But questions asked of group members like 'What were your feelings when you first opened your envelope?' ought to get answers like 'What on earth can I make of these bits?' That sort of answer is itself an indication that a person's first thoughts are usually, and quite naturally, about his own predicament. Concern for the group comes later, and in the first moments of bewilderment and uncertainty a certain inward-looking attitude is to be expected. So a discussion of personal feelings can lead to an examination of the difficulties of cooperation (which is what the exercise is about) without necessarily having one particular dramatic event to start it.

Considering this issue emphasises once again that the tutor must think very carefully about what exactly he is seeking to communicate. If he is, perhaps unconsciously, trying to duplicate an experience that he observed once in the past and found illuminating, then he may very well fail. If he concentrates instead on the principle then he may find that it is brought out by a different event, but brought out just as clearly. Open concern for the event that impressed him may lead him to ignore one that is just as good. The idea can be conveyed diagrammatically by showing a Situation, which is set up by the tutor and is common to all the groups that he handles in the same way. Because of the Situation, the students find themselves faced with a Problem. They can React in various different ways, all of which can be linked to the problem that caused them. A tutor who sees his job as provoking and studying just one reaction may not see the others, or may not recognise them, or may not be quick enough to employ them in discussion. His job is to focus attention upon 'Forms of human behaviour in a particular situation' not just a single form. Figure 8:1 will illustrate the point.

Some of these exercises are very good, and generate a lot of interest, so it is easy to allow the material itself to take over in one's mind. One then sees 'running such-and-such an exercise' as the objective, and it becomes difficult even to make a statement about the purpose of doing it. One tends to run the exercise first, and then declare as one's objectives the things that came out of it on that occasion. So it may be helpful to suggest some of the purposes for which the simpler be-

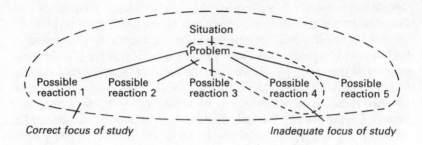

Figure 8:1   Forms of human behaviour in a particular situation

havioural games might be chosen. A list could include making students more deeply aware:

1   How human beings make assumptions about a situation, without realising that they have done so.
2   How heavily human beings are influenced in their judgements by their own background and conditioning.
3   What extremes of behaviour they will exhibit in order to avoid any risk of looking ridiculous.
4   How closeness and unity within one group will tend to make its members perceive outsiders as 'them' or even 'the enemy'.
5   How very difficult human beings find it to listen to views they disagree with without intruding their own views and so setting up a confrontation.
6   How seriously disoriented they can become when an event does not turn out to be similar to their expectations of it.
7   How dramatically their behaviour differs between moments when they feel sure of what to do and moments when they are uncertain.
8   How difficult they find it to say or do anything that is contrary to normal practice.
9   How very highly they value psychological comfort.

These are ideas that managers need to grasp, because they modify the way they treat people, the way they expect people to react and the way they judge the actions that others have taken.

To distribute

The requirement here is to provoke a lively discussion, so the exercise chosen must have many different angles and allow as many people as possible to contribute with confidence. While being centred on the chosen subject area it must not define this narrowly and there must be no fully correct right answer, so that a person grasping it early on would be able to dominate the group. It is the essence of management games to provide a consequence, of course, and by that consequence to pass judgement on what was done. But the objective of distributing knowledge calls for judgement that is not condemnatory: it should encourage further contributions rather than terminate them. It ought to be possible to attribute the result to more than one cause, so that a person who has adopted a reasonable line, albeit one that did not work in the exercise, is not left defenceless. The point can be illustrated by comparing a maze with a programmed simulation. The former merely provides a consequence for each action in the form of an altered situation – thus inviting a new decision without any back-tracking. The latter reveals the 'right' answer at each point, thus clearly labelling the others as 'wrong'. Enquiry studies are a good vehicle for the objective of distributing knowledge, for the consequence is not a right/wrong judgement but merely the acquisition of this or that information.

To examine

Some basic aspects of human behaviour have been mentioned under the objective 'to demonstrate', and some specific forms of individual behaviour will appear later as skills that may be practised. There is an intermediate area in which the tutor is probably seeking to study behaviour generally, but in the context of work situations: to move on from the structured experience which encapsulates a principle without bothering too much about background. The logical step is to an organisation game of a fairly simple type that mirrors the divisions between people created by hierarchies or specialisms. There is no point in moving the whole distance to a detailed study of one organisation, for the principles will get lost in the mass of data, but there are several rather stylised exercises that are nevertheless excellent for this purpose. An example is the one that sets up a three-tier organisation making greetings cards. The nature of the product is common knowledge, and the ways in which it might be made in a training room situation are easy to see. Therefore a credible working organisation can be set up in quite a short time and its performance becomes available for study. This particular exercise is one in which a physical product is manufactured, but that is not an essential feature. Exercises that use symbols or tokens will do quite well provided only that there is room for the separation of roles and responsibilities.

To stimulate thought

An objective not often stated for management games is 'to make people think'. It is impossible to demonstrate success in regard to this objective, so it has become rather discredited. The attitude seems to be, 'You are only claiming that thinking has been stimulated because you have no other, measurable, achievement that you can show us.' Nevertheless, encouraging a person to think, and helping him to do so, is probably the best service that can be rendered to him or his employer. A management game can meet this objective by presenting to students a problem of which they have no specific knowledge but which will yield to the application of such general knowledge as they do possess and to the force of logic. This, after all, is the basic technique for tackling all new problems: to reason outwards from the known to the unknown.

A game used for stimulating thinking does not have to be related to the student's own job. Indeed a game that is totally unrelated to current work is often the best type for this purpose. Current experience of a thing limits a person's ability to see all its angles: people get conditioned to certain responses and tend to make assumptions that 'such-and-such must be so' when the only real evidence is that it has been so for a long time.

In this sort of use, the effectiveness of a game depends very much on the fact that the umpiring device is unknown to the players. They are given a number of variables that they can manipulate and know that certain results will be related to these variables in some way. The steps that they must take are fairly obvious. They must examine their own limited knowledge of the subject of the game to form an opinion about just what relationships might exist. Then they must use their newly formed ideas about what the relationships might be to enter a set of decisions that they hope will produce satisfactory results. In due course they get the results back, and commence the critical process of examining them to see to what extent they support the hypothesis about the relationships in the model. A revised hypothesis will then be formed.

As the process repeats (decision-making, umpiring) the players will collect more and more data and become more and more skilled at making sense of it. That is to say, they will become better and better at thinking.

The sort of game needed for this purpose obviously has to be a model-based game, and ideally the sort in which the players can get to grips with the model without too much preliminary work. Just how complex the model needs to be is going to depend on the quality of the players, but there is a danger of using one that is too complex. The tutor is, in fact, inviting the players to attempt to break the model and it ought to be possible to do so.

To assess

Because a game creates a dynamic situation with opportunities for showing mental and behavioural skill it can be used for staff assessment. However, there is a difference between making judgements based on the *results* achieved in the game and judgements based on the *manner* in which a person is seen to tackle its problems. The former would seem to be invalid, for the circumstances of each play will be different, and the quality of the opposition, and in any case it has been agreed that no simulation can be totally real. On the other hand the assessment centre approach seems much more satisfactory. In this, trained observers watch a participant at work and make judgements on the skills and abilities that he displays. Such an observer can make statements about whether a player shows, for instance, more or less 'determination' or 'throughness' or whatever quality is to be observed. It is a statement about the person himself and can be disassociated from the specific results that the behaviour achieves in the game. In looking for games to be used for this purpose, the starting point must obviously be the quality which one hopes a person will possess. Possible games must be examined to see whether they contain opportunities to demonstrate it.

To practise skills

The same comment applies when the objective is to allow the practice of skills; there must be an opportunity for them in the game. If, say, the intention is to give students a chance to use forecasting techniques, then all the necessary data must be provided. Suitable games for this sort of practice are likely to be the more complicated type, for extensive data seems incongruous in a game that features one aspect of business only.

It does not stand up to examination and is seen as a classroom exercise rather than a worthwhile game. So to go deliberately searching for a game that deals with a technique is probably a fruitless quest. It is better to look for games about the general subject to which the technique is known to be relevant and examine a few of them to see whether there is enough in them to allow its application. Thus it would be unhelpful to spend a long time looking for a market-forecasting game but it would be sensible to search among marketing games in general for one that requires the use of forecasting techniques.

There is also the point that some techniques are applicable in more than one situation. A good example is the problem of stockholding, ordering and reordering. A game with scope for the appropriate techniques might be found amongst production games (the stocking of adequate raw materials), marketing games (the amount of stock to be held in a warehouse or in stores) or financial games (the amount of money that could reasonably be left tied up in stock).

So the principle to be observed is: Decide where the technique you wish to consider normally has applications and then look in those areas. Look at sophisticated games rather than simple ones. The search can be a long one, but will prove worthwhile in the end. This is because the most difficult part of acquiring a new skill is recognising the opportunity to use it. Both in working and in training situations people frequently fail to see that some technique of which they are perfectly well aware would be just the right thing to use. Simulation of such moments during a game, with the scope for discussion that exists, can increase the chance of such opportunities being recognised and used.

A general skill often stated as a training objective is that of 'working together'. So far as this implies expertise in a particular cooperative task, there is a need for an exercise directly similar to the real thing. The related objective of team-building is discussed later.

With regard to behavioural games, the opportunity to exercise a particular skill arises partly from the situation modelled and partly from the in-game behaviour of individuals. The intention could be, for instance, to let an organisational subordinate practise the skill of making a case to his manager. There would clearly be a need for two hierarchical levels in the simulation and there would be rules as to what issues each person was able to decide for himself. There would also have to be conscious choice of the individual to play the manager's role, for some people are so easily influenced that an interview with them is no test at all while others are so stubborn that failure is a foregone conclusion.

The type of game required is in fact fairly obvious once the skill to be tackled has been defined. One list of management skills from the behavioural science field includes the following items among its total of 51:

1 Persuading others when you do not have formal authority
2 Building on the contributions of others
3 Listening with understanding to subordinates
4 Adapting or changing policy in the light of new experience

Such lists are useful, for not all students are accustomed to analyse their activities in detail and the question 'What do you mean by management skills?' is quite common. Those listed above show the need for defined roles in an exercise designed for their practice, and a sufficient body of background data to allow realistic role-playing. A good starting point is to ask 'In what real-life situation is that sort of skill obviously needed?' it may then be possible to identify and reproduce it. It is probable that with behavioural games the answer will be the creation of a new exercise or the adaptation of a familiar one, rather than the immediate use of something new and strange.

Decision-making skill

A special case often cited as an objective by users of games and simulations is decision-making. To judge the effectiveness of games in this area one must first ask how well they simulate the circumstances of decision-making, and one is led inevitably to ask: What is decision-making anyway? What are its constituent parts? For the mental process must be known before it is possible to say whether an exercise is able to evoke it. The following analysis concentrates upon the mental activities required. At first sight it appears an academic exercise, but it is relevant in relation to the planning of a training activity. It helps to analyse what it is that a person cannot do now but will, hopefully, be able to do after training. Six stages can be distinguished.

1 Determination of objectives/identification of problem

It is very important for the person or group that is facing a problem to identify its objective clearly. This is not a hard thing once the question has been formulated in down-to-earth terms such as: What is it that we really want to achieve? Unfortunately, there are many occasions when it is not asked at all, possibly because the people concerned have seized on some obvious but intermediate objective. An example might be the loss of certain customers to a competitor. At the moment of crisis there would be some who identified the objective as 'to win those customers back', when a more far-sighted approach would identify it as 'to restore our share of the market to an acceptable level' or 'to replace the loss of revenue suffered'. A helpful technique is to ask, about each suggested objective, 'Why do we want to achieve it?' When a satisfactory answer has been given (that does not itself invite the question: Why?) the true objective has been found. Examination of the problem leads naturally to the consideration of acceptable ways of solving it. A person asks himself: What outcomes would I regard as satisfactory? These may be more in number than at first appear, and may differ considerably in their nature. If this is so then the actions required to reach them will differ too. This step is likely to widen the scope of a person's thinking. It is a thought process depending on imagination.

2   Collection and/or analysis of information

Frequently the data immediately available are inadequate to solve the problem. They include both items that are relevant and irrelevant: they do not include all the items that are necessary. There is a sorting process to be carried out, which implies both assessing the relative value of each item and classifying it as being useful or not. This calls for logic. Then there is the much tougher problem of deciding what information not presently available might be useful and might be discovered by research, and the consequent problem of doing that research. This is primarily an imaginative task.

3   Definition and/or comparison of alternative courses of action

The previous steps, properly carried out, will have given a person all the data he needs to formulate some courses of action. He must then find a means of comparing the alternatives, possibly by weighing the desirability of each solution and the probability of reaching it successfully. Thus the 'ideal' solution might well be discarded because the chances of reaching it were low. He must attempt also to identify the likely side-effects.

4   Action

The action stage of decision-making relies on the quality of the previous steps and the extent to which the various parties have accepted them. It can only be tested in those games where there is some division of responsibility and a real chance that individuals will not, when the crunch comes, do quite the same thing as their colleagues expect them to do. Practical simulations are very good in this respect, and the sort of behavioural game that has an action phase tacked on to the end of it. Often these can show that a player will stray from the agreed plan, or fail to execute it with due determination and so permit it to collapse. Typical reasons can be that he has encountered other problems which strike him as more important, or that he has failed to grasp the reasoning behind the agreed plan and therefore cannot properly assess the priority to be given to it. The action phase is a vital one, and there is at times a distressing tendency to suggest that success or failure is decided at the planning stage only without regard to the determination and commitment with which the plan is carried out. History is full of situations in which a rather bad plan has succeeded gloriously and situations in which a rather good plan has failed. The qualities needed are determination, thoroughness and enthusiasm.

5 Review of results

This is the stage at which the results are examined for indications of whether the original decision was or was not good, and to seek ways in which it can be improved. A key concept here is that of 'feedback', defined by J. B. Biggs as 'the transmission of information from the end result of a process to a centre controlling the process'. Feedback frequently has to be sought for, and always requires to be carefully evaluated. There are certain characteristics that feedback has to possess if it is going to fulfil its function:

It has to be recognisable. That is to say, the result appearing must be seen to be attributable to one or more of the actions previously taken. Alternatively it must be seen to be unrelated to any such action and therefore not a direct comment upon it. (This would apply to a completely new development, such as changes in legislation that affected the sales of a company's product. A new development would need to be taken into account in the future but does not imply a judgement on past policy.) The critical point is that the result should be *correctly* attributed to its cause.

It has to be controllable. It must be possible for the person controlling the process to take some action which will, in the future, alter the nature of the result.

It has to be acceptable. When a result turns out to be other than what a person sought, the inference that his behaviour was in some way wrong must be so presented that he is willing to make use of it and try again. If it is too harsh, or not justified by the circumstances, it will be rejected.

Only if it satisfies these conditions will the information 'transmitted to a centre controlling the process' be properly used (in this case the centre is the human mind).

	Determination of objectives	Collection and/ or analysis of information	Definition and/ or comparison of alternative courses of action	Action and review (feedback cycle)
Traditional model-based	5	5	5	5
Puzzle	0	8	4	8
In-basket	5	5	5	5
Maze	0	0	10	10
Programmed simulation	3	0	7	10
Enquiry study	4	8	4	4
Encounter game	2	2	8	8
Adult role – playing game	6	4	8	2
Structured experience	6	3	3	8
Organisation game	2	4	7	7
Organisational simulation	Depends entirely on the purpose of the individual exercise			
Exploratory game	0	0	8	12
Practical simulation	2	4	7	7

Figure 8:2   Guide to the emphasis that particular types of game give to various aspects of decision-making

If, then, an exercise is to be useful in the sense that it makes a student better able to solve real-life problems, and if it is accepted that these are the habits of thought needed for such problem-solving, then each form of the exercise should stimulate and exercise these habits in one or more ways. How do they do it? What sort of problem does each present and is there scope in it for the exercise of the process described? If there is, what feedback is offered on a person's performance and is it acceptable?

Figure 8:2 attempts to show the extent to which each form of game emphasises one step or another in the decision-making process. The action and review stages have been combined in this table, because they are so intimately connected with each other. For each type of game, 20 points have been distributed between the stages. A high number in one square thus indicates that the game concerned is relatively powerful in regard to that particular decision-making step when compared with the other steps. If an instructor particularly wishes to concentrate on one step, the table should prove a helpful guide.

When considering an event in which he sees himself as having some sort of authoritative role, the tutor can go a long way to deciding what material he needs by asking and answering two very simple questions.

1 Am I trying to make a point or to provide an opportunity?
2 Is the subject more concerned with business (economic) relationships or with human behaviour?

Making a point calls for material that allows him to show the 'best' answer, while providing an opportunity means that it should be open-ended. Business and economic relationships usually mean a lot of facts and figures, while human relationships are mainly a matter of words. So a matrix can be set out as below:

	Business relationships	Human behaviour
To make a point	Has an answer. Uses facts and figures as its 'currency'	Has an answer. Uses words as its 'currency'
To provide an opportunity	Is open-ended. Uses facts and figures as its 'currency'	Is open-ended. Uses words as its 'currency'

This is not an infallible guide, and by no means covers all cases, but it is a great help when one is in doubt about what to do.

To preview

This is an objective for which 'to demonstrate' would be a perfectly sensible title, if that had not been pre-empted earlier. The difference is that the former description envisaged a tutor demonstrating well-accepted knowledge, while this envisages a chief executive using a model of his organisation to say to his people 'This is how I see things going'. The person who has a vision of what he wants to achieve and seeks to put this across to organisation members has a considerable communications task. One way of doing it is to build a simulation in which the decisions he favours will lead, by reasonable and logical paths, to good results. This could be described as propaganda – building a 'bent' model to mirror a particular concept of what the world is like. But is this an unreasonable strategy? Chief executives will in any case insist on the implementation of their policies, so is it not better that the purpose of those policies, and the reasons for them, and the hoped for results, should be properly understood? And is such a model any less satisfactory from an intellectual point of view than one that reflects accepted current theory? Models are always selective, so they do not mirror that theory perfectly anyway, and since the world changes rapidly the theory is always in danger of being out of date. The model produced by a skilled and conscientious chief executive might very well be better than the product of the established wisdom. A game of this sort has a great advantage as a communication tool because it allows time for consideration and has a repetitive cycle in which people can see a cause-effect linkage emerging. It is a sound way of demonstrating 'What I believe we can do if we go about it in such-and-such a way'.

In this sense the word model takes a different gloss again, for engineers have been using models for centuries to show their prospective clients 'How it will work'. The sort of exercise chosen for this purpose is naturally going to be dictated by content. It has to contain the variables and the results that the chief executive wants to consider. It may well be custom-built.

To build a team

This is an objective that might be undertaken at the behest of some authority, or might emanate from the team members themselves. It has already been argued that deeper personal knowledge of one's colleagues will probably lead to greater mutual respect and to better cooperation. Where this concept of 'knowing each other' is the objective then the activity undertaken is better not related in any way to the work situation. It will have a greater chance of revealing qualities in those participating that would not come to light in their everyday work. Where the performance of the team must be directly related to its work, of course, the content of the game becomes the criterion for choice instead.

Objectives that do not imply a controlling authority

Most of the general objectives described above imply an authority who has decreed the activity and is conducting it. Other uses of games and simulations were suggested in Chapter 1 under the headings 'To examine performance' and 'To experiment'. They do not imply an authority in the same sense. Instead they emphasise the idea that the study is of common interest to all, and that all have something to offer in interpreting the results. It is envisaged that everybody will be learning – not just a group labelled 'students' – though when the learning has been done there may still be some decisions taken by an authority. Are there any sub-heads of these objectives, and can anything useful be said about finding material that is suitable?

To examine performance

This calls for a simulation of reality that is as accurate as possible, and the idea can be illustrated by thinking of an extreme case – a drill, in the military sense. A prepared drill, for alerting a camp in the event of an attack, or evacuating a building when a fire is reported, or responding to unexpected customer demand by rushing in more stock – all these are in fact simulations. They take place apart from the real event but demand that people should act as if that event was happening. A drill can be run through for examination purposes to see 'what we are doing now' and to give clues as to 'where we went wrong'. Most of the activities an organisation wants to examine will not, of course, be as tightly defined as this. For some matters there will be generally agreed procedures, but for others it will be necessary to ask the people involved 'what do you actually do in such-and-such a case'. It will be the same process as suggested under the heading 'organisational simulations', because there may be no standard practice or there may be one, but it is disregarded. Any simulation built for this purpose must be carefully scrutinised so that it models 'what is' rather than 'what is supposed to be'.

To experiment

This is an objective that can be considered at first as an extension of to examine, for looking at current practice invites the question 'How would it be if we did so-and-so instead?' and at that point the experiment is beginning. But while 'examine' has connotations of the past, 'experiment' explicitly looks to the future and implies a dynamic state of affairs in which the environment might change as well as the subject. Examination goes with phrases like 'What happened?' while experiment goes with phrases like 'If so and so happens, what will we do?'. This may seem a fine distinction, but it has a major effect on the type of material needed since looking backward means considering events already known. A simulation prepared for that purpose can draw upon existing knowledge in the minds of the people who will use it. If the intention is to experiment, there must be an opportunity for novel events to occur, and the element of familiarity has then gone. The nature and implications of the new event somehow have to be communicated to those using the simulation. The device that is used for such a purpose is probably going to appear less real than one used for examination for the very sound reason that it is *not* modelling the present reality. It is modelling instead some person's concept of future reality, or the products of his imagination. So abstract representation and the use of symbols is much more likely: they are a highly flexible and very obvious way of illustrating different ideas and different threats or opportunities. The type of activity required of the people using the simulation has also changed. Examination of present performance in response to familiar developments is more likely to require close scrutiny of what one does and alterations in matters of detail. It should be done slowly and carefully because one is not gathering new data but re-organising one's response to the old. Experimenting means encountering new events and offering a series of alternative responses to them from every one of which new data will be gathered. The first need is to gather this data, so the device used has to be volatile and dynamic: it is going to look much less like a drill and much more like a game played for fun. It will be based on definite rules, so that it is playable, but for each group of experiments the rules can be altered. There will be a great many plays, and when people have become reasonably familiar with the new situations and the possible responses, then they can begin to work out preferred tactics. These requirements point to a game using maps, charts and symbols or to a visual display on a computer screen.

Another use of the word experiment is that which goes with research. Games are useful tools for research on decision-making because they can generate situations that can be controlled and repeated. There is valuable comment in a paper entitled 'Board wargames for decision making research' by Dale F. Cooper of Southampton University and Jonathan Klein of Royal Holloway College. They find much to be said for games that are easy to learn, move fast and generate a high level of player interest. They comment 'it seems likely that other commercially available games, and particularly business games, could be adapted similarly for research purposes'.

Acceptance of the activity by players

The arguments so far presented concern the theoretical matching of objectives to types of game. They assume, by ignoring the issue, that there is no problem in persuading players to commit themselves to the game, to take a constructive attitude to it, and to persevere with it long enough to gain some benefit. This is by no means the case, and games will sometimes fail disastrously because of player rejection. A game may have characteristics that are apparent at an early stage and which, because they are unwelcome, inhibit any closer scrutiny. The wrong vocabulary, for instance, can make players feel that the game is too advanced for them, or else that they have been insulted by something that is too easy. If it is too abstract for the more practical students it can be rejected, just as it can by intellectual students who see it as over-specialised and lacking in general application. Another characteristic is appearance: what does it look like to the person who is being asked to play? Will it seem appropriate in the light of his expectations? Will he be prepared to invest time and effort in participating? The outward forms tend to evoke images and comparisons in the minds of players. Some of these are reasonably predictable.

Board games

These are frequently associated with the board games used in leisure activities – by children as much as by adults – and may be seen as not offering a serious intellectual challenge. The expectations raised by the sight of a board game probably include that it will contain an element of chance, that it will be a great simplification of reality, and that it will not go on too long. They are not generally seen as a vehicle for 'heavy' learning or involving a great deal of hard work, though there are many that can be used that way if people are willing. The benefits usually expected are a lively discussion with colleagues and a limited number of important but conceptually simple lessons. The options for the tutor are to fall in with the expectations that he believes his students will have, or to attempt to change them by discussion.

Within the category of board games, there are differences relating to presentation and to subject. The more glossy and colourful a game is, the more it will be mentally equated with leisure activities, and the more romantic the subject the more the same effect will occur. Two interesting examples are Wildcat, from Guardian Business Services (which is about North Sea Oil and Gas) and Contributor, from Chris Elgood Associates Limited (which is about running a factory). Wildcat has a delightful, gaily coloured board and is about a romantic subject. Contributor has a simple black-and-white board and is not. Books get written, and films made about adventures among North Sea oil rigs: they do not get written and made about plant depreciation. So the image created in a student's mind is different. Both games are excellent in the right setting, but that setting will not be the same.

Games that make use of tokens and symbols

These have the same sort of problem to face, because tokens are equated with childhood and the world of make-believe. They can be seen as an open acknowledgement of 'not-realness'. By contrast, adults tend to see serious learning as coming from educated pursuits like studying papers or listening to an expert lecturing. There is something slightly uncomfortable about picking up once again the learning tools of childhood. So there may be a barrier to overcome, and the most successful way of tackling it is always to demonstrate the objective of the game and to show that the medium used is suitable. Once people are convinced on these points any objections will fade away. Sometimes it can be a matter of explanation, but the subject matter of the game is again relevant because some carry their own, obvious message. For instance The Green Revolution Game from The London School of Hygiene and Tropical Medicine, uses cut-out symbols for items like 'fertiliser' and 'pesticide spray' which are stuck into slots on a base representing an acre of land. The whole subject of the game is clearly serious, so the symbols are going to be more readily accepted. By contrast, some of the structured experiences – the more abstract ones – may lead the tutor to hand out symbols that do not seem to have any great meaning and cannot be related *at that moment* to a worthwhile objective. Once again, neither method is better or worse than the other *except in relation to a specific intention by the user.*

Games that involve subjects apparently unrelated to work

Some such exercises are deemed irrelevant by potential players because an outward discrepancy in subject matter conceals their true value. This mainly happens with people who have difficulty in thinking in abstract terms and look for all their training to be obviously and directly job-related. The exercise about manufacturing greetings cards, which has already been described, is one that can fail in certain circumstances for this reason. It sets up a model of a human organisation, with specialist functions and different levels in a hierarchy, and provides excellent material for the study of how people in organisations behave. Not all students can see that this abstraction is valid: some can only see that it is quite unlike their own factory (which does not make greetings cards) and are therefore inclined to condemn it. They are unable to see that certain aspects of human behaviour are concerned with the relationship between people rather than with the task for which that relationship exists. This is a pity, for exercises like the greetings card one are elegant and economic in that they reduce the need for an elaborate scenario: they work by drawing on concepts that already exist in the mind and need little explanation. This gives them an advantage over some of the more specialised simulations. Another delightful example is the game called Managed Croquet from John R. Cooper which studies the management of specialists by taking the conventional lawn game of croquet and splitting the player role into several specialist functions. Like the greetings card game, it draws upon existing knowledge so that no detailed instruction is needed. It also draws strength from the fact that players are automatically involved in an enjoyable outside activity. The argument that could be brought against it is the traditional and rather narrow one that it is not outwardly like 'work'.

Personal computer games

Here, the field is in a fascinating state of change because direct personal interaction with one's own computer is becoming a respectable form of learning. The division between what is seen as serious and what is seen as frivolous appears to be connected with the image of the equipment and with the form of presentation. An exercise that presents knowledge in word or number form through the medium of an IBM Personal Computer is probably serious and one that presents it in the form of a colourful chart on a machine primarily sold for fun is not. For the tutor who must determine what exercise to use there is no need to consider the desirability of this state – all that is necessary is an awareness of the students' expectations so that a sound choice can be made. For the specialist in educational methods, it is a matter for urgent study because it impinges on the work/leisure barrier. The value that seems to be attached to leisure activities comes from their dramatic eventfulness, their success in creating early involvement by the player and their economy in presenting necessary information. Contributing to these benefits are colour and movement and shape. These features could surely be exploited more fully than is currently the case in serious business education.

A particularly interesting exercise when considering the work-fun interface is Free Enterprise from Science Research Associates Limited, of which it is clearly stated in the notes that 'the most popular use of Free Enterprise is just for fun in the home'. (The text goes on to describe teaching uses.) It has a facility that allows a player to call up one or more simulated players to oppose him – their decisions being provided by the computer program. The end result is that the game can be a one-person self-operated learning tool or a competitive device played between several teams. This is clearly a game that bridges the work-fun gap.

Games that call for extensive reading

Most of the dangers so far pointed out have related to the possibility of a game not being taken seriously. The opposite danger applies when contemplating some of the complex games which first appear to the player as a mass of small print some twenty pages thick. Such things are seen by almost everybody as serious, but may also be seen as totally de-motivating. They imply a long period of study before one knows what is required, and there may even be a further period when one is doing it wrong and getting depressing results. On the other hand such games will not seem de-motivating to those whose natural environment is the printed word, and figures in tabular or matrix form. To them, the game will seem entirely legitimate.

Playability

It seems likely that a deduction is made from the appearance of a game not only about its acceptability but also about its 'playability' – meaning the amount of effort that seems to be necessary to interact with the game set against the quality and quantity of the response that one is likely to get. In some games it is not immediately possible to see what action is called for: even to get that information will need an hour or two of reading. A player thus sees an unacceptable figure on the cost side of the equation and rejects the deal without further thought. In other cases it is perhaps apparent what must be done but the feedback offered on the action seems meagre or uninteresting and again there is rejection. A third case might call for a very reasonable investment of time and effort, and offer interesting feedback, but the time interval between experiments might seem too long. Again, the result would be rejection. The contrasting ends of the spectrum might be the twenty page script and a shooting-down-spaceships video-game. In the latter it is immediately obvious what one must try to do, and what form the feedback will take. It is also obvious that the feedback will be immediate, that one can make many attempts in a very short time and that one can discontinue the experience whenever one wishes to. It has high playability, but the benefit to be gained may well be assessed as meagre. The twenty-page text may be presumed to offer more serious learning, but the nature of that learning is not clear and playability is low. It must rely on motivation already existing in the player, because there is little in the material itself. It might be argued that one should be able to assume student motivation anyway: that management games take place as part of serious training courses, are work rather than fun, and that there is no need to make them appear enjoyable. This would seem to be closing the door on an additional energy source which is more likely to help the learning process than hinder it.

Checklist for assessing the usefulness of a game

Summarising, there are some questions that ought to be asked about a management game that will give a good idea whether it will serve a particular purpose:

1 What does the game material look like, physically?
2 How long will it be before the players are able to take some positive in-game action?
3 What decisions do the players have to make? How many of them are there and on what subjects?
4 What results are given back to the players after umpiring (if such exists)? How long must players wait to get them?
5 How many of the decision variables contribute to each result? (This is a good measure of the complexity of the game. The more factors influencing each result, the more difficult the game will be.)
6 What steps do the players have to take to convert the results they are given into results that mean something in terms of winning or losing?
7 Is there a single problem that has to be solved, or is it subdivided?
8 How many 'roles' are there?
9 Is there scope within the game for the development of an organisational structure?
10 Is there an obvious and sensible way of deciding a winner?
11 Is there any sort of chance element?
12 Does the game go into great detail about any one functional area?
13 How much mathematical calculation is called for from the players?
14 What will the players be doing, physically, while the game is in progress? (writing? debating? throwing dice? building a card-house?) Will it affront their self-image to be doing this?

Considerations when writing a game

Some of the decisions that relate to the writing of a game also give clues about choosing and using them. For instance, early questions that a writer will ask are 'What sort of people is this exercise for? What is their intellectual level? What message is it supposed to put over? How much time is to be allowed for it?' Intellectual ability is relevant not just because there may be mathematical work involved but because not all likely students are capable of conceptual thought. The sort of game in which numbers written down on a form are taken to represent an operational decision does require conceptual, or abstract thinking – and student groups from supervisory levels in the older, experienced based industries sometimes have difficulty with it. They are not comfortable unless they are discussing something they can relate directly and closely to a familiar aspect of their everyday work. One gets comments like 'This form is completely useless: it has no similarity to our normal quarterly return. The person who wrote this knows nothing about our information system.' In such circumstances the practical simulation is apt to be a better bet because the players readily understand what is happening and can see the point of it all.

The culture of the organisation will also make a difference. Is it the sort of organisation in which relationships are very formal, and the outward symbols of position emphasised, and personal dignity very important? Or is it an organisation where the formalities are hardly apparent, people talk to each other quite freely across boundaries of rank and nothing really matters except getting a good result? In the former it is sensible to stick closely to whatever is seen as a 'proper' form of presentation and avoid any interactions or results which will embarrass the players. This may mean an exercise that looks a bit dull, but it is probably better than something that is too far advanced for the environment and just assures rejection. In the latter sort of organisation any type of game is accepted provided there are sound reasons and these reasons are apparent. Games with descriptive material of the utmost simplicity – looking more like a primary school text book than anything else – have worked successfully in a highly intellectual environment because that medium was the best one for communicating swiftly with the playing group. The distinction given between two extreme types of organisation tends to correlate with their experience of behavioural work. Organisations that are familiar with this have a large area of study available to them which those at the other extreme do not even acknowledge. Naturally, they also have the language that goes with it and an understanding that human behaviour is a universal phenomenon to be found outside the work environment as well as within it. They therefore do not need to have everything set out in the language of their organisation.

A less common but interesting effect of organisational culture is the standard of presentation appropriate to a game. There are cases where 'our image' is a factor of great concern and no amount of technical excellence will make a thing acceptable if the outward appearance is not prestigious.

There will also be some sort of brief for a game writer to follow, for anyone commissioning such work is sure to have an image in his mind of what he expects to happen. He will be able to state objectives in terms of the hoped-for effect of the game. Words commonly used are 'I want them to understand that . . .' or 'I want them to be able to . . .' or 'I want them to have the experience of . . .' or 'I want to emphasise the importance of . . .'. With a little questioning it will become clear whether the objective relates to intellectual/analytical skill or skill in the area of interpersonal behaviour. The answer will point to one end or the other of the game spectrum. The person commissioning a game will also have some idea what he expects to be going on while the game is in progress. This can be a useful starting point: it will lead back to why he wants a game at all (often because of some previous experience) and what particular advantages he feels it can offer. The objective is always the most critical factor and it may take a lot of work to define it adequately.

9

Conducting a management game

The tutor's preparation

The first requirement for successful conduct of a management game – one that can never be over-emphasised – is a proper understanding by the tutor of the method in general and of the particular device that he intends to use. Any sort of simulation is both similar to and different from reality. Therefore, players who are asked to commit themselves to it will encounter some uncertainty in knowing where the boundaries lie. In what respects can they assume that it is 'real' (and therefore permits them to draw on real life for clues) and to what extent is it a fabrication that they will have to learn from scratch? This is a characteristic of the method, and one which the tutor will be wise to recognise openly and discuss with the players so that their frustration is minimised. He must also examine his own role in the event and the extent to which it requires him to be authoritative. There is a common belief that a training event will be seen as having 'gone well' (or otherwise) partly by reference to the tutor showing control of the situation – which he does by being constantly right. This is not an easy thing to achieve, for games invite an exploratory approach and it is possible that a player will come up with some proposition that has not been thought of by the tutor or even by the game designer. Naturally, experience of running a particular game makes a tutor increasingly aware of the wrinkles and less likely to be caught out – but the authoritarian stance remains a difficult one to adopt and not to be favoured without good reason. One usually gets a better response from the players by presenting a game as having some degree of uncertainty for all parties – but justified because of its other merits.

Accepting that one is unlikely to be secure against all possible error does not mean that one should give up trying, and the tutor should certainly make himself as familiar as possible with the material he intends to use. It is often not possible to learn enough just by reading some descriptive text, for games tend to reveal unforeseen strengths and weaknesses. This is probably because game writers become frustrated by the frequent lack of reality and respond by including rather more than they originally intended. It is easy for a writer to feel that such-and-such a feature increases the credibility of his creation without making it unduly complicated, so it might as well go in! These choices are personal, they might not seem logical to somebody else, and are not an integral part of the main design; so they may not appear in a formal description and a tutor can be unaware of them till his activity is up and running. There is no adequate substitute for working through the material in private or with colleagues and trying to envisage exactly what will happen with a group of students.

Explaining what is required

The most common human reaction when contemplating a game is to ask 'What have I got to do? What sort of action is required of me?' The tutor needs to answer this question for his students, and while some games are quite easily understood there are two types that present a problem – those that appear to have almost no rules, and those that appear to have far too many.

In the first category are some of the simpler structured experiences, especially those that are primarily designed to provoke human behaviour which then displaces the initial subject matter as the main focus of study. For example, the rules for the pairing exercise described in Chapter 6 (a variation of a concept often referred to as The Prisoner's Dilemma) are meagre. They state how the game is to be carried on, but they give no indication of the purpose behind the actions – what sort of goals are to be aimed at or how success is to be judged. They are very different in this respect from the ordinary sort of game, which states quite clearly that 'the object of the players is to . . . etc.' The difference is deliberate, so that the decisions about objective which the players eventually make will be clearly their own and cannot be attributed to any external influence. So the problem here is that providing elaborate rules will probably defeat the overall purpose – but their absence can be frustrating for the students. A similar state of affairs can be seen in an exercise known as 'The . . . Memorial Fund' – the blank being filled in with the name of someone famous and recently deceased. The scenario here is that the team have been given a large sum of money and have to decide how it should be spent. The exercise is for looking at the way in which people import their own beliefs and values into an arena without being fully aware that they have done so. The hope is that the team will eventually get round to debating the *purpose* of such a fund rather than examining a succession of ideas without any criterion by which to judge them – but if this hope is expressed as part of the rules, the exercise might as well not be run. So the tutor, when asked to supply rules, is really unable to do so. The best answer is the truth: 'I cannot give you more precise rules without spoiling the exercise. Trust me for a while, do what *you* think is right, and I will explain as soon as it is over.' As mentioned before, the chance is then present that there will be a sequence of events which does *not* demonstrate the points the tutor seeks to make. If it happens, he must either be prepared to examine constructively whatever *did* happen or pass on to another experience on the basis that 'you cannot win them all'.

The other end of the scale is represented by the traditional model-based game played, possibly, with a group of students to whom the concept of a management game is new and who have no idea how it is carried on. A helpful way of starting is to explain the decision-result cycle and use a diagram like Figure 9:1.

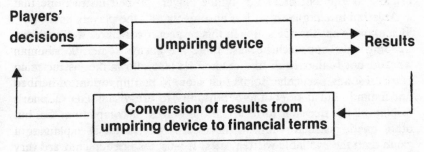

Figure 9:1   Cycle of activities in a game

It may also be worthwhile to display one typical graph, such as the price/sales graph in Figure 9:2 as an indication of how the umpiring is carried out.

Two problems will thus have been dealt with, for a frequent question is: How are these results worked out? There can be annoyance when it is discovered that the umpiring device cannot cope with every level of

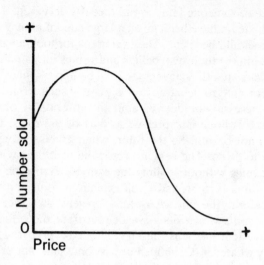

Figure 9:2   Typical model of a sales/price relationship used in umpiring

decision and it helps to make the limitations clear beforehand.

Another decision is whether there should or should not be a verbal briefing to supplement a study by the players of their instructions.

A verbal briefing more or less ensures that all the players have some idea about what the rules are. In this respect it compares well with the 'reading only' approach because there are always some idle students who do not bother to do the reading. It also allows the instructor to emphasise any particular points that seem to him important or hard to understand, and it offers the opportunity to use visual aids such as a display of the decision form in various stages of completion. On the other hand, instructors are not necessarily any better at explaining a game than the available written rules. It must also be remembered that there is bound to be some sort of discussion of the rules before the game starts in order that the instructor can answer questions. Much depends on the probability of careful study beforehand.

A particular reason for emphasising this point is that in model-based games a team's decisions have to be written down on a decision form in order to be umpired. For the umpire to give the correct results it is necessary that this should be completed accurately. It cannot be done if the rules are not understood.

Getting the game under way

Whatever explanatory efforts are made, full understanding will not be achieved except by the experience of playing. In the early stages there will be questions in abundance, and at least these have the advantage of being put for immediate 'need to know' reasons. Some of the problems may relate to the decisions for the first round, and where a game has a cold start quite generous guidance is in order. A 'cold start' means that the game sets the boundaries within which decisions may be made but gives no obvious clue as to what decisions are sensible. There will certainly be information from which a policy can be deduced, but a team of limited ability may not be able to make proper use of this and may make early, bad decisions from which it is hard to recover. This danger can be minimised by a 'warm start', meaning the provision of a 'most recent' decision taken by a notional previous management team. This also has the advantage of forcing the teams to work through any 'interpretation of results' phase using data known to the tutor. This allows him to check their figures and ensure that at least one part of the activity has been properly understood. Generally, every sign of procedural misunderstanding or error should receive attention at an early stage because rectification becomes steadily harder as the game goes on. The tutor becomes burdened with umpiring tasks; the students are constantly building on past records and therefore have a serious re-writing task if an error goes uncorrected for several time periods.

Staff resources

The number of staff needed will naturally vary with the game used, but games can in some cases be labour-intensive. Annoying though this may be, there is a danger in economising because the competitive nature of a game can make the players very demanding and very critical of the service that they get. Inconvenience and frustration can damage their attitude to the experience, and make it less useful. To consider a bad case – from the staff requirement point of view – an elaborate model-based game might need the following roles:

Chief umpire To have overall control

Assistant umpires In a ratio, say, of one to every two teams. Their duties would be to answer questions, check for form-filling and accounting errors (a policing role), and be intermediaries between

the team and the umpiring centre
Computer operators/calculators To work the umpiring device
Process observers One for each team to study the internal decision-making process and possibly intervene in an attempt to improve it
Market research staff Games frequently include an opportunity for teams to buy information from such an agency, which must be staffed to supply it accurately and without delay.

Staffing at this level is frequently not practicable, and some of the roles may have to be doubled up or sacrificed: but there is apt to be some degree of risk attached. If there is more work than the staff can cope with, the build-up of pressure soon shows in delays and hurried answers and in major or minor errors.

Composition of teams

One of the duties of the tutor is to decide the number of teams that there are to be, how many people are to be in each and which individuals these are to be. A packaged game will normally state certain limits to the number and size of teams, but these are flexible and the tutor will have a definite number of people to accommodate. There are plenty of games which can be played by one-man teams, but in such a case there is none of the interpersonal discussion which contributes so greatly to the learning process and which is so characteristic of real life. A three-man team is the smallest in which these features really appear. At the other end of the scale, a team of more than eight people has to spend so much effort on its own organisation that its actual decisions are often delayed and imperfect.

Therefore, the points that the tutor must consider are the complexity of the game and the time that is to be allowed for it. The number of teams need not be much of a problem: only two are needed to create some degree of competition and, at the other end of the scale, a much larger number can always be organised into two separate 'leagues'. This does, of course, require more staff. One possible difficulty with a small number of teams is that some interacting games require decisions from a minimum number of teams – often four – before the model will produce realistic results. This can be solved by the tutor putting in one or more dummy decisions. The composition of teams can be a very important factor. For example, it is best to avoid a situation in which a team is completely dominated by one man. This can happen because of strength of personality or higher status in the organisation: either way it leads to the other team members learning little and quite often, to the one individual making a fool of himself. On the other hand, a team of unenterprising individuals will produce few ideas and achieve poor results. The aim should be to balance the team members in terms of personality and in terms of the specialised knowledge that each will be able to contribute.

Objectives within the game

The tutor must decide what to tell the competing teams about objectives. One of the problems of a game is that people instinctively see it as a thing to be won or lost and look for the criterion which is going to be used. Such an attitude can obscure the true objectives of all those involved, which is to learn. But is it possible to say to students, 'Play the game in the manner that will enable you to learn most'? In one sense this is a very commendable attitude, recognising the active role demanded of the student if training is ever to be of real, practical usefulness. It can, however, cause problems if a team spends too much of the time on such arguments as interest its members and fails to get on with the job. Further, the tutor has his own obligations in terms of the learning process. Just because he is the tutor, and not a student, it can be assumed that he has something worthwhile to offer, and it may be that his message will never be appreciated unless the players tackle the game in a disciplined way. Much depends on the purpose for which the game is being used, as discussed in Chapter 8.

A useful approach is to ask players to define their objectives for themselves, in terms of a statement of company policy which has to be filed with the umpire. This usually results in a discussion about the true purpose of business in society, which can be very fruitful. It still leaves a measurable financial criterion because all players eventually agree that if a firm is to continue to exist it has to be moderately profitable. On the other hand this approach has two disadvantages: it takes up more time and it may lead to a type of play that fails to explore the complexities of the game. This means that it will fail to reveal some of the learning inherent in it. For instance, one objective that is frequently put forward is 'to offer stable employment to the maximum number of people'. Though this objective is inseparable in the long run from maximum financial success it takes a long time for this to become obvious and it can lead to some very unadventurous play.

Organisation within teams

This is a matter of intense concern to those who study individual and group behaviour. It is touched upon in the discussion of behavioural games but cannot be adequately dealt with in a book of this type. The most that is possible is to give some brief pragmatic advice.

To a large extent the organisation within each team is best left to the players themselves, the most helpful guidance by the instructor being a statement that the formal rules of a meeting do not have to apply. This is worth mentioning because people who are thrust into a new situation often identify with some particular role in order to provide themselves with a standard by which to behave. Thus it is quite possible to have members sitting round a table, addressing each other as Mr Chairman, Mr Production Manager, and so on, and taking notes of what is said, and altogether losing a great deal of time because of extreme formality. Such behaviour contains an element of fear, because to abandon formality means that sooner or later some individual must assume a leadership role, not because of some external circumstance (such as election or nomination) but because he truly believes that in his present situation he is fitted for it. To adopt this role is at once to put oneself at risk and possibly to antagonise other members of the group. The danger of formality is greatest when players are, in their normal working lives, accustomed to rule unchallenged in their own areas and not to have much involvement with interfunctional bargaining. It can be seen to a marked degree among foremen in the more traditional industries such as the older types of mechanical engineering. The reverse, completely informal argument and acceptance of defeat from time to time as a matter of course is typical of high-level students such as graduate entrants to a firm. To them status matters less than reason: they have no established position within an organisation that needs to be defended.

Carrying on the comparison made above, foremen are likely to be very much slower than graduate entrants in the way they tackle a game. They will have more difficulty with the roles thrust upon them and more difficulty with the conventions of the game. On the other hand, they will be extremely thorough and likely to learn a great deal from a game. Graduate entrants are faster and take the conventions of the game in their stride, but against this they frequently grasp only the principal issues of the game and pass over the details.

Including a behavioural scientist as a process observer will always add a dimension to the game, but this has to be seen in the context of the overall objective. Such a person needs time and a suitable climate in order to contribute fully, and to tie this idea on as an extra is usually a mistake. It has to be done properly or not at all. There must be clear thinking at the start about what a game is intended to cover and what is to be left out.

A problem that almost always arises is a different rate of progress shown by different teams. It is especially serious in an interactive game, when none of the results can be handed back until all the teams' papers have been considered. There will be one team that is ready long before the others and one that holds things up. Two tactics are available to the umpire. He can stick faithfully to his advertised timing and if a team has not given in its decision he can use the same figures that they entered last time. This will get rid of the immediate problem and get the other teams moving along at a decent pace, but it will not be a lot of use to the team that is in difficulties. The probable reason for their being so is that they cannot handle the data available to them already – and the effect of this tactic is to give them another lot of data (the results from the next decision period) on top of something that has already proved too much for them. An alternative tactic is to put in a 'staff' manager and send the team off into a corner to reorganise their decision-making procedures. While they are away, the staff manager just feeds in middle-of-the-road decisions and keeps the paperwork up to date.

Technical problems

There are a number of even smaller problems: the technical ones. Nothing can ruin a session so quickly as discovering too late that the plug on an item of electrical equipment will not fit the socket, or the room will not black out for the showing of a slide, or that there are lorries constantly unloading outside the window and hence nothing that anybody says can be easily heard.

Starting at the lowest level, there have to be sufficient copies of the players' instructions (if the game requires such things) for everybody to have one, and likewise sufficient copies of the various decision forms. Possibly the game will generate records of performance, so there should be chalkboards or flipcharts in each room, and something to write on them with. There should also be graph paper and rulers, and students should be encouraged to bring calculators.

There should be, if possible, a separate room for each team, and it ought to be large enough for working papers, graphs and tables to be spread out. It should have space enough for the setting up of at least one 'subcommittee'. The team rooms ought to be close together, ideally be connected by telephone, and there should be a separate room for the umpires and a separate room for consultations and contingencies. All too often it is not possible to meet these requirements but something can be done by means of a large hall divided up by screens. Management games are an unconventional form of education and tend to have to be run in some place other than the organisation's own regular training area. This can lead to all sorts of complications, such as having locations that are distant from one another, thus presenting communication problems, or locations that are not continuously available. It is not unknown for a team of players to go off to dinner eager to plan the strategy of their next round and come back afterwards to find that their room has been locked up by the caretaker and all their papers left inside it.

An even more humble consideration is heating. The organiser, when shown a possible room by his host, sees it on a warm sunny afternoon and forgets that the circumstances in which he is going to use it may be different. Management games encourage a degree of freedom, and a team that finds itself stuck in unacceptable conditions will just migrate to a better environment: the organiser will find himself searching desperately for a lost team.

Teaching within the game situation

There are opportunities in the game situation for the instructor to improve the quality of the learning achieved. Learning ought to be connected with doing, and for a student to say, 'Yes, I understand the point being made', is not a satisfactory response. It should provoke from the instructor the attitude, 'I am pleased that you understand it. Can you apply this knowledge successfully to the appropriate business situation?' The instructor has a duty to monitor the way in which students are making use of a game situation, and experience of any particular game will give him a very good idea of the points at which he should intervene to guide the discussion or to make a 'knowledge input'. A useful technique is to schedule sessions into the playing programme at which players can be questioned about what they have done so far and offered ideas and techniques that will enable them to do better. This is in fact the natural sequence in which knowledge and skill are transmitted by a skilled practitioner to a learner. The practitioner performs the operation: he does this slowly, in front of his apprentice, explaining at each stage what he is doing, and why he is doing it, and how he is doing it. He then gives his apprentice a simple example to attempt and goes off to do something of his own. From time to time he comes back to check on the progress of his apprentice, to answer any questions and check on any errors. From time to time he takes the tool/pen/paint brush/chisel from the apprentice and makes corrections himself. By a constant repetition of this process the apprentice, given the necessary innate ability, acquires the skill of the master. An instructor can use a management game as the background for a very similar process, calling the teams together at chosen moments to tell them things that are relevant, explain techniques that might be useful, show the impact on group effectiveness of various types of individual behaviour and describe mental approaches to the problem that might be enlightening. The following comments are examples of what might be offered:

> The market for consumer variables is considerably affected by the current legislation on consumer credit. (An item of new knowledge that would be highly relevant in a game built around these products.)

> There is a technique known as marginal costing which can give you a great deal of help about the cost of each of your products and what you should charge for it and whether you should make more of it or less of it. Here is how it works. I want you to apply it in the company you are running.

> I want each of you to decide on a rating, between 0 and 5, which will answer the question: To what extent does my group listen to the contributions I make to the discussion? Write your rating on a piece of paper, and the number of the group you are in, but *not* your name. (This is a way of making use of the behaviour that the game has aroused. The instructor works out an average figure for each group and tells them what it is. The individuals who have given a high rating – those who have monopolised the discussion – will be shocked to find that some of their colleagues obviously feel they are not getting a fair chance. Hopefully this will modify their behaviour.)

> I want you to consider the type of person who makes the decision whether or not to buy your product. Don't think just about the man who is going to use it, but the man who is going to make the final decision about whether his company will or will not place an order.

It is obvious that to use a game as an educational tool in this way is going to demand a considerable degree of skill in the instructor. He must himself be competent in the subject areas that he intends to explore and he must be prepared for a great deal of hard work. It is, however, rewarding: a management game, well run, allows a professional training specialist to use a simulated situation instead of the real one and to employ within it the techniques of on-the-job training.

Administrative and educational considerations are both well served by the tactic of running one preparatory session a day or more before the 'proper' event. It has been argued in Chapter 3 that the decision forms and accounting forms, if well designed, can themselves be a significant source of learning. An instructor may choose to employ these as a 'static' exercise, having as his object to get each student, by the end of the session, to understand the meaning of the form and to be able both to make the required decisions and to enter them in the right manner. When the event proper begins he can say, 'You know how to make decisions and present them: now do it for real'. This does, of course, depend very heavily on the logic of the game being a true reflection of business life: if it is not, then the 'learning to play' session will not stand up as a piece of training valid in its own right.

If it is recognised that the instructor should make use of the game as opposed to just 'running' it there are other things characteristic of real life that can be done. One of these is to offer practice in the art of management by getting one individual to come into a game of which he has no previous knowledge and assume a management role. This might involve, say, taking control of three teams as a general manager with a brief from the board that calls for an increase of 20 per cent in turnover within four playing periods. To structure a situation like this highlights the distinction between really being a manager (getting things done through other people) and being personally involved in the work. The person thrust into this role will have no deep knowledge of the actual work done by his subordinates, though they will themselves have plenty of knowledge. Instead he will be called upon to act as a resource for them: listening to their views, pondering what they tell him, making comparisons, looking at outside circumstances that they, perhaps, cannot see and making suggestions that he feels may prove helpful. It is a most demanding experience, and there is great variation in the success with which different people tackle it.

Practical simulations require a special note because they are difficult to administer and can easily subside into chaos. For a start, they occupy a great deal of time and, unless some teams are to be denied the chance to see their plans put into effect, a basically similar performance has to take place twice. The conventional approach is to have an even number of teams, two, four or six, and cause each one of them to carry out, as a management team, the designing, costing, pricing and marketing part of the exercise: everything short of the actual production of goods in quantity. Then one team acts as the workforce and is directed by their partners as they manufacture the latter's product or products. After the 'run' has succeeded or failed, the teams change round. (Often the manufacturing time allowed to a team is limited.) This arrangement is psychologically good because all the students have a chance to put their planning to the test. It is bad because of the duplication involved and the time and materials consumed. The time factor matters a great deal, for while lessons can be learnt in a dramatic way they are not apparent to everybody with the same frequency or the same force. A real-life foreman, thrust into the position of general manager and making all the mistakes for which he regularly curses his own boss, learns a lot: the person sitting at a table for an hour or more cutting simple shapes out of plastic foam may just get bored. Although he probably sees mistakes going on all round him, he already knows theoretically that such mistakes do get made. He does not have the shock of realising that he himself is making them. Such a person can very well argue that the exercise is a ridiculous waste of time.

The alternative to more than one 'run' is to choose one team only whose plan is to be put into effect. This goes well while all are in the planning stage and the choice has still to be made, but once a team is identified the others are likely to lose interest. If there are more than two teams then at least one is unable to participate in the 'live run', even as workers, and must just look on. This is not a satisfying role, for to give the management team a reasonable chance of success the shopfloor must be kept free from observers, and to see clearly what is going on can be difficult. Closed-circuit television is a help, but even this does not wholly solve the problem. So far as it can be solved, the secret is to be very careful about the students with whom it is to be used and the circumstances that will surround it. If the attitude they take is pleasant and cooperative then it will probably be seen as an extremely useful exercise from which everybody claims to have learnt some fundamental lesson. If the attitude is critical, well, there are plenty of things to be critical about.

Obviously, practical simulations present problems in terms of materials and accommodation. If the event is not planned well in advance there can be surprising problems in getting enough 'raw material', enough 'manufacturing plant' and a room sufficiently big to work in. Most training establishments are set out on the assumption that education takes place with students sitting in nice neat rows – and it is not easy to make much of a production line out of the modern sort of conference chair which just has a flap swinging round on a pivot so that the student has a surface for his notebook. A large, solid table is needed, and preferably one that can stand a few marks on it without the authorities screaming too loudly. (Model-makers' knives make deep scratches.)

Behavioural games present two special problems. One arises from their very simplicity. The tutor finds himself thinking 'It is all in my head, really, apart from a map that they will need (say) and twenty-four coloured counters'. Ten minutes before the session is due to start he finds that a colleague has borrowed map and counters and failed to return them: because the resources needed were minimal he took them for granted. The natural reaction of the players will be increased if the exercise is suspect anyway. The sort of comments overheard are 'Not only does he want us to carry out some ridiculous activity that has nothing to do with our work – he can't organise it properly either'. The outward appearance of competence really does matter.

The review session

There has been no formal mention of what is variously described as the review session, post-mortem or de-brief. It seems to feature in almost all training programmes, is seldom questioned, but enjoys no general agreement about how it should be conducted. Badly handled, it can appear as an attempt by the organiser to reassert his control of the situation, to trick students into asserting that they have learnt something, and to emphasise points that should have become obvious during the play but have failed to do so. It is not a subject on which firm rules can be given, for so much depends on the beliefs that each tutor holds about the learning process and on the circumstances in which he is working. However, brief comment under the headings of 'objective setting' and 'student habits' may be useful.

Objective setting

It can reasonably be argued that a review session is less important if the objectives of the activity have been thought through carefully beforehand, explained to the participants and related to the different events as and when they arise. The value of the training session itself will have thus been increased, there will be less to be cleared up afterwards, and the matters that do get raised will be more fundamental. Briefly, 'Make a good job of the main session and there will be less tidying-up to do afterwards'.

Student habits

This refers to habits of learning which may be so deeply ingrained that there is no hope of changing them. The two ends of the spectrum are the lookers-for-authority and the reflective learners. The former expect a very traditional form of instruction and either want or need to have it emphasised several times. It is for these people that one hears training staff repeating the military adage 'I tell them what I am going to tell them, and then I tell them, and then I tell them what I have told them'. There are other learners who commonly spend time reflecting on what they have heard and trying to integrate it with what they know already, possibly altering their overall concept of reality as a result. Provided they have understood the content of the training session, these are probably going to get value from it whether or not there is an extended review. They are likely to discuss the experience privately among themselves and may also raise it formally at a later time.

PART TWO
Directory of British management games

Introduction to the Directory

Copyright

Management games develop in the hands of each user, and the assignment of a particular game to a particular individual or organisation does not necessarily imply that copyright is claimed. One or two organisations have made the point that the origin of the games they can offer is untraceable.

Number of players and teams

The information given is to be regarded as a guide. The circumstances in which a user finds himself often require that a game be adapted to provide a different number of roles, or roles that are either more or less taxing. In most cases this is possible.

Breaks for umpiring

Where this heading appears, it must be regarded as an indication only. The entries submitted by contributors naturally describe a particular use of a game, and this can affect the extent to which the calculation of results holds up play. For instance, a break for umpiring of fifteen minutes would hold up a game if the intention was to play several periods continuously, but it would have no effect if the game was played at discrete meetings on different days.

Indexes

In an attempt to direct the reader's attention to the games that most nearly meet his requirements, every one has been classified by:

1   The type of game it is (model-based, encounter game, structured experience, etc.)
2   Its scope (functional, company, business or environment)
3   The working environment against which it is set (manufacturing industry, retail trading, general, etc.)

The description 'model-based' means the traditional type, the others being distinguished by name. In each description the term *'feedback'* has been used to describe the form in which the student is made aware of the consequences of his decisions and or actions.

Index of backgrounds

This index lists the different working environments, where this is clearly apparent from the description given. In such cases it is assumed that the parameters used in the game, and often the range of values, will be consistent with the background and that the game will be readily comprehensible to players in the same sort of business. Where a game is set against a generalised background, or where the background does not make a significant difference, the game does not feature in this index.

Index of functional areas

This lists the different functional areas of management (production, distribution, etc.) and shows under each heading the games that concentrate upon it. The index does not list games in which the subject is considered in conjunction with others.

Alphabetical index of games with description and classification

Action Plan

Management situation: Junior management of several functions in a manufacturing and selling company.

Suitable for: Fifth form and sixth form schoolchildren; undergraduates.

Subjects: Industrial marketing; production organisation; purchasing; stockholding; pricing; industrial relations.

Description: Players assume the roles of junior functional managers in the company. They make 'routine' types of decision related to the throughput of the product which commit them to a four-week forward plan. Against this background they are faced with a series of current problems and have to choose a solution from three possible ones provided. The choice has an effect on their business situation.

Decisions: Production to be scheduled; materials to be ordered; response to be chosen to each problem from the different options allowed.

Data available initially: Costs of materials; costs of production; fixed sales price; market forecast.

Feedback: Experience of the impact of the chosen solution to a current problem upon the planned business activity.

Interactive or noninteractive: Noninteractive.

Number of players: 3–16.

Number of teams: 1–4 (3–4 per team).

Duration: 3–4 hours.

Umpiring device: Computer assists in administration and records and compares progress of teams.

Form: Self-contained kit.

Terms: On application.

Available from: Manager, Management Resources, Guest, Keen & Nettlefolds Limited, Group Head Office, Smethwick, Warley, West Midlands B66 2RZ.
Editor's classification: Encounter game. Company. Manufacturing Industry.

The Airways Challenge

Management situation: The management of an airline under conditions of vigorous competition.
Suitable for: Undergraduates; postgraduates; DMS students; foremen/ supervisors; junior managers; middle managers; senior managers.
Subjects: Service capacity; sales promotion; pricing; corporate planning.
Description: The playing teams all have independent access to a computer model that simulates the competitive market for transatlantic air travel. A team can therefore conduct experiments in which they enter not only their own policy but also the policies that they believe their competitors are likely to adopt. In this way they become sensitive to the strengths and weaknesses of various policies in various different market situations.
Decisions: Seats to be provided; price; advertising.
Data available initially: Limited documentation only, since the computer model provided for experiment supplies all necessary data.
Feedback: Financial success of a team's own airline, and of competing airlines.
Interactive or noninteractive: Interactive.
Number of players: 3–60.
Number of teams: 1–10 (3–6 per team).
Duration: 2–4 hours.
Umpiring device: Computer.
Form: Presentation by consultant.
Terms: By negotiation.
Available from: M. A. P. Willmer, Manchester Business School, Booth Street West, Manchester M15 6PB.
Editor's classification: Encounter game. Business. Airline operation.

Alfreds of Alfriston

Management situation: Management of a department store.

Suitable for: Middle managers; senior managers.

Subjects: Financing a business; sales planning; sales promotion; stock-holding.

Description: An exercise that requires players to prepare a sales budget. They must then take operating decisions that will allow them to achieve it profitably.

Decisions: Advertising; merchandising; staff changes; staff pay changes; mark-ups; special sales features.

Data available initially: General description of previous years results; balance sheet; trading account.

Feedback: Monthly balance sheet; trading account; staff report; stock report; semi-net statement; sales (by departments); staff costs. A comparison is made with the same month the previous year.

Interactive or noninteractive: Noninteractive.

Number of players: 2–25.

Number of teams: 1–5 (2–5 per team).

Duration: 6–9 hours.

Umpiring device: Micro-computer.

Form: Presentation by consultant.

Terms: By negotiation.

Available from: A. I. S. Debenham, 9 Roland Way, London SW7 3RF.

Editor's classification: Model-based. Business. Retail trading.

Allied Engineering Contractors

Management situation: A batch production engineering company.

Suitable for: Middle managers; senior managers; postgraduates.

Subjects: Economic environment; financing a business; corporate planning; domestic, consumer goods marketing; sales promotion; production planning; company organisation; distribution.

Description: A computer-based game in which teams manage their own company, and set and implement a strategy for it. Decisions are involved on finance, production, marketing, labour relations, purchasing and inventory control, in relation to the needs of shareholders, management, customers and workforce. Companies compete for finance and markets.

Data available initially: Briefing booklet containing necessary information; first-period decisions.

Feedback: Production, distribution, sales figures; profit/loss and cash-flow statements; share prices of all companies; economic data.

Interactive or noninteractive: Either.

Number of players: 8 upwards.

Number of teams: 2 upwards (4–8 per team).

Duration: 1½–2½ days (including umpiring time).

Umpiring device: Micro-computer (supplied).

Breaks for umpiring: 15 minutes after each decision period of 75 minutes.

Form: As self-contained programme, including services of consultants or by leasing.

Terms: By negotiation, approximately £15.00–£30.00 per participant per day.

Available from: Doug Wood, Manchester Business School, Booth Street West, Manchester M15 6PB.

Editor's classification: Model-based. Business. Consumer durables.

Allocate

Management situation: The provision of social services in the United Kingdom.

Suitable for: Undergraduates; postgraduates; DMS students; foremen/ supervisors; junior managers; middle managers; senior managers.

Subjects: Economic environment; work group organisation; committee work.

Description: A structured role-playing exercise containing preparation stage, team meetings, social services committee meeting, second team meeting, second committee meeting and review. Players work through a decision-making procedure using data provided by the game. Outcomes are thus generated by the game itself.

Decisions: For each role-player, how to present his case, or respond to the statements of others, when discussing general areas of social service, individual case histories, and budgets.

Data available initially: Present scale of operations; particular services offered; past expenditure.

Feedback: Outcome of the final meeting. Relationship between budgets requested and money allocated.

Interactive or noninteractive: Interactive.

Number of players: 5 upwards.

Number of teams: 1 upwards (5–10 per team).

Duration: 6 hours.

Form: Self-contained kit or presentation by consultant.

Terms: On application.
Available from: Maxim Consultants Limited, 6 Marlborough Place, Brighton, East Sussex BN1 1UB.
Editor's classification: Organisational simulation. Environment. Social services.

Alpha

Management situation: Producing and selling complex industrial equipment through a technical sales force.
Suitable for: Postgraduates; DMS students; middle managers; senior managers.
Subjects: Economic environment; corporate planning; industrial marketing; sales planning; production; organisation; stockholding; management accounting; pricing.
Description: The game simulates the operations of companies producing and selling complex industrial equipment in a competitive home market through technical sales staff. Each company has to decide the size of plant it will construct, and then operate it.
Decisions: Production scheduling; pricing; hiring and training of sales staff; advertising; information acquisition; research and development; financial management; new capital investment.
Data available initially: Starting situation of company; market condition; available capital.
Feedback: Units sold, from which teams must prepare financial statements.
Interactive or noninteractive: Interactive.
Number of players: 6–30.
Number of teams: 2–5 (3–6 per team).
Duration: 5–10 hours.
Umpiring device: Manual calculation.
Breaks for umpiring: 15 minutes per playing period.
Form: Presentation by consultant.
Terms: Approximately £150.00 per day.
Available from: B. D. Najak, Durham University Business School, Mill Hill Lane, Durham DH1 3LB.
Editor's classification: Model-based. Business. Industrial equipment.

Alpha Displays Limited

Management situation: Managing a series of genuine industrial situations that have been transposed from their original settings to a 'model' company.

Suitable for: Undergraduates; postgraduates; DMS students; junior managers; middle managers; senior managers.

Subjects: Corporate planning; international marketing; industrial marketing; management accounting; pricing; company organisation; committee work; personnel policies and practices; communication; licensing; product evolution; design management; research and development.

Description: The exercise makes use of a well-documented 'model' company that has been built up by the incorporation of real world events as and when this seemed desirable. The model company therefore has its own history which unrolls for the student as the exercise progresses. The problems posed for the students are problems that actually occurred, so the action taken and the results of that action are known. Alternative actions are handled according to the judgement of the umpire. The exercise is adaptable, and the model company adds to its history with new events. The exercise is particularly useful for stimulating innovation and entrepreneurship. There are a total of eight separate stages.

Decisions: How to handle a series of situations, each of which draws upon the known facts about the model company. The situations include relations with a consortium, setting up a Research and Development department, controlling the evolution of a product and varying the company organisation.

Data available initially: Such knowledge of the history and affairs of the company as is appropriate to the stage of the exercise being conducted.

Feedback: Umpires comments on the decisions made, actions taken or recommendations put forward, based upon his knowledge of the real case from which the event is drawn and on his general judgement.

Interactive or noninteractive: Noninteractive.

Number of players: 4–28.

Number of teams: 1–4 (4–7 per team).

Duration: 18–36 hours in three-hour sessions.

Umpiring device: Umpires assessment, based on case knowledge.

Form: Presentation by consultant.

Terms: By negotiation.

Available from: H. V. Beck, 6 Manland Way, Harpenden, Hertford-

shire AL5 4QS.
Editor's classification: Encounter game. Business. Electronics industry.

Alsirat Limited

Management situation: Financial analysis, cash-flow and profitability.
Suitable for: Middle managers; senior managers.
Subjects: Financing a business; management accounting; pricing.
Description: Alsirat Limited starts as a case study about the interpretation of accounts. It continues as an interactive simulation of a manufacturing and marketing company.
Decisions: Sources of finance; production; price; advertising; credit policy.
Data available initially: A full set of published accounts, analysed during the case study phase.
Feedback: Company's sales; total market size; price, advertising and credit policies of other companies.
Interactive or noninteractive: Interactive.
Number of players: 4–16.
Number of teams: 2–4 (2–4 per team).
Duration: 8–12 hours.
Umpiring device: Manually operated mathematical model.
Form: Presentation by consultant. Component of training course.
Terms: By negotiation.
Available from: Management Training Services, 14 Claytons Meadow, Bourne End, Buckinghamshire.
Editor's classification: Model-based. Business. General.

Annales '76

Management situation: Local authority: district council.
Suitable for: Undergraduates; postgraduates; junior managers; middle managers; senior managers.
Subjects: Economic environment; corporate planning.
Description: A team assesses the basic data and the game then progresses in cycles, representing the financial year of the local authority. The results of decisions taken are fed back to each team, together with the local newspaper, which revises the national and regional scenario and provides information on available options.

Decisions: Local authority finance; community issues (social and economic and physical planning); planning applications.

Data available initially: Description and detailed statistics on the area of the district authority; financial information and priorities for the authority; description of national/local economy.

Feedback: A range of social and economic indicators of success (employment, housing, amenities, development) characteristic of the responsibilities of local government.

Interactive or noninteractive: Noninteractive.

Number of players: 4 upwards.

Number of teams: 1 upwards.

Duration: ½–1 day plus preparation time.

Umpiring device: 'Nexus' accounting system.

Breaks for umpiring: 15–25 minutes after each cycle of play.

Form: Self-contained kit.

Terms: £40.00 per set, inclusive of postage and packing. Includes permission to photocopy materials for organisational use.

Available from: Dr. Margaret Hobson, 15, Malmesbury Park, Hawthorne Road, Edgbaston, Birmingham B15 3TV.

Editor's classification: Model-based. Environment. Local government.

Argal

Management situation: Conduct of a repetitive job.

Suitable for: Undergraduates, postgraduates, DMS students, foremen/supervisors, junior managers, middle managers, senior managers.

Subjects: Personnel policies, industrial relations, management style, management structure, communication.

Description: Argal is designed to simulate experientally such factors as boredom, frustration and lack of purpose which are found in many jobs. As a result, participants feel typical reactions and are affected in terms of their motivation and morale and show different attitudes to productivity, industrial relations and organisational effectiveness.

Decisions: How to conduct oneself under conditions of boredom and frustration and, sometimes, injustice while in paid employment.

Data available initially: Knowledge of the immediate work to be done.

Feedback: There is no formal feedback, since one point of the exercise is that the workforce does not receive the quality of treatment that this would imply.

Interactive or noninteractive: Interactive.

Number of players: 12 upwards.
Number of teams: 2 (6 upwards per team).
Duration: 1½–2½ hours.
Additional resources: Radio, tape recorder or record-player: £2.00 worth of 1p coins: Film, *People and Organisations,* is useful but not essential.
Form: Self-contained kit or presentation by consultant.
Terms: £30 per kit. Consultancy presentation by negotiation.
Available from: Instructional Technology Unit, Dept. of Education Services, Sheffield City Polytechnic, 36 Collegiate Crescent, Sheffield S10 2BP.
Editor's classification: Structural experience. Functional – employee relations.

Atlas

Management situation: Administrative and managerial problems in a marketing and sales division.
Suitable for: Undergraduates; junior managers; secretaries.
Subjects: Company organisation; administration; organisation and methods; management principles and practice; communications; recruitment.
Description: An opening situation is described to the players and a succession of interrelated problems are fed in by the tutors. The solutions chosen affect the teams capability in regard to future developments. The exercise highlights the responsibilities of key personnel and their place in the organisation structure. It demonstrates O & M principles and gives practice in creating job specifications and personnel specifications. It shows management principles and practice in a crisis situation.
Decisions: Verbal commitment to a particular decision on each successive office management problem.
Data available initially: Description of existing circumstances at the start of the game.
Feedback: Experience of the opportunities or limitations created by previous decisions when a new problem arises. Assessment of actions by the tutor at de-briefing.
Interactive or noninteractive: Noninteractive.
Number of players: 15–36.
Number of teams: 3–6 (5–6 per team).

Duration: 6–9 hours.
Umpiring device: Instructor's assessment.
Form: Presentation by consultant.
Terms: By negotiation.
Available from: Ian Machorton, TSL (Training Services) 235 High Holborn, London WC1V 7DN.
Editor's classification: Encounter game. Functional – company organisation.

Basegame

Management situation: Running a company that employs physical, human and financial resources to create and sell a product/service in a changing environment.
Suitable for: Middle managers; senior managers.
Subjects: Economic environment; financing a business; corporate planning; marketing; production organisation; purchasing; management accounting; pricing; distribution.
Description: A generalised framework that treats a business as a system, having inputs and outputs and operating in a changing environment. The computer program allows adjustments to the importance of likely variables and to the degree to which they interact with each other. In this manner the basic concept of the game can be customised to reflect the situation of different organisations.
Decisions: Quantity and quality of inputs to be acquired; quantity and quality of product/service to be offered; scope of distribution; promotional methods to be used; level of investment in each.
Data available initially: Cost, availability and capability of resources; current market state; current financial position of company.
Feedback: Goods the company was able to make/level of service it was able to provide; market demand for the product/service; up-date of economic conditions.
Interactive or noninteractive: Interactive.
Number of players: 8–36.
Number of teams: 4–6 (2–6 per team).
Duration: 1 day.
Umpiring device: Micro-computer.
Form: A specialist service requiring credible data about the company concerned so that the model will reflect its work. The finished exercise is

presented on the first occasion by a consultant.

Terms: Depending on the complexity of the company. From £2000.00.

Available from: Chris Elgood Associates Limited, The Studio, Cranbrook Road, Hawkhurst, Kent TN18 4AR.

Editor's classification: Model-based. Business. General.

Beta

Management situation: Production and sales of an industrial product in an inflationary environment.

Suitable for: Undergraduates; postgraduates; DMS students; middle managers; senior managers.

Subjects: Economic environment; financing a business; corporate planning; industrial marketing; stockholding; management accounting; pricing.

Description: A complex game about producing and selling industrial products in a competitive home market. The problems of inflation are simulated by the umpire's ability to alter input prices for materials, labour, fuel etc.

Decisions: Production scheduling; raw material purchases; marketing and pricing; investment/borrowing; information acquisition; basic research; applied research; directors' salaries; new investment in plant; dividend declared (annually).

Data available initially: Performance of company over the previous two years; profit and loss account; balance sheet.

Feedback: Sales achieved; orders lost; research breakthroughs; prices for raw materials next quarter; cash-flow; stock position; profit and loss account; balance sheet.

Interactive or noninteractive: Interactive.

Number of players: 6–45.

Number of teams: 3–9 (2–5 per team).

Duration: 2½–4½ hours excluding introduction and review.

Umpiring device: Computer.

Breaks for umpiring: 12 minutes per team playing.

Form: Presentation by consultant.

Terms: Approximately £250.00 per day.

Available from: B. D. Najak, Durham University Business School, Mill Hill Lane, Durham DH1 3LB.

Editor's classification: Model-based. Business. Manufacturing industry.

Birkaton

Management situation: Running a company that makes and sells a tonnage material (Birkaton) used in the manufacture of synthetic rubber.

Suitable for: Undergraduates; DMS students; junior managers; middle managers; entrants to an open competition run by Birklands Management Centre.

Subjects: Economic environment; financing a business; corporate planning; industrial marketing; sales promotion; purchasing; stockholding; management accounting; pricing.

Description: A game that uses a limited number of decision variables (10) but links these together, and links them to related costs, in a way that generates comprehensive financial statements about the position of the business. Operating decisions are thus set in the context of their strategic consequences and students are encouraged to take an overall view of the enterprise.

Decisions: Price; expenditure on marketing; expenditure on improvement of quality; expenditure on improvement of plant efficiency; expenditure on plant capacity; material quantity to be purchased; whether or not to build a new plant; capacity of any new plant; whether or not to sell to competitors; whether or not to raise or repay loans.

Data available initially: Raw material costs; variable costs, related to material used; standing charges, related to the plant capacity; price and quality of a competing substitute material; accounting conventions for the game that allow players to make forward estimates of total cost; current state of the market.

Feedback: Total market; market share for all companies; own sales; competitors' prices and qualities; operating statement; profit/loss account; statement of assets and liabilities; statement of realisable cash reserves.

Interactive or noninteractive: Interactive.

Number of players: Flexible.

Number of teams: 2–5.

Duration: Dependent on circumstances of use.

Umpiring device: Micro-computer. (380Z).

Form: Presentation by consultant. Component of training course. Basis of an open competition.

Terms: By negotiation.

Available from: S. T. Lunt, Birklands Management Centre, The Hatfield Centre for Management Studies, 330 London Road, St.

Albans, Hertfordshire AL1 1ED.
Editor's classification: Model-based. Business. Materials industry.

Bissim

Management situation: Management of a manufacturing company.
Suitable for: Undergraduates; postgraduates; DMS students; junior managers; middle managers; senior managers.
Subjects: Economic environment; financing a business; corporate planning; marketing; sales planning; sales promotion; production organisation; purchasing; stockholding; management accounting; credit control; management services; distribution.
Description: A realistic and detailed simulation of a manufacturing company. It is flexible, allowing participants to move from the simple to the complex and from the known to the unknown.
Decisions: Pricing; market research; promotional expenditure; staffing levels; wage rates; production schedules; capital expenditure; bank borrowing; research and development; productivity; overtime rates; quality; industrial relations problems; market segmentation; distribution channels; media selection; trade discounts; sales force size and administration; equity and loan financing; dividends; credit policy; after-sales service.
Data available initially: Full details of the starting position of the company are contained in the participants notes.
Feedback: A print-out of the profit/loss account and balance sheet.
Interactive or noninteractive: Interactive.
Number of players: 3–100.
Number of teams: 1–10 (3–10 per team).
Duration: 10–24 hours.
Umpiring device: Micro-computer.
Form: Self-contained kit including program in BASIC for Tandy, Apple or Pet. Custom-built versions available also.
Terms: £900.00 plus VAT for basic kit. £9000.00 plus VAT for full custom-built version for individual clients.
Available from: Management Games Limited, 2 Woburn Street, Ampthill, Bedford MK45 2HP.
Editor's classification: Model-based. Business. Manufacturing industry.

Boss-man

Management situation: Personnel and staff relations aspects of a business at junior management level.
Suitable for: Foremen/supervisors; junior managers.
Subjects: Industrial relations; communication; motivation; company procedures.
Description: Teams assign a member to each of the subject areas mentioned. Movement of its token on a board causes a team to receive cards which pose problems related to these subjects. The problems are answered in writing and scored by the tutor. Maximum marks are normally obtainable only when a specialist answers questions on his own specialism, but non-specialists are permitted to answer, and there may be group answers. There are also hazard cards and crisis cards.
Decisions: For a team manager, which of his members should handle a problem. For all members, what answer to give to the specific problem posed by a card.
Data available initially: None.
Feedback: The scores attributed to each written answer by the tutor.
Interactive or noninteractive: Noninteractive except in so far as acquisition of a hazard card may enable a crisis to be imposed on the opposing team.
Number of players: 8–16.
Number of teams: 2 (4–8 per team).
Duration: 1–1½ hours plus a review session.
Umpiring device: Subjective judgement of tutor.
Form: Self-contained kit.
Terms: £35.00 per set inclusive of postage, packing and VAT.
Available from: Guardian Business Services, 119 Farringdon Road, London EC1R 3DA.
Editor's classification: Encounter game. Functional – use of authority. General.

Bridge Builders Limited

Management situation: Building a bridge.
Suitable for: Undergraduates; postgraduates; DMS students; foremen/supervisors; junior managers; middle managers; senior managers; administrators.
Subjects: Purchasing; planning; work-group organisation; communica-

tion; delegation.

Description: Knowing what materials the umpire has available, teams are required to design a bridge, purchase the chosen material, and complete the structure to an acceptable standard – profitably.

Decisions: What design to adopt; what materials to buy; how to organise the construction activity; how to cost it; how to schedule the stages; how to ensure acceptable quality.

Data available initially: The nature of the task; the present state; the nature and cost of materials; the allowable actions.

Feedback: The experience of success or failure in completing the structure in achieving the declared cost target and in completing on time.

Interactive or noninteractive: Noninteractive.

Number of players: 4–8 per team.

Number of teams: 2 upwards.

Duration: 3½–4 hours.

Umpiring device: None. The physical progress of the task performs this function.

Form: Self-contained kit. Component of training course.

Terms: Kit, £25.00 for Instructors Manual plus £12–50 (VAT extra) for game materials. Training courses, by negotiation.

Available from: Verax. 60 High Street, Odiham, Hampshire RG25 1LN.

Editor's classification: Practical simulation. Business. Civil engineering.

The Brighton Conference Game

Management situation: The organisation of a major conference.

Suitable for: Undergraduates; postgraduates; DMS students; foremen/supervisors; junior managers; middle managers; senior managers.

Subjects: Financing a business; sales planning; sales promotion; management accounting; pricing; company organisation; workgroup organisation; committee work; conference organisation.

Description: A game that simulates the organisational difficulties of arranging a major conference by setting teams the practical task of gathering information and preparing proposals.

Decisions: Size of planned conference; nature and subject of conference; resources to be made available.

Data available initially: Handbook describing the issues involved and the sort of conference to be planned.

Feedback: Comparison of different resources discovered and chosen by different groups; comparison of different programmes prepared; experience of instructors assessment.
Interactive or noninteractive: Interactive.
Number of players: 4 upwards.
Number of teams: 2 upwards (4–6 per team).
Duration: 6 hours.
Form: Self-contained kit. Presentation by consultant.
Terms: On application.
Available from: Maxim Consultants Limited, 6 Marlborough Place, Brighton, East Sussex BN1 1UB.
Editor's classification: Organisational simulation. Functional – administration. Conference organisation.

Buildem

Management situation: Management of the production side of an engineering business.
Suitable for: Undergraduates; postgraduates; foremen/supervisors; junior managers; middle managers.
Subjects: Production methods; production organisation; purchasing; stockholding; maintenance; quality control.
Description: A game that concentrates on the economics of the production function and the interface between minimising cost and maintaining a good delivery performance.
Decisions: Order quantities; production level; machine loading; overtime; pricing; location of inspection points; expenditure on quality control; maintenance priorities; maintenance frequency and general investment in maintenance.
Data available initially: Description of production conditions in the factory in terms of cost and performance. Description of the market, including a forecast price/demand schedule.
Feedback: Sales, based on price and delivery performance.
Interactive or noninteractive: Interactive.
Number of players: Unrestricted.
Number of teams: Unrestricted (2–5 per team).
Duration: 6–12 hours.
Umpiring device: Formal rules administered by the instructor.
Form: Self-contained kit, comprising Instructor's Manual, 20 sets of participants' notes and all necessary forms.

Terms: £500.00 per set.
Available from: Management Games Limited, 2 Woburn Street, Ampthill, Bedford MK45 2HP.
Editor's classification: Encounter game. Functional – production. Engineering.

The Building Game (Garston)

Management situation: Groups organising the building of a brick and concrete project.
Suitable for: Undergraduates; postgraduates; junior managers.
Subjects: Production organisation; workgroup organisation; supply considerations; effect of design upon the work program.
Description: Players take the role of a builder who has contracted to construct the shell of a two-storey brick and re-inforced concrete structure. They have details of all the activities needed and the capability and cost of the resources involved. They have to schedule the work on a resource allocation chart. They have to make choices without being able to fully foresee the consequences. The final results show variations in contract duration and contract cost. The game includes two designs for the structure, showing how design affects constructional efficiency.
Decisions: Choice of design; whether to subcontract; number of men required; number of machines required; start and finish dates of different parts of contract.
Data available initially: The alternative designs; quantities of materials needed; capabilities and costs of the different resources; sequential order of operations in cases where there is no flexibility.
Feedback: Experience of opportunities and difficulties in completing the contract, these being partly a consequence of the programme to which a team committed itself. Comparison with the results of other groups.
Interactive or noninteractive: Noninteractive.
Number of players: 1 upwards.
Number of teams: 1 upwards.
Duration: 6 hours–2 days.
Umpiring device: The automatic consequence of known rules. Each decision has a known consequence, but the mix of consequences resulting from several decisions is complex, and therefore makes the future state hard to foresee. It only becomes clear as time moves on.
Form: Self-contained kit. (One required for each playing team.)

Terms: £1 per kit including postage.
Available from: Publication Sales Office, Building Research Establishment, Garston, Watford, Hertfordshire WD2 7JR.
Editor's classification: Encounter game. Functional – production scheduling. Construction industry.

Building Societies' Management Game

Management situation: Building society operations.
Suitable for: Undergraduates; postgraduates; DMS students; junior managers; middle managers; senior managers.
Subjects: Economic environment; financing a business; corporate planning; domestic marketing; stockholding; management accounting; personnel policies.
Description: Each team represents a building society and starts from the same position represented by the opening building society balance sheet. For each of the five accounting periods of a round, decisions have to be taken as to the employment of available resources by the building society. Detailed building society situations, with attendant problems, risks and consequences of strategies adopted, are presented by a computer. This enables participants to appreciate fully the corporate nature of planning and control and the complex nature of the building society decision-making process.
Decisions: Typical decisions related to the successful operation of a building society, including share rate; mortgage rate; commission rate; quotas; premium share rate; maximum percentage share balance; marketing; staff remuneration; training; recruitment; equipment; additional branch development; investment strategy.
Data available initially: Opening balance sheet; economic situation; present scale of operations; objectives to be pursued; limits on allowable actions.
Feedback: The game is normally played on a postal basis, and teams receive a computer print-out that constitutes a very detailed management report, including revenue statements, functional accounts and balance sheet.
Interactive or noninteractive: Interactive.
Number of players: Effectively unlimited.
Number of teams: Effectively unlimited.
Duration: A game played on a postal basis starting in February and finishing in November.

Umpiring device: Computer.
Form: Self-contained kit, allowing purchaser to take part in the game, which is centrally administered.
Terms: £55.00 plus VAT per team entering.
Available from: The Chartered Building Societies Institute, Fanhams Hall, Ware, Hertfordshire SG12 7PZ.
Editor's classification: Model-based. Business. Building society.

Burnham Bus Company

Management situation: Management of a public transport company.
Suitable for: DMS students; junior managers; middle managers.
Subjects: The economics of pricing and resource allocation in a transport company.
Description: The exercise is designed to give participants practice in decision-making in the public transport industry. Participants are divided into teams to run a bus company which has a monopoly of certain routes but which is in competition for other types of business. The exercise concentrates on the problem of costing and pricing, the allocation of resources, the evaluation of investment decisions and the financing of a public undertaking.
Decisions: Allocation of resources; prices; advertising; capital investment.
Data available initially: Resources of the company; economic environment.
Feedback: Load factors and sales; decisions made by other companies.
Interactive or noninteractive: Mainly interactive.
Number of players: 12–20.
Number of teams: 4.
Duration: 1–1½ days.
Umpiring device: Manual computation.
Breaks for umpiring: 10 minues after each decision period.
Form: Presentation by authors.
Terms: By negotiation.
Available from: Nicholas Rints and Derek Hayes, The Management Centre, Slough College of Higher Education, Wellington Street, Slough, Berkshire.
Editor's classification: Model-based. Business. Public transport.

Business Management Exercise

Management situation: Managing a company under competitive conditions.

Suitable for: Undergraduates; postgraduates; DMS students; junior managers; middle managers; senior managers; bankers; accountants.

Subjects: Financing a business; corporate planning; domestic marketing; sales planning; sales promotion; production organisation; stockholding; management accounting; pricing; workgroup organisation; communication.

Description: Competing teams decide their own objectives and policies and prepare forecasts, plans and cash-flow projections. They must then seek to achieve their stated objectives by recording successive sets of operating decisions which are umpired and returned to them. The exercise can be integrated with inputs from the umpires relating to business functions or to the behavioural aspects of group cooperation.

Decisions: Buying plant; ordering materials; investing money; hiring and deploying salesmen; advertising expenditure; research and development expenditure; selling price; purchase of market information; acquiring and using capital.

Data available initially: All the companies start from a 'green fields' situation and work from the detailed statement of opportunities and costs that is given in their brief.

Feedback: Materials purchased; materials in stock; units produced; units sold; units in stock; revenue; profit/loss account; balance sheet. Teams can buy market information and calculate their own market share.

Interactive or noninteractive: Interactive.

Number of players: 12–28.

Number of teams: 3–4 (4–7 per team).

Duration: 1½–5 days.

Umpiring device: Programmed forms administered by the umpires.

Breaks for umpiring: Limited breaks for umpiring, but players continue their analysis while this is done.

Form: Presentation by consultant.

Terms: By negotiation.

Available from: Midland Management Exercises, 349 Clarence Road, Sutton Coldfield, West Midlands B74 4LY.

Editor's classification: Model-based. Business. Manufacturing industry.

Buster Trucks

Management situation: The task of identifying and obtaining the information required to solve business problems.
Suitable for: Undergraduates; postgraduates; DMS students.
Subjects: Economic environment; financing a business; corporate planning; domestic marketing; industrial marketing; sales planning; sales promotion; production organisation; stockholding; management accounting; pricing; company organisation; industrial relations; management services; distribution; communication.
Description: Players start with published accounts for the business, which is a manufacturer in the heavy truck sector. The task of the groups is to isolate and request such information as will help them to identify, analyse and evaluate the company's problems. This 'paper chase' leads them through each of the functional areas. Each group operates independently of the others and prepares a presentation of their findings. The umpire can analyse the differences in their findings and relate these to the quality of their information-seeking activity.
Decisions: What information to seek; how to frame enquiries. When the information gathering stage is over, how to use it in the analysis of the company's problems.
Feedback: For each enquiry, the information revealed by the umpire. Generally, the realisation of skill or lack of skill in formulating enquiries – as shown by the value of the information received. Further feedback in this area comes from the comparison of a group's analysis of the situation with that presented by others.
Interactive or noninteractive: Noninteractive.
Number of players: Up to 42.
Number of teams: Up to 6 (5–7 per team).
Duration: 4–6 hours.
Umpiring device: Subjective judgement of the umpire who role-plays the managing director of the company and supplies the answers to the enquiries.
Form: Self-contained kit.
Terms: £100.00 per set.
Available from: R. L. Ritchie, Business Studies Department, North Staffordshire Polytechnic, Brindley Building, Leek Road, Stoke-on-Trent, Staffordshire ST4 2DF.
Editor's classification: Enquiry study. Business. Motor industry.

C & D Breweries

Management situation: Managing a brewery with sales to the trade and sales through tied outlets.
Suitable for: Junior managers; middle managers; senior managers.
Subjects: Financing a business; corporate planning; consumer goods marketing; sales planning; sales promotion; pricing.
Description: A computer-based game about marketing a single product in two different forms and through two different channels.
Decisions: Number of outlets to be maintained; bulk sales price; retail sales price.
Data available initially: A full description of the general situation, the constraints, and the range of allowable decisions.
Feedback: Bulk sales achieved, retail sales achieved.
Interactive or noninteractive: Noninteractive.
Number of players: 4–16.
Number of teams: 2–4 (2–4 per team).
Duration: 4–6 hours.
Umpiring device: Micro-computer.
Form: Presentation by consultant.
Terms: By negotiation.
Available from: A. I.S. Debenham, 9 Roland Way, London SW7 3RF.
Editor's classification: Model-based. Functional – sales/marketing. Brewery.

Can You Run A Business?

Management situation: Running a television rental company.
Suitable for: Junior managers; middle managers.
Subjects: Financing a business; sales planning; stockholding; management accounting; pricing.
Description: A self-administered exercise in which, having made decisions, players have direct access to the model and calculate their own results.
Decisions: Price; advertising; stock levels; finance.
Data available initially: Costs; availability of finance and other resources. The game being self-administered, there is data about a 'dummy' company to make the procedures of playing clear.
Feedback: Sales; market share.
Interactive or noninteractive: Noninteractive.

Number of players: 1 upwards – a self-administered game for personal use at players own pace and convenience.
Duration: At individual players discretion.
Umpiring device: Manual calculation method provided for each player.
Form: Self-contained kit.
Terms: By negotiation.
Available from: Management Training Services, 14 Claytons Meadow, Bourne End, Buckinghamshire.
Editor's classification: Model-based. Functional – marketing, television rental.

CAP That!

Management situation: Negotiating terms prior to entry to a common market.
Suitable for: Undergraduates; postgraduates; DMS students; middle managers; senior managers; administrators.
Subjects: Economic environment; communication.
Description: A role-play that promotes understanding of the Common Agricultural Policy by re-creating the problems of British entry to the EEC. Four teams adopt the roles of The British Government, The Commission, The National Farmers Union and The Commonwealth. Each has a separate brief from which they prepare a case and negotiate with the others.
Decisions: Negotiating positions to be adopted by the different parties.
Data available initially: All relevant facts are supplied in the briefs.
Feedback: Success or lack of it in the negotiating activity of the game. Comparison of the agreed result in the role-play with what happened in reality.
Interactive or noninteractive: Interactive.
Number of players: 20–60.
Number of teams: 4 (5–15 per team).
Duration: 6–8 hours.
Form: Presentation by consultant.
Terms: By negotiation.
Available from: D. V. Marshall, Department of Law, North Stafford-shire Polytechnic, Brindley Building, Leek Road, Stoke-on-Trent, Staffordshire ST4 2DF.
Editor's classification: Organisational simulation. Functional – economic relationships. International relations.

The Card Game

Management situation: Problem-solving by a group.
Suitable for: Undergraduates; postgraduates; DMS students; foremen/ supervisors; junior managers; middle managers; senior managers.
Subjects: Behaviour.
Description: By using a specially designed set of cards, a team is set a problem requiring each member to be satisfied with his part of it before the overall problem is considered complete. This involves considerable interaction between the members and the modification of personal desires and opinions to meet group goals.
Feedback: Evaluation of performance of a group by instructor and colleagues.
Number of players: 1–80.
Number of teams: Any number of groups of 3–8 players.
Duration: 1–2 hours.
Form: Presentation by consultant.
Terms: By negotiation.
Available from: Urwick Management Centre, Baylis House, Stoke Poges Lane, Slough, Berkshire.
Editor's classification: Structured experience. Functional – group effectiveness. General.

Career Development Exercise

Management situation: Personnel decisions relating to appointment, transfer and promotion.
Suitable for: DMS students; middle managers; senior managers; trainee personnel officers.
Subjects: Personnel policies.
Description: Each team is presented with an organisation chart and details of the personnel. Additional data is obtained by 'interviewing' the personnel (tutor). Each round simulates one year. The teams make decisions on personnel administration and the computer feeds back performance consequences. The tutor decides on leavers.
Decisions: Appointments; transfers; promotions; inducements; terminations.
Data available initially: Basic job and personnel characteristics; personnel policies.
Feedback: Experience levels; work output; leavers. At game review:

evolution of strategies, data handling and individual decisions, implications.
Interactive or noninteractive: Noninteractive.
Number of players: 8–42.
Number of teams: 2–6 (4–7 per team).
Duration: 4–5 hours.
Umpiring device: Computer and instructor's assessment.
Form: Self-contained kit, presented in first instance by supplier.
Terms: By negotiation.
Available from: F. Wedgwood-Oppenheim, Institute of Local Government Studies, Birmingham University, Birmingham B15 2TT.
Editor's classification: Model-based. Functional – company organisation. General.

Cereal Marketing Game

Management situation: The storage and selling of cereals.
Suitable for: Undergraduates; postgraduates; DMS students; junior managers; middle managers; senior managers; farmers.
Subjects: Domestic marketing; sales planning; management accounting.
Description: Players are given a tonnage of grain to sell over six time periods. They decide whether to sell spot or forward contract, at given prices, or offer to sell spot at their own price. Together, the players represent an independent market with the possibility of import if prices are too high or supplies not available. Their objective is to maximise their final cash balance.
Decisions: Quantity to try to sell; price and conditions to quote.
Data available initially: Grain stock; market situation; range of permitted conditions of sale.
Feedback: Tonnage sold; market prices; own cash-flow position.
Interactive or noninteractive: Interactive.
Number of players: 25–35, playing as individuals.
Duration: 2–3 hours.
Umpiring device: Predetermined formulae administered by umpire. Micro-computer version imminent.
Breaks for umpiring: 10–15 minutes between each round.
Form: Self-contained kit.
Terms: Two copies of instructional manual, £5.00.
Available from: B. E. Cox, 21 Shrewsbury Road, Edgmond, Newport, Salop.

Editor's classification: Model-based. Functional – marketing. Produce marketing.

Collective Bargaining

Management situation: A negotiation between management and trade union.
Suitable for: Junior managers; middle managers.
Subjects: Overtime regulations; discipline; subcontracting conditions; redundancy; conditions of service.
Description: A two-part exercise which allows the participants to simulate the atmosphere and conditions attaching to the negotiation of a new agreement on wages and conditions of service. It emphasises that each person at the bargaining table has an individual viewpoint and an individual set of values. Programmed case studies precede a role-playing simulation.
Decisions: What strategy to adopt in negotiations. What words and manner to choose in interacting with others. How to respond to the contributions of others. Whether to accept or reject proposals.
Data available initially: Ideas gleaned from the preceding case studies. Details about the subjects of negotiation set out in brief.
Feedback: Response of the other parties in the negotiation to one's own contributions. Outcome of the negotiation itself.
Interactive or noninteractive: Interactive.
Number of players: 4–20.
Duration: 3–5 hours.
Umpiring device: Model answers (for the Programmed case studies) and scores based on original objectives (for the Role-play).
Form: Self-contained kit comprising Instructor's Manual, 20 sets of Participant's instructions and a supply of decision forms and score sheets.
Terms: £150.00 per set.
Available from: Management Games Limited, 2, Woburn Street, Ampthill, Bedford MK45 2HP.
Editor's classification: Role-play. Functional – industrial relations. General.

Commercial Negotiations

Management situation: Buying and selling a set tonnage of 'idium cores'.
Suitable for: Postgraduates; junior managers; middle managers; purchasing officers; salesmen.
Subjects: Economic environment; industrial marketing; sales planning; purchasing; negotiating.
Description: Participants are divided into teams, and each team is designated as a supplier or a purchaser of 'idium cores'. Each team has a brief, outlining its particular circumstances and the strengths and weaknesses that are peculiarly its own. Each team considers its position and there follows a negotiating session in which purchasers discuss with suppliers the terms of possible bargains. This is followed by a moment of decision when the teams write down 'firm' policies (including the placing of definite orders). The instructor assesses the outcome of these decisions and informs the participants. They are then able to work out the financial implications of what has happened prior to playing another round.
Decisions: Selling price; delivery reliability (by supplier). Identification of supplier most likely to fulfil purchasing requirements (by purchaser).
Data available initially: Production cost; premium production cost; transport cost; quality; delivery reliability (all in basic form).
Feedback: Actual achievement in terms of transport costs, production costs, premium production costs; quality of product and delivery reliability.
Interactive or noninteractive: Interactive.
Number of players: 12–40.
Number of teams: 4–10 (3–4 per team).
Duration: 4–6 hours.
Umpiring device: A set of rules (graphs and tables, etc.) enabling the instructor to assess the outcome of the combined buying/selling decisions and determine the extent to which each is fulfilled.
Breaks for umpiring: No playing time lost.
Form: Self-contained kit.
Terms: £150.00 per set for 20 participants.
Available from: Management Games Limited, 2, Woburn Street, Ampthill, Bedford MK45 2HP.
Editor's classification: Encounter game. Business. Material supply.

Communicate!

Management situation: Groups tackling a communication problem.
Suitable for: Undergraduates; postgraduates; DMS students; foremen/
supervisors; junior managers.
Subjects: Work-group organisation; communication.
Description: Two teams are located in separate rooms and are linked
only by an intercommunication system. They have to communicate
effectively without personal or visual contact.
Decisions: Decisions within the groups about what to say, and how to
interpret what is said to them. Instant decisions by the speaker about the
precise words to be used and the tone of voice to adopt.
Data available initially: Subject matter for communication, provided
with the game.
Feedback: Experience of success or failure when reviewing the exercise
with the other group, and reflecting upon it.
Interactive or noninteractive: Interactive.
Number of players: 6–14.
Number of teams: 2 (3–7 per team).
Umpiring device: None.
Form: Self-contained kit, including audio tape.
Terms: £60.00 per set including postage and packing.
Available from: M. Lynch, Northgate House, Perrymead, Bath, Avon
BA2 5AX.
Editor's classification: Structured experience. Functional – communica-
tion. General.

The Component Game

Management situation: Manufacture and sale of a motor car component.
Suitable for: Undergraduates; postgraduates; DMS students; middle
managers; senior managers.
Subjects: Corporate planning; industrial marketing; consumer marketing; sales promotion; production; purchasing; management accounting;
pricing; company organisation.
Description: A game that presents production and marketing problems,
both of which must be tackled before the overall position of the
company will improve. While the need to balance production and sales
is obvious, this becomes difficult to achieve if progress in the two areas is
not constantly reviewed. In both areas there is considerable room for

the practice of analytical skill and management techniques. Loss of time through umpiring is avoided by means of a time-lag feature.

Decisions: Size of production capacity; number of working hours to be scheduled; maintenance expenditure; R & D expenditure; material to be ordered; number of salesmen and amount of advertising in regard to four different markets; pricing; priority of supply between the four markets.

Data available initially: Full data about the previous month's activity and firm plans for the first month of the game.

Feedback: Production hours achieved; production rate; scrap rate; orders won in each of the four markets.

Interactive or noninteractive: Interactive.

Number of players: 9–48.

Number of teams: 3–6 (3–8 per team).

Umpiring device: Micro-computer program or charts and tables.

Form: Self-contained kit. Presentation by consultant.

Terms: Kit £120.00 per set. Presentation by negotiation.

Available from: Chris Elgood Associates Limited, The Studio, Cranbrook Road, Hawkhurst, Kent TN18 4AR.

Editor's classification: Model-based. Business. Manufacturing industry.

Computer Life Line

Management situation: Relationships between governments and multinational companies.

Suitable for: Undergraduates; postgraduates; DMS students; junior managers; middle managers; senior managers; administrators.

Subjects: Economic environment; financing a business; corporate planning; management accounting; company organisation; industrial relations; communication.

Description: Players are split into three groups that represent a national government, a company, and the trade unions. By negotiations between them, they seek to establish a formal set of conditions which will allow all of them to achieve their major objectives.

Decisions: For each group, what negotiating position to adopt and how to respond to the requirement of the other parties.

Data available initially: All three groups receive a common descriptive brief about the overall situation. They also receive separate briefs about their own circumstances and objectives.

Feedback: The experience of reaching or not reaching a working agreement. Discovery in the review session of the extent to which the three groups achieved their objectives.

Interactive or noninteractive: Interactive.

Number of players: 20–60.

Number of teams: 1, comprising the three role-groups.

Duration: 6–8 hours.

Form: Presentation by consultant.

Terms: By negotiation.

Available from: D. V. Marshall, Department of Law, North Staffordshire Polytechnic, Brindley Building, Leek Road, Stoke-on-Trent, Staffordshire ST4 2DF.

Editor's classification: Organisation game. Functional – negotiation. International business development.

Contractors International

Management situation: Contracting, especially the construction industry.

Suitable for: DMS students; junior managers; middle managers.

Subjects: Economic environment; financing a business; sales planning; management accounting; pricing; tendering in a competitive situation.

Description: Teams bid for contracts and sell resources in a market place. The game illustrates a contracting industry and has special relevance to construction and civil engineering. Time periods represent three months.

Decisions: Resource allocation; tendering; pricing.

Data available initially: Current situation; accounts for previous years.

Feedback: Sales and financial performance of companies.

Interactive or noninteractive: Interactive.

Number of players: 9–25.

Number of teams: 3–5 (3–5 per team).

Duration: 9–12 hours.

Umpiring device: Manual calculation.

Form: Presentation by consultant.

Terms: By negotiation.

Available from: Nicholas Rints and Derek Hayes, Slough College of Higher Education, Management Centre, Wellington Street, Slough, Berkshire.

Editor's classification: Model-based. Business. Contracting.

Counterpaint

Management situation: Management of a multi-product manufacturing company.
Suitable for: Postgraduates; DMS students; senior managers.
Subjects: Economic environment; corporate planning; domestic marketing; production methods; production organisation; management accounting; pricing; distribution.
Description: A detailed computer-based simulation in which companies handle several different products, marketing them in a competitive environment.
Decisions: All operating decisions appropriate to the company simulated.
Data available initially: General description of company and its situation backed up by extensive management information.
Feedback: Operational data necessary for managerial control of the company.
Interactive or noninteractive: Interactive.
Number of players: 24–54.
Number of teams: Minimum of 3.
Duration: 7–10 days.
Form: Presentation by consultant.
Terms: By negotiation.
Available from: D. J. Moul and P. R. Woolliams, PhD, Anglian Regional Management Centre, Duncan House, High Street, Stratford, London E.15.
Editor's classification: Model-based. Business. General.

CRAPID (Commercial Research and Production Interactive Device)

Management situation: Production – research interface.
Suitable for: Undergraduates; postgraduates; junior managers; middle managers; senior managers; production specialists; research specialists.
Subjects: Conflict of attitudes and priorities between people in different functional areas; reasons for such conflicts and strategies for moderating their effects.
Description: Two production units and a central research unit are formed. Time is provided for familiarisation and their initial training. Production takes place in two phases, the break giving research an opportunity to communicate its ideas and seek production approval.

Pilot projects can be run to prove ideas. It is necessary to obtain a labour force, such as fifth or sixth form schoolchildren seeking to learn about industry.

Decisions: Production: what action to take in response to such operating problems as arise; how to respond to projects floated by research. Research: how to communicate with and influence production so that research concepts can be attempted in practice.

Data available initially: Participants' instructions; customer needs and specifications; supplier's catalogue; in-tray data; research unit brief; research aid.

Feedback: Quantity and quality of units produced; financial results.

Interactive or noninteractive: Interactive.

Number of players: 13–24.

Number of teams: Up to 5.

Duration: 10–12 hours.

Umpiring device: Outside stimuli controlled by organiser – otherwise none.

Form: Presentation by consultant.

Terms: By negotiation.

Available from: John R. Cooper, 7 St. George's Avenue, Rugby, Warwickshire CV22 5PN.

Editor's classification: Practical simulation. Functional – research/production interface. Manufacturing industry.

Crimos

Management situation: Achieving the correct definition of a problem in conditions of uncertainty.

Suitable for: Undergraduates; postgraduates; DMS students; foremen/supervisors; junior managers; middle managers; senior managers.

Subjects: Situation analysis; formation of objectives; experiment and the assessment of data. Set against the background of a security problem.

Description: The subject matter of the exercise is a pilfering situation which demands that action be taken. The learning is to do with understanding the real nature of the problem so that the actions chosen are related to the underlying causes rather than to assumptions based on habit or external influence. Incorrect identification of the problem makes it difficult to learn from the results of the policies adopted.

Decisions: How to cope with pilfering. Variables include the level of policing; deployment of security staff; prosecution policy and sentencing policy. An integral part of the decision-making is agreement on the objective a policy is intended to reach. The situation permits more than one.

Data available initially: Past four months figures for offenders caught, pilfering methods used, money spent in dealing with offenders, policing costs, pilfering loss, and total cost of pilferage.

Feedback: Up-dated figures under the headings given for data available initially, plus a notional figure called the 'equivalent monthly payment' which measures overall success.

Interactive or noninteractive: Noninteractive.

Number of players: 4–21.

Number of teams: 4–7 (1–3 per team).

Duration: ½–1 day.

Umpiring device: Computer.

Form: Presentation by consultant.

Terms: By negotiation.

Available from: M. A. P. Willmer, Manchester Business School, Booth Street West, Manchester M15 6PB.

Editor's classification: Model-based organisation game. Functional – security. General.

Culture and Commerce

Management situation: International trade negotiations.

Suitable for: Managers and experts in international firms; development assistance officials and experts; international business students.

Subjects: The impact of differences in national cultural approaches on the success of international trade.

Description: Players are divided into 4–5 teams belonging to different countries. Each team has both business objectives as well as culturally determined practices, habits and values, which must be respected. After an initial phase of 'tourism', in which one or two players from each team visit the others, teams start trading. Success depends on both business skills and cultural insight.

Decisions: What to offer and to demand, where and how to do it.

Data available initially: Population size and per capita GNP of all countries; products of all countries; own trading objectives.

Feedback: Multiplicity of actual objectives in an intercultural business situation; relativity of own business approach; tension between achievement of own goals and respect for others' cultures.

Interactive or noninteractive: Interactive.
Number of players: 10–30.
Number of teams: 4–5 (2–7 per team; teams of unequal size).
Duration: 3 hours.
Form: Self-contained kit.
Terms: On application.
Available from: IRIC (Institute for Research on Intercultural Cooperation), Velperweg 95, 6824 HH Arnhem, the Netherlands, telephone (85) 612647.
Editor's classification: Organisational simulation. Functional – marketing. International trading.

Dart Aviation Limited

Management situation: Management of an aircraft manufacturing company.
Suitable for: Fifth form and sixth form schoolchildren.
Subjects: Methods of manufacture; work allocation; quality control; pricing; advertising.
Description: Buying raw material from the umpires, competing companies make and sell paper aircraft. Market share is determined by pricing and advertising decisions of different teams judged in relation to one another. For goods to be accepted, aircraft must be at least 17 cm long and 8 cm wide and fly at least 4 metres.
Decisions: How to design and make the product. What materials to buy. Price; advertising.
Data available initially: Conditions of the game. Availability and cost of materials.
Feedback: Orders received; products accepted; profit or loss on sales.
Interactive or noninteractive: Interactive.
Number of players: Flexible.
Number of teams: Flexible.
Duration: 4 hours.
Umpiring device: Tutors judgement, within guidelines.
Form: One representative item in a packaged set of 'Five Simple Business Games'. (With Gorgeous Gateaux. Fresh Oven Pies. The Island Game. The Republic Game.)
Terms: On application.
Available from: Careers Research and Advisory Centre, Bateman Street, Cambridge CB2 1LZ.

Editor's classification: Practical simulation. Company. Manufacturing industry.

Decision

Management situation: The application of disciplinary rules and procedures in employment.
Suitable for: DMS students; foremen/supervisors; junior managers; middle managers; senior managers.
Subjects: Industrial relations.
Description: Players are given six specific items of information about a disciplinary problem and are asked to decide on the action they would take. Depending on the choice, and the reasons given, they receive one of a limited number of overkey cards which varies one or more of the items they previously possessed. The process is repetitive, and players steadily improve their understanding of the issue.
Decisions: What action to take, in the light of the data available at each stage, and how to justify it.
Data available initially: Information on the current problem in the form of six specific items.
Feedback: Discovery of new information as a result of the choice made.
Interactive or noninteractive: Noninteractive.
Number of players: 6–20.
Number of teams: 2–4 (3–5 per team).
Duration: 30–60 minutes.
Umpiring device: Tutor's judgement about what card to give as a result of the decision and the explanation.
Form: Self-contained kit.
Terms: £35.00 plus VAT.
Available from: Supervisory Management Training Limited, Peak House, 66 Croydon Road, Beckenham, Kent BR3 4AA.
Editor's classification: Enquiry study. Functional – use of authority. General.

Delivered on Time

Management situation: Job scheduling.
Suitable for: Undergraduates; postgraduates; DMS students; foremen/supervisors; junior managers; middle managers; senior managers;

students from age 15 upwards.

Subjects: Production methods; production organisation; stockholding; management accounting; interaction between sales order requirements and capacity variables.

Description: The game can be played in two versions. A simple 'static' game illustrating the basic guidelines to follow when scheduling jobs that depend on one another and a more complex 'dynamic' game. This introduces unplanned events into the scheduling as well as allowing for cost penalties in the assessment of results. Each team is given a scheduling board, details of the job to be completed, and any restrictions applying. They must then plan production in such a way as to achieve stated goals.

Decisions: Resource allocation; planning; scheduling; utilisation; costing; storage (work-in-progress and finished goods); delivery.

Data available initially: Resource capacity; orders; time requirements.

Feedback: Resource utilisation; work-in-progress; finished goods in store; machine situation; batch splitting; early and late delivery.

Interactive or noninteractive: Interactive.

Number of players: Up to 20.

Duration: 1–3 hours.

Form: Self-contained kit.

Terms: £55.00 plus VAT.

Available from: Supervisory Management Training Ltd., Peak House, 66 Croydon Road, Beckenham, Kent BR3 4AA.

Editor's classification: Encounter game. Functional-production scheduling. Manufacturing industry.

Devex Chemical Company Limited

Management situation: Managing an R & D project. Choosing projects for an R & D portfolio.

Suitable for: Middle managers; senior managers (in R & D and marketing).

Subjects: Corporate planning; industrial marketing; pricing; company organisation; communications.

Description: A two-stage exercise starting with the opportunity to examine the record of the Devex Chemical Company in regard to a particular R & D project. Players are allowed to submit five questions to the instructor about the conduct of the project, which are answered in writing. Because of the restriction on the number there is heavy emphasis on the quality of the questions put. This is done individually, and the answers are considered by students in groups, each group then reporting its findings. A similar device is employed in the second part of the exercise, which is concerned with choosing between the three new R & D projects.

Decisions: What questions to submit to the umpire, and how to frame them.

Data available initially: Detailed brief about the existing situation. Diary of events over four years relating to the initial project studied. Details of further projects available.

Feedback: Usefulness of the questions formulated, as revealed by the value that can be drawn from the answers.

Interactive or noninteractive: Noninteractive.

Number of players: 9–20.

Number of teams: 3–4 (3–5 per team).

Duration: 8–12 hours.

Additional resources: Photocopier.

Form: Presentation by consultant, or part of training course.

Terms: By negotiation.

Available from: Urwick Management Centre, Bayliss House, Stoke Poges Lane, Slough, Berkshire.

Editor's classification: Enquiry study. Functional – R & D. Chemicals.

Disclose

Management situation: A business enterprise.

Suitable for: Undergraduates; postgraduates; DMS students; foremen/ supervisors; junior managers; middle managers; senior managers; functional specialists; trade unionists; school pupils.

Subjects: Financing a business; sales planning; production methods; production organisation; management accounting; company organisation; workgroup organisation; personnel policies; industrial relations; behaviour and motivation.

Description: Teams are formed and briefed. Each sets itself up as a company, with an organisation suitable for the manufacture of a particular physical product using resources that have been specified and observing some given constraints. Each team takes its turn at putting the planned organisation into practice, using workers drawn from the other teams. A few players are selected beforehand to be observers. Measured results, and observed behaviour, are analysed at the review stage.

Decisions: Number, type and quality of end product to be made; organisation and methods to be used; relationship to be sought with workforce, suppliers and customers.

Data available initially: Participants instructions; syndicate instructions; customers needs and specifications; suppliers catalogue.

Feedback: Quality and quantity of products completed; financial results; behaviour of workforce; own feelings; reports of observers about the behaviour of all parties.

Interactive or noninteractive: Interactive.

Number of players: 10–60.

Number of teams: 2–6 (5–10 per team).

Duration: 10–16 hours.

Form: Presentation by consultant.

Terms: By negotiation.

Available from: John R. Cooper, 7 St. George's Avenue, Rugby, Warwickshire CV22 5PN.

Editor's classification: Practical simulation. Company. General.

Discost

Management situation: A construction industry project.

Suitable for: Undergraduates; postgraduates; foremen/supervisors; junior managers; middle managers; senior managers; construction industry personnel.

Subjects: Financing a business; management accounting; company organisation; workgroup organisation; personnel policies; industrial relations; tendering; project management.

Description: The exercise structures a central management team and a site management team and several project teams. The project teams compete by tender for the execution of a construction project. The contract is awarded to one or two of them by the client. Unsuccessful project teams are made redundant and join a labour pool. Construction and installation are carried out by the site management team, advised by the project team that was successful. When construction is finished, there is testing and final acceptance by the client. A review is held after the game to consider and examine the views and experiences of all parties (including observers).

Decisions: Details of scheme offered; tender price and conditions of contract; negotiating procedure; personnel policies; deployment of team members.

Data available initially: Participants' instructions; client's brief; client's specifications; materials and plant catalogues; contract forms.

Feedback: Physical progress of a contract, including time taken, costs incurred and degree of conformity to specification; observable behaviour of the parties.

Interactive or noninteractive: Interactive.

Number of players: 9–25.

Number of teams: 3–5, always including one management team (3–5 per team).

Duration: 8-10 hours.

Form: Presentation by consultant.

Terms: By negotiation.

Available from: John R. Cooper, 7 St. George's Avenue, Rugby, Warwickshire CV22 5PN.

Editor's classification: Practical simulation. Company. Construction industry.

Dislocate

Management situation: A production environment.

Suitable for: Undergraduates; postgraduates; DMS students; foremen/supervisors; junior managers; middle managers; senior managers; functional specialists; trade unionists; school pupils.

Subjects: Production methods; workgroup organisation; personnel policies; industrial relations; motivation and demotivation.

Description: An exercise that sets up a simulated factory and allows each team in turn to manage it, using another team as the workers. A third team observes. Conditions are so structured that workers commence the activity with high motivation: any diminution of this is due to management action. Results are measured, recorded, analysed and compared. Observers' reports, and the feelings described by managers and workers, are then discussed. The exercise creates an excellent environment for the study of organisations.

Decisions: How to deploy and utilise a well motivated workforce.

Data available initially: Participants' instructions and constraints; work programme; customers' specifications; factory lay-out, machines and processes; job descriptions.

Feedback: Measured data relating to quantity and quality of output and utilisation of resources, especially human resources; observed and/or

expressed motivational state of workers.
Interactive or noninteractive: Interactive.
Number of players: 10–45.
Number of teams: 2–6. Optimum 3 (5–7 per team).
Duration: 5–8 hours.
Form: Presentation by consultant.
Terms: By negotiation.
Available from: John R. Cooper, 7 St. George's Avenue, Rugby, Warwickshire CV22 5PN.
Editor's classification: Practical simulation. Company. Manufacturing industry.

Distribution Management Game

Management situation: Import, packing, distribution and sale of a toy.
Suitable for: Undergraduates; postgraduates; DMS students; junior managers; middle managers; senior managers.
Subjects: Financing a business; corporate planning; domestic marketing; consumer goods marketing; sales planning; production organisation; stockholding; management accounting; pricing; distribution; location of plant and depots; vehicle scheduling; replacement parts.
Description: The game studies the relationship between the functional roles of production, marketing and distribution, emphasising the value of distribution as a marketing tool through the variables of plant and depot location and vehicle scheduling. The teams study the information provided and formulate a strategy. Then, in successive time periods, they make decisions on pricing, production levels, vehicle scheduling and similar matters. The decisions are recorded on forms and umpired by computer. The results are made known through a computer print out. After a sufficient number of rounds have been played a feedback session terminates the exercise. The game has optional decision areas involving trade unions, bank negotiations and tenders for contracts.
Decisions: Leasing or terminating the lease of factories or depots in suitable locations; hiring or firing workmen, drivers and · salesmen; buying and selling of vehicles; maintenance of vehicles; ordering unpacked toys; scheduling packing of toys; scheduling trunking of toys from factory to depot; scheduling distribution of toys to sales areas; pricing.
Data available initially: Capital resources available to the project; indication of the costs of each activity; data about the population

distribution in the geographical area covered.

Feedback: Goods, vehicles and labour on strength at each factory and depot at the end of the time period; information on prices charged by and locations of factories and depots of competitors; sales made and orders gained in each sales area; balance sheet; statement of assets; warning of purchases not made because of insufficient overdraft facilities.

Interactive or noninteractive: Interactive.

Number of players: 12–30.

Number of teams: 4–6 (3–5 per team).

Duration: 4–8 hours.

Umpiring device: Computer.

Breaks for umpiring: Limited breaks between decision periods.

Form: Self-contained kit, with computer program supplied on cards or tape. (Equipment required is computer with Fortran IV compiler, at least 24K of CPU and back-up storage – preferably discs – for sequential access files.)

Terms: By negotiation.

Available from: C. D. T. Watson-Gandy, 12, Thorney Hedge Road, Chiswick, London W4 5SD.

Editor's classification: Model-based. Functional – marketing/distribution. Consumer goods.

Down The Line

Management situation: Delegation of work within a company.

Suitable for: DMS students; foremen/supervisors; junior managers; middle managers.

Subjects: Delegation.

Description: A maze exercise in which players work through a text, taking one decision after another as the problem develops. Players experience consequences appropriate to their choices.

Decisions: Which of certain options to choose when dealing with problems arising over the delegation of work.

Data available initially: Details about the company concerned, the staff situation, and the circumstances surrounding the delegation problem.

Feedback: Experience of the consequences attached to the choice made (predetermined but previously unknown to the players).

Interactive or noninteractive: Noninteractive.

Number of players: Flexible. Exercise is used by individuals or small

groups and large numbers only require additional copying of material.
Duration: 25–50 minutes plus discussion time.
Form: Self-contained kit in the form of a reproducible master.
Terms: £45.00 per kit.
Available from: Supervisory Management Training Limited, Peak House, 66 Croydon Road, Beckenham, Kent BR3 4AA.
Editor's classification: Maze. Functional – delegation. Office management.

Economania

Management situation: Production of 'desirable goods and services' within a simulated economic environment.
Suitable for: Undergraduates; postgraduates; DMS students; foremen/supervisors; junior managers; middle managers; senior managers.
Subjects: Economic environment; financing a business; production; management accounting; pricing; industrial relations; customer purchasing patterns.
Description: A practical simulation in which players are assigned roles as bankers, managers or workers and have to organise the manufacture of a number of extremely simple products. Each management/worker team makes a different product and every player also has a second role as an individual customer. In this role he is required to assume a defined 'purchasing preference' in regard to the products that are being made. All these individual preferences are different. Money starts in the hands of the bankers, passes to the managers as capital and thence to managers and workers as salaries and wages. It then returns to the companies through the roles of the individuals as purchasers. The game as a whole offers a dramatic representation of economic affairs. It is played in rounds.
Decisions: As appropriate to the different roles: amount of capital to be borrowed/lent and interest to be asked; assessment of likely purchasing power of public and amount that might be won by each team; production to be attempted; relative rewards to be promised to managers/workers; cost of production expected and sales price to be set; whether to acquire new production machinery and how to share out any benefits that it may bring.
Data available initially: Amount of money in the economy; number of products on the market; cost of raw materials. To each individual, his own 'purchasing preference'.

Feedback: Practical experience of production and sales achievement as compared with that which was expected.

Interactive or noninteractive: Interactive.

Number of players: 20–48.

Number of teams: 5–8 (4–6 per team).

Duration: 6–12 hours.

Umpiring device: A set of rules governing the order in which available goods are purchased by individuals.

Form: Presentation by consultant.

Terms: By negotiation.

Available from: Chris Elgood Associates Limited, The Studio, Cranbrook Road, Hawkhurst, Kent TN18 4AR.

Editor's classification: Practical simulation. Environment. General.

The Electronic Local Authority

Management situation: Different groups of personnel within a local authority exploring the implications of information technology.

Suitable for: Postgraduates; DMS students; foremen/supervisors; junior managers; middle managers; senior managers; administrators.

Subjects: Economic environment; corporate planning; industrial relations; motivation; communication; information technology; local government.

Description: A role-playing exercise which sets up four groups: senior elected members and chief officers, technologists, middle-range professionals, and clerical/administrative staff (including trade union representatives). The groups identify coming events in information technology, assess the impact upon them and report to a plenary session. They next consider differences that seem likely to arise between their group and other groups because of differing viewpoints. Then there is interaction between the groups to search for an agreed strategy in regard to information technology. The final phase is in separate groups again, considering what progress has been made towards an agreed strategy and examining the forms of behaviour which helped or hindered progress.

Decisions: Personal and group decisions about attitudes to be adopted in negotiation and about how to respond to others. Adjustment or opposition to the interests of other groups in a situation that implies both a need to cooperate, and some degree of conflicting interest.

Data available initially: A scenario describing a local authority in which computing staff have proposed to senior officers and elected members that investments be made in new technology. Information about relevant technology is available from the tutors.

Feedback: Effect on others of individual and group behaviour, as judged from their response. Greater or lesser success in promoting personal or group viewpoint. Greater or lesser success in reaching an agreed strategy. Tutor's comments.

Number of players: 12–30.

Number of teams: 4–5 (3–6 per team).

Duration: 3 hours to 3 days.

Umpiring device: Direct response of other parties. Self-assessment. Instructors assessment.

Form: Presentation by consultant. Component of training course at Institute of Local Government Studies. Self-contained kit following briefing by supplier.

Terms: By negotiation.

Available from: Simon Baddeley, Institute of Local Government Studies, University of Birmingham, P.O. Box 363, Birmingham B15 2TT.

Editor's classification: Organisational simulation. Functional – negotiation. Local government.

Energy Strategy Exercise

Management situation: UK energy policy to the year 2000.

Suitable for: Postgraduates; DMS students; middle managers; senior managers.

Subjects: Economic environment; corporate planning; public policy.

Description: The exercise models public policy-making as an interactive, interorganisational process. The teams take the roles of energy industries, the environmentalist lobby and the British Government.

Decisions: Policy for own industry or group; alliances and negotiations with other industries; recommendations for government energy policy and action.

Data available initially: Up-to-date information on energy supply and demand; fuel mix for UK; forecasts and plans of energy industries.

Feedback: Experience of agreements reached or not reached in negotiations; plenary review by Deputy Secretary for Energy or International Energy Consultant.

Interactive or noninteractive: Interactive.

Number of players: 15–66.
Number of teams: 5–6 (3–11 per team).
Duration: 6–7½ hours.
Form: Self-contained kit.
Terms: By negotiation.
Available from: Professor Bernard Taylor, Henley – The Management College, Greenlands, Henley-on-Thames, Oxfordshire RG9 3AU.
Editor's classification: Organisational simulation. Functional – public relations. Energy industry.

The Esso Students' Business Game

Management situation: Directing a company that manufactures and markets music centres.
Suitable for: Undergraduates; postgraduates; junior managers; fifth and sixth form schoolchildren.
Subjects: Financing a business; corporate planning; consumer goods marketing; sales planning; production organisation.
Description: Each team starts with a factory with capacity for six production lines, and borrows money from the bank to install lines and cover initial production and marketing expenses. Planning ahead is required since two periods must elapse before the decision to produce can result in a sale. The volume of production must be scheduled one period in advance and the cost of the materials purchased varies with the scale of production scheduled. Each line employs eight staff and each company must decide how much to pay them. Companies are subject to wage demands, and companies paying less than competitors tend to incur strikes.
Decisions: Production capacity; production quantity; wages; quality; sales staff and advertising in each of six areas; price.
Data available initially: Full details of the options open to the teams, and their cost. Indication of likely market.
Feedback: Sales demand.
Interactive or noninteractive: Interactive.
Number of players: 12–36.
Number of teams: 4–6 (3–6 per team).
Duration: 1 day.
Umpiring device: Calculation by umpires. Computer program now also available.
Breaks for umpiring: Manual version only, 20 minutes.

Form: Self-contained kit.
Terms: Approximately £25.00 (Manual version).
Available from: The Careers Research and Advisory Centre Limited, Bateman Street, Cambridge CB2 1LZ.
Editor's classification: Model-based. Business. Consumer goods.

Exaction

Management situation: Developing agricultural industries.
Suitable for: Professionals in development; government administrators (finance and rural development); students in economics, development studies, geography etc.
Subjects: National economic management; rural development; small farmers' decision making; urban/rural terms of trade; international terms of trade; trading intermediaries.
Description: An extension of the Green Revolution Game, to include an urban/industrial sector, domestic and international currency and a role for government.
Decisions: Farming investment decisions; industrial investment decisions; marketing structures; trading policy; government pricing; exchange rate; money supply.
Data available initially: Village resource allocation; urban resource allocation; production functions, both urban and rural; money supply; external prices.
Feedback: Extensive debriefing on individual farm parameters, industrial production data, population data, money supply/inflation data, ruses and results of trading intermediaries, activities of bankers, access to and use by government of information.
Interactive or noninteractive: Interactive.
Number of players: 24–36.
Number of teams: 11–20.
Duration: 2 hours (introduction), 6 hours (playing), 1½ hours (debriefing).
Form: Self-contained kit, in addition to Green Revolution Kit.
Terms: By negotiation.
Available from: Swarmhurst Limited, 36 St Andrew's Road, Cambridge CB4 1DL.
Editor's classification: Organisational simulation. Business. Farming.

Executive Team

Management situation: Managing a company in competitive conditions.
Suitable for: Postgraduates; DMS students; middle managers; senior managers.
Subjects: Economic environment; financing a business; management accounting; pricing; workgroup organisation.
Description: A competitive and interacting game about production and marketing that can be operated at simple or advanced level. Optional features include a negotiating exercise and the financial restructuring of the business.
Decisions: Selling price; marketing expenditure; production plans; plant and transport investment; research and development investment. Wage negotiations and equity problems may be introduced if desired.
Data available initially: Past pricing; sales costs; loan limits; previous market strategies.
Feedback: Market share; production costs; profit/loss account; balance sheet.
Interactive or noninteractive: Interactive.
Number of players: 6–42.
Number of teams: 2–7 (3–6 per team).
Duration: 1 day or 9 one-hour sessions.
Umpiring device: Computer.
Form: Self-contained kit. Presentation by consultant.
Terms: Kit, £450.00. Presentation, by negotiation.
Available from: Alameda Software (Micro-computers in Business Education), Friern Lodge, The Avenue, Ampthill, Bedford MK45 2NR.
Editor's classification: Model-based. Business. General.

Exercise Albatross

Management situation: Management of a company in the motor retail business.
Suitable for: Junior managers; middle managers.
Subjects: Economic environment; financing a business; corporate planning; sales planning; stockholding; management accounting; pricing.
Description: An exercise designed to give participants understanding of the management of a single garage with a new and used car department,

a service department and a department responsible for the sale of petrol and parts. Teams compete for sales in each of these departments and are also concerned with the interdependence of individual aspects of the business, especially as the service department is involved in PDI and warranty work. Teams are provided with a financial reporting system which enables them to investigate the profitability of various activities and to ensure the profitability/survival of the business.

Decisions: Stock levels of new and used cars; mark-ups; promotion; employment of salesmen; operating decisions on service department, on forecourt and on spares department; financing the business.

Data available initially: Present level of operations.

Feedback: Sales of cars, petrol, parts and service hours; cars traded-in and their value; labour turnover in service department.

Interactive or noninteractive: Interactive.

Number of players: 9–20.

Number of teams: 3–4 (3–5 per team).

Duration: 14–18 hours.

Umpiring device: Manual computation.

Breaks for umpiring: 10 minutes after each decision period.

Form: Presentation by authors.

Terms: By negotiation.

Available from: Management Training Services, 14 Claytons Meadow, Bourne End, Buckinghamshire.

Editor's classification: Model-based. Business. Motor trade.

Exercise Alborak

Management situation: Small company operation.

Suitable for: Undergraduates; foremen/supervisors; junior managers.

Subjects: Economic environment; financing a business; domestic marketing; production organisation; management accounting; pricing; industrial relations.

Description: Teams make decisions on the major function of a small company. These decisions cover three months in the life of the business.

Decisions: Production levels; marketing decisions; wage levels; financing the business.

Data available initially: Present resources; company accounts; past sales.

Feedback: Market share; productivity.

Interactive or noninteractive: Interactive.

Number of players: 6–24.
Number of teams: 2–6 (3–4 per team).
Duration: 6–8 hours.
Umpiring device: Manual calculation.
Form: Presentation by consultant.
Terms: By negotiation.
Available from: Management Training Services, 14 Claytons Meadow, Bourne End, Buckinghamshire.
Editor's classification: Model-based. Business. General.

Exercise Chelone

Management situation: Financial control in a manufacturing company.
Suitable for: Postgraduates; DMS students; junior managers; middle managers; senior managers.
Subjects: Financing a business; corporate planning; purchasing; stockholding; management accounting; pricing; cash-flow; micro-economics.
Description: Teams make operational decisions in circumstances which are structured to highlight the financial implications. Decisions cover three months in the life of the business and each set of decisions is designed to illustrate different financial techniques.
Decisions: Production and marketing decisions with an emphasis on financial aspects.
Data available initially: Resources; financial results of earlier years.
Feedback: Sales, financial results.
Interactive or noninteractive: Interactive.
Number of players: 6–24.
Number of teams: 2–6 (3–4 per team).
Duration: 9–12 hours.
Umpiring device: Manual calculation.
Form: Part of three day training course – 'Finance for non-financial managers'.
Terms: By negotiation.
Available from: Nicholas Rints and Derek Hayes, The Management Centre, Slough College of Higher Education, Wellington Street, Slough, Berkshire.
Editor's classification: Model-based. Functional – finance. General.

Exercise Citran

Management situation: Operation of a city bus company – public sector.
Suitable for: Postgraduates; DMS students; middle managers; senior managers.
Subjects: Economic environment; financing a business; corporate planning; management accounting; pricing; industrial relations; politics.
Description: The exercise takes place against a predetermined five year economic and political background. Each team is required to examine the market situation and the social need in its city and to take decisions on resource allocation and fares that will achieve the politically and economically desired objectives.
Decisions: Number of buses; number of drivers; deployment of buses and drivers on routes; fare policy.
Data available initially: Results of last year's operations; inventory of available resources.
Feedback: The extent to which a team has met preset business and social objectives. Some feedback items are apparent after each yearly playing period, others are apparent at the end of the game.
Interactive or noninteractive: Noninteractive.
Number of players: 9–16.
Number of teams: 3–4 (3–4 per team).
Duration: 4–4½ days.
Umpiring device: Instructor's model.
Breaks for umpiring: ¾ hour.
Form: Presentation by consultant.
Terms: By negotiation.
Available from: T. R. Garrison, MA(OXON), MA(BRUNEL) I.M.P., 10 Tunmers End, Chalfont St. Peter, Buckinghamshire SL9 9LW.
Editor's classification: Model-based. Company. Public transport.

Exercise Cobbler

Management situation: The strategic response of domestic producers to the import of cheap foreign products. Based on the shoe industry.
Suitable for: Postgraduates; DMS students; middle managers; senior managers; employees in the private sector shoe industry.
Subjects: Economic environment; international marketing; domestic marketing; consumer goods marketing; production methods; management accounting; pricing; industrial relations; implications of

automation for an industry.

Description: A game for four teams in which three operate as domestic producers and one as an importer. Decisions are made by all teams on volume, range of styles, marketing mix, prices, and the technology to be used. The model shows how it is possible to fight back when conditions have apparently changed for the worse.

Decisions: Overall business strategy; technology to be used; production/ import quantities; range of styles; prices.

Data available initially: Extensive background picture of the past operation of the competing teams. Economic and market place scenario.

Feedback: Marketing and financial performance, from which teams calculate profit and loss accounts and balance sheets.

Interactive or noninteractive: Interactive.

Number of players: 12–20.

Number of teams: 3–4 (4–5 per team).

Duration: 3½ days.

Umpiring device: Instructors model.

Breaks for umpiring: 1 hour between each of the five rounds of the game.

Form: Self-contained. Presentation by consultant.

Terms: £300.00 per day for consultant. Game free of charge.

Available from: T. R. Garrison, MA(OXON), MA(BRUNEL) I.M.P., 10 Tunmers End, Chalfont St. Peter, Buckinghamshire SL9 9LW.

Editor's classification: Model-based. Business. Shoe industry.

Exercise Goldcrest

Management situation: Marketing a consumer product.

Suitable for: Undergraduates; DMS students; junior managers.

Subjects: Consumer goods marketing; sales promotion; pricing.

Description: A short simulation in which teams aim to maximise profits by marketing consumable products. The effects of competitive marketing are dramatically demonstrated and the exercise provides a vehicle for teaching managerial economics with particular emphasis on the economies of oligopoly.

Decisions: Price; advertising; promotion – type and expenditure.

Data available initially: Company resources.

Feedback: Sales; total market; marketing decisions of competitors.

Interactive or noninteractive: Interactive.

Number of players: 3–27.
Number of teams: 3–9 (1–3 per team).
Duration: 2–3 hours.
Umpiring device: Manual computation.
Breaks for umpiring: 5 minutes after each decision period.
Form: Presentation by authors.
Terms: By negotiation.
Available from: Nicholas Rints and Derek Hayes, The Management Centre, Slough College of Higher Education, Wellington Street, Slough, Berkshire.
Editor's classification: Model-based. Functional – marketing. Consumer goods.

Exercise Lemming

Management situation: Management of a company in the consumer durable market.
Suitable for: Postgraduates; DMS students; junior managers; middle managers; senior managers.
Subjects: Economic environment; financing a business; corporate planning; international marketing; domestic marketing; sales planning; production; stockholding; management accounting; pricing; industrial relations; capital investment.
Description: This exercise provides a vehicle through which the student can identify the need for, and can practise, management planning and control techniques – with special emphasis on financial and cost control. Teams manage a company producing and marketing a consumer-durable product in the UK, and as the exercise progresses opportunities arise to diversify into additional markets. There is also scope to develop a technically improved product, to direct cost-reduction exercises and to introduce labour productivity schemes.
Decisions: Production: size of labour force; single/double shift/ overtime; pay level; stockholding; capital investment. Marketing: pricing; advertising; size and pay of sales force. Research and development: launch of new models; raising finance.
Data available initially: Balance sheet; details of resources; sales and environmental data for past three years.
Feedback: Sales (home and export); labour turnover; results of R & D, cost reduction and productivity expenditure. Information about competitors – prices, advertising, etc. – and about the environment –

price index, wages and earnings, bank rate and hire-purchase controls, etc. Company share prices.
Interactive or noninteractive: Interactive.
Number of players: 4–30.
Number of teams: 2–6 (2–5 per team).
Duration: This exercise is the basis of a 4½ day residential management course.
Umpiring device: Manual computation.
Breaks for umpiring: 10 minutes after each decision period.
Form: Presentation by authors.
Terms: By negotiation.
Available from: Nicholas Rints and Derek Hayes, The Management Centre, Slough College of Higher Education, Wellington Street, Slough, Berkshire.
Editor's classification: Model-based. Business. Consumer durable.

Exercise Phoenix

Management situation: Management of a department store.
Suitable for: Junior managers; middle managers; senior managers.
Subjects: Financing a business; corporate planning; sales planning; sales promotion; purchasing; stockholding; management accounting; pricing; allocating resources.
Description: Participants manage the operations of a medium-sized department store. Decisions are required on pricing policy, stock levels and promotional activity, and floor space has to be allocated and staffed. The exercise concentrates on the financial implications of the decisions and provides a vehicle for understanding management reporting systems.
Decisions: Stock levels; margins; advertising; allocation of floor space; size and allocation of sales staff; clearances.
Data available initially: Present scale of operations; previous year's sales by quarters and by departments; accounts for previous year.
Feedback: Sales by departments; turnover of labour; information about other stores represented in the exercise.
Interactive or noninteractive: Interactive.
Number of players: 6–16.
Number of teams: 3–4 (2–4 per team).
Duration: 12–15 hours.
Umpiring device: Manual computation.

Breaks for umpiring: 10 minutes after each decision period.
Form: Presentation by authors.
Terms: By negotiation.
Available from: Management Training Services, 14 Claytons Meadow, Bourne End, Buckinghamshire.
Editor's classification: Model-based. Business. Retail trade.

Exercise Playabout

Management situation: Operation of a public sector leisure centre.
Suitable for: Postgraduates; DMS students; middle managers; senior managers.
Subjects: Economic environment; financing a business; corporate planning; management accounting; pricing; industrial-relations; politics.
Description: A game that concentrates on the problem of meeting social and financial and political objectives in a public sector enterprise. Each team has a dual role, one as a political group setting objectives for another group of leisure centre managers and one as a leisure centre management group itself responsible to a political group.
Decisions: Size of centre; sports facilities offered.
Data available initially: Size and socio-economic nature of city concerned; political background – local and national; economic situation.
Feedback: Extent to which each leisure centre management team has met the business and social objectives established for it. Some feedback items are apparent after each playing period, others are apparent only at the end of the game.
Interactive or noninteractive: Interactive.
Number of players: 9–16.
Number of teams: 3–4 (3–4 per team).
Duration: 3½–4½ days.
Umpiring device: Instructor's model.
Breaks for umpiring: ¾ hour.
Form: Presentation by consultant.
Terms: By negotiation.
Available from: T. R. Garrison, MA(OXON), MA(BRUNEL) I.M.P., 10 Tunmers End, Chalfont St. Peter, Buckinghamshire SL9 9LW.
Editor's classification: Organisational simulation. Company. Leisure facilities.

Exercise Prospect

Management situation: Establishing a common understanding within a group when tackling a complex task.
Suitable for: Undergraduates; postgraduates; DMS students; junior managers; middle managers; senior managers.
Subjects: Communication; interpersonal relations; logical decision-making.
Description: The exercise simulates a search for minerals in which layers of rock are represented by coloured counters. The only way to find the colour of a lower layer is to remove the one on top. Players are provided with a clue which can be interpreted in several different ways, thus supporting several different arguments about the best method of exploration. Players frequently do not appreciate that different interpretations are being made, and therefore have difficulty in understanding the logic of each other's proposals.
Decisions: Successive decisions about which counter to remove as the exploration progresses.
Data available initially: The top (visible) colour in each of the mining locations, and the clue.
Feedback: On each removal of a counter, the colour of the one found underneath it and the support (or contradiction) that it offers to the theory being followed.
Interactive or noninteractive: Noninteractive.
Number of players: 3–6.
Number of teams: 1 (Each group requires one set of the equipment).
Duration: 30–45 minutes plus discussion time.
Form: Self-contained kit.
Terms: £25.00 for first set. Thereafter £20.00 per set.
Available from: Chris Elgood Associates Limited, The Studio, Cranbrook Road, Hawkhurst, Kent TN18 4AR.
Editor's classification: Encounter game. Functional – communication. General.

The Expedition

Management situation: Planning a desert expedition.
Suitable for: Undergraduates; postgraduates; DMS students; foremen/supervisors; junior managers; middle managers; senior managers.
Subjects: Workgroup organisation; planning; communication;

delegation.

Description: Teams undertake the organisation and planning for an expedition, recording their strategy and their operational decisions on a checklist. This is scored by the umpire who compares it with a master-list of his own. Events characteristic of such an expedition are then described, so that it can be seen how well the plans made by the teams would enable them to cope.

Decisions: Identification of the requirements for an expedition and decisions on how to meet them.

Data available initially: A brief describing the conditions of the expedition and the constraints within which the teams must work.

Feedback: Comparison of a team's checklist with the model held by the umpire. Realisation by the teams that, due to inadequate planning, they might not be able to cope with some of the events described to them.

Interactive or noninteractive: Noninteractive.

Number of players: 4–28.

Number of teams: 4 (1–7 per team).

Umpiring device: Model checklist held by the umpire, and knowledge provided for him of likely events during such an expedition.

Form: Self-contained kit.

Terms: £99.00 per set plus postage and packing.

Available from: M. Lynch, Northgate House, Perrymead, Bath, Avon BA2 5AX.

Editor's classification: Encounter game. Functional – planning. Exploration.

Experimark

Management situation: Using a market model to test out alternative strategies.

Suitable for: Undergraduates; postgraduates; DMS students; junior managers; middle managers; senior managers.

Subjects: Consumer goods marketing; sales promotion; pricing; management accounting; financial planning.

Description: The scenario postulates the opening of a chain of shops in a new territory. Teams are given access to a computer model of market behaviour in six locations that are broadly similar to those in which the new ones may be located. Head Office insist that all shops should adhere to a common policy, so teams have to test out a range of alternative marketing strategies to see which would have the greatest overall success. It is not essential to use all locations – if the best results come from a policy that uses only some of them, that is acceptable.

Decisions: Each strategy to be tested comprises decisions on staffing; training; range of goods; mark-up percentage; advertising.

Data available initially: Details of the experimental range that the computer model can cope with. No additional data is necessary because experiments are unrestricted.

Feedback: From each experiment, the 'Contribution to overheads' resulting from the use of the chosen policy in the chosen location.

Interactive or noninteractive: Noninteractive.

Number of players: 4–7 per team.

Number of teams: 1 upwards, but every team needs a micro-computer.

Duration: 4–6 hours.

Umpiring device: Micro-computer.

Form: Presentation by consultant.

Terms: By negotiation.

Available from: Chris Elgood Associates Limited, The Studio, Cranbrook Road, Hawkhurst, Kent TN18 4AR.

Editor's classification: Encounter game. Functional – marketing. Retail stores.

Fast Buck

Management situation: Coping with financial problems connected with the international trade cycle.

Suitable for: Undergraduates; postgraduates; DMS students; junior managers; middle managers; senior managers.

Subjects: Economic environment; corporate planning; international marketing; sales planning; production organisation; purchasing; management accounting; pricing; arbitrage; competition law.

Description: The exercise sets up conditions of limited competition in which teams are cast as suppliers of material to manufacturers or as manufacturers themselves. The ultimate source of material is role-played by staff members, as are the customers to whom the manufacturers are seeking to sell. Within this context, the teams have to determine their own objectives and seek to achieve them. The environment is volatile and there are temptations to questionable commercial behaviour.

Decisions: What official sales price to publish; what specific deals to make with suppliers and customers (possibly varying the price); what agreements to seek with other parties in order to safeguard one's interests against competition and a changing environment.

Data available initially: Commercial and economic statements about the two countries concerned; market forecasts (at a cost); exchange rates; existing cost data so that teams are able to determine prices.

Feedback: The negotiations with suppliers and customers have a definite result, which enables financial performance figures to be calculated.

Interactive or noninteractive: Interactive.

Number of players: 40–200.

Number of teams: 10–20 (4–10 per team).

Duration: Flexible.

Umpiring device: None. Results are supplied by the outcome of negotiations with staff, but the economic environment and its changes are pre-determined.

Form: Presentation by consultant.

Terms: By negotiation.

Available from: D. V. Marshall, Department of Law, North Staffordshire Polytechnic, Brindley Building, Leek Road, Stoke-on-Trent, Staffordshire ST4 2DF.

Editor's classification: Organisational simulation. Functional – Public relations. High technology.

Finance

Management situation: The accounting function at a non-technical level.

Suitable for: Non-financial managers.

Subjects: Accounting practices; ratios; profit margin; stock turnover; current assets; liquidity.

Description: A simulation designed to help non-financial managers improve their skills with financial information so that they are able to make better decisions in their own areas.

Decisions: At each stage, which option to choose when faced with a number of possible interpretations offered for some accounting data presented.

Data available initially: The simulation is in two parts. The first explains the construction of the profiting and budgeting function and enables the student to tackle the problems presented in the second part.

Feedback: Discovery of the choices made by the other participants. Experience of reaching a consensus. Discovery of the choice recommended by the author.

Interactive or noninteractive: Noninteractive.
Number of players: 3–24 (optimum 9–12) participants as individuals or as teams.
Duration: 4-6 hours or equivalent in separate sessions.
Umpiring device: Programmed text.
Breaks for umpiring: None.
Form: Self-contained kit, comprising Instructor's Manual, 20 sets of Participant's workbooks and 20 sets of Answer sheets.
Terms: £400.00 per set.
Available from: Management Games Limited, 2, Woburn Street, Ampthill, Bedford MK45 2HP.
Editor's classification: Programmed simulation. Functional – finance. General.

Financit

Management situation: Manufacture and sale of products in a changing market.
Suitable for: Undergraduates; foremen/supervisors; junior managers; middle managers.
Subjects: Economic environment; corporate planning; production organisation; purchasing; stockholding; management accounting; pricing.
Description: A game that concentrates on the expected life-cycle of a product and shows the need for profitability in the present so as to be able to re-equip for making the products of the future. The game uses a playing board and symbols to express the decisions made.
Decisions: How many of the three possible products to make and sell. For each of them, quantity of material to purchase; number of units to make; price to be asked.
Data available initially: Material costs; probabilities attaching to the manufacturing facility; market forecasts.
Feedback: Quantity produced; quantity demanded by customers.
Interactive or noninteractive: Interactive.
Number of players: 9–32.
Number of teams: 3–8 (3–4 per team).
Duration: 2–4 hours.
Umpiring device: Micro-computer program or manually operated formulae.
Form: Self-contained kit or presentation by consultant.

Terms: Self-contained kit £120.00 per set. Presentation by consultant, on application.
Available from: Chris Elgood Associates Limited, The Studio, Cranbrook Road, Hawkhurst, Kent TN18 4AR.
Editor's classification: Model-based. Business. General.

Finansim

Management situation: Financial management in a company manufacturing a consumer durable.
Suitable for: Undergraduates; junior managers; middle managers; accountancy students.
Subjects: Financing a business; corporate planning; consumer goods marketing; sales promotion; production organisation; stockholding; management accounting; pricing.
Description: A model-based game that places special emphasis on the calculation and use of financial measures such as dividends, return on assets and gearing ratio. It deals with the relationship between commercial success and the ability to raise capital. It provides an introduction to corporate financial analysis for the non-specialist and helps the professional accountant to understand the impact of management decisions on the accounts.
Decisions: Pricing; marketing research; promotion; credit; production quantity; production capacity; share issues; bank borrowing and repayment; dividends; payment to suppliers.
Data available initially: Detailed description of the business situation to be encountered.
Feedback: Sales, response to share offers.
Interactive or noninteractive: Noninteractive.
Number of players: 4–24.
Number of teams: 2–6 (2–4 per team).
Duration: 6–15 hours.
Umpiring device: Circular slide rule or mini-computer program.
Breaks for umpiring: Not significant.
Form: Self-contained kit, comprising Instructor's Manual, 20 sets of participants' notes, slide rule, and all necessary forms.
Terms: £500.00 plus VAT per set.
Available from: Management Games Limited, 2 Woburn Street, Ampthill, Bedford MK45 2HP.
Editor's classification: Model-based. Company. Consumer durable.

Finmark

Management situation: A newly created company set up to manufacture and sell two versions of a new type of consumer durable.
Suitable for: Undergraduates; postgraduates; junior managers; middle managers.
Subjects: Financing a business; consumer goods marketing; production; stockholding; management accounting; pricing.
Description: The game is designed to highlight financial and marketing problems in a manufacturing business. It usually occupies eight quarterly decision periods. In addition to the normal problems thrown up by the game, extra ones are supplied for use at the instructor's discretion.
Decisions: Price fixing; subcontracting; use of plant; advertising expenditure; cash discounts; market forecasts; production forecasts.
Data available initially: Working capital; likely demand and possible prices; costs of production; credit limits.
Feedback: Total sales of each model and individual company sales of each model.
Interactive or noninteractive: Interactive.
Number of players: 6–25.
Number of teams: 3–5 (2–5 per team).
Duration: 5–7 hours.
Umpiring device: Nomographs and charts.
Breaks for umpiring: 15-20 minutes between decision periods.
Form: Self-contained kit.
Terms: £500.00 per set.
Available from: Management Games Limited, 2 Woburn Street, Ampthill, Bedford MK42 2HP.
Editor's classification: Model-based. Business. Consumer durable.

Fire! At Mansfield

Management situation: Responding to an outbreak of fire in a factory.
Suitable for: Administrative and security staff who are concerned with emergencies.
Subjects: Effects of an outbreak of fire; appropriateness of possible actions at different stages of the emergency.
Description: Players are taken through the scenario by listening to tape recordings. These confront them with choices of action at certain

strategic moments and the choices lead them to open numbered envelopes. The envelopes contain comments on what they have done. The tape recordings are supplemented by a simulated Alarm Panel, having pages that indicate what the real panel would look like at different moments. At a certain point the choices made by the players cause them to get different results, so that some survive the emergency better than others.

Decisions: Successive limited choice decisions about how to respond as the emergency develops.

Data available initially: The kit contains detailed plans of the factory and its fire control system.

Feedback: In the early stages the choices result only in written comment and all players resume at the same point. As the exercise progresses, they influence the emergency and so provide direct feedback by results.

Interactive or noninteractive: Noninteractive.

Number of players: Flexible.

Number of teams: Flexible.

Duration: Dependent on the intentions of the user.

Form: Self-contained kit.

Terms: Available only by agreement with Factory Mutual International.

Available from: FM Insurance Company Limited, Southside, 105 Victoria Street, London SW1E 6QT.

Editor's classification: Maze: Functional – emergency services. Manufacturing industry.

Fluted And Squared

Management situation: The management of a manufacturing company over several simulated weeks.

Suitable for: Undergraduates; postgraduates; DMS students; foremen/supervisors; junior managers; trainee systems analysts.

Subjects: Financing a business; corporate planning; industrial marketing; sales planning; production organisation; purchasing; stockholding; management accounting; pricing; company organisation; industrial relations; management services; distribution; communication.

Description: Delegates play the role of managers running a company. A computer, sometimes aided by the team's adviser, plays the roles of all people with whom the team interacts: e.g. shop steward, foreman, auditor, supplier, customer, bank manager. Each week the team can quote for orders, order its raw materials, produce and sell products and obtain or repay bank loans. 'Hazards' can be introduced to complicate the running of the company, and these require decision and action by the managers. At the end of each week the team must produce 'company accounts'. These are 'audited' by reference to computer-produced analyses.

Decisions: Selling price; advertising strategy; purchase quantities; production quantities; quotations to be offered; delivery priorities; how to organise the group itself; how to handle industrial relations problems; how to measure performance.

Data available initially: Present scale of operations; past pricing strategy; economic situation; material costs; supplier information; current cash and stock position; current order book; customer information; production costs.

Feedback: Units produced; sales made; expenses incurred; purchases made; size of order book; stockholding; profit and loss account; evaluation of systems developed.

Interactive or noninteractive: Noninteractive.

Number of players: 4–7 per team.

Number of teams: Dependent on number of micro-computers and umpires.

Duration: 4–6 hours.

Umpiring device: Micro-computer and Instructor's assessment.

Form: Self-contained kit (Apple II microcomputer required). Presentation by consultant. Component of training course at BL Systems Limited.

Terms: By negotiation.

Available from: BL Systems Limited, Grosvenor House, Prospect Hill, Redditch, Worcestershire.

Editor's classification: Model-based. Business. Manufacturing industry.

Free Enterprise

Management situation: Management of a company competing with one or more others in world markets.

Suitable for: Undergraduates; postgraduates; DMS students; junior managers; middle managers.

Subjects: Economic environment; financing a business; corporate planning; international marketing; industrial marketing; management accounting; pricing.

Description: The computer program for this game is written in such a way that the computer can itself supply playing teams. The game can thus accommodate any mix of human and non-human teams up to a total of six. It is therefore playable as a single-person study experience or as a competitive team game. There are three levels of difficulty, the simplest one demanding only two decisions from the players and the computer supplying the rest. The intermediate and advanced levels release successively more variables to player control.

Decisions: Selling price; cost of sales; plant improvement; research and development investment; loans to be taken or repaid; dividends to be paid.

Data available initially: Descriptive scenario; news bulletins; stock market reports; industry reports; market surveys; sales analysis by areas; production reports; sources and employment of finance; profit/ loss account; balance sheet.

Feedback: Up-dates of the initial data consequent upon the decisions made.

Interactive or noninteractive: Interactive.

Number of players: 1–36.

Number of teams: 1–6 (1–6 per team).

Duration: 1–2 hours.

Umpiring device: Micro-computer.

Form: Presentation by consultant or by licensing agreement. (Equipment provided would be Manual and Diskette – Apple II or IBM PC.)

Terms: By negotiation.

Available from: Science Research Associates Limited, Newtown Road, Henley-on-Thames, Oxfordshire RG9 1EW.

Editor's classification: Model-based. Business. General.

Gambit

Management situation: The process of building design.

Suitable for: Undergraduates; postgraduates.

Subjects: Economic environment; ecological environment; building design; relations between specialists; relations between suppliers and users.

Description: A simulation of building design that features integrated teams of specialists (e.g architects, quantity surveyors, etc.) and concentrates on thermal design structure and cost. It pays special attention to solar gain storage and control. Physical materials are used to simulate proposed structures.

Decisions: For each group of specialists, the best way of employing their expertise within the broad structure proposed, and reaching compromise solutions with other specialist groups involved.

Data available initially: The rules of the exercises; current thought in the specialist areas; ideas drawn from the physical materials provided.

Feedback: The visible evidence of the structure finally agreed by the group, as shown by a model.

Interactive or noninteractive: Interactive.

Number of players: 6–30 depending on the number collectively assigned to a role.

Duration: 8 hours.

Umpiring device: Principally, peer group assessment.

Form: Presentation by consultant, or handbook from which a kit can be prepared.

Terms: Presentation, by negotiation. Handbook, £15.00.

Available from: Cedric Green, Department of Architecture, University of Sheffield S10 2TN.

Editor's classification: Organisation game. Functional – design. Building design.

Global

Management situation: Management of a multinational company.

Suitable for: Postgraduates; DMS students; senior managers.

Subjects: Economic environment; corporate planning; international marketing; domestic marketing; consumer goods marketing; industrial marketing; sales planning; production methods; production organisation; purchasing; stockholding; management accounting; pricing; company organisation; committee work; capital investment; diversification.

Description: A multi-tasking, multi-access portable micro-computer based simulation with data base and management decision-making aids facilities.

Decisions: The full range of decisions appropriate to the situation simulated.

Data available initially: Background data provided by a major case study. Extensive management information also provided as the basis for decision-making.

Feedback: Information printouts and real-life environmental data.

Interactive or noninteractive: Interactive.

Number of players: 27–54 in three teams.

Duration: 5–10 days.
Form: Presentation by consultant.
Terms: By negotiation.
Available from: D. J. Moul and P. R. Woolliams, PhD, Anglian
Regional Management Centre, Duncan House, High Street, Stratford,
London E15.
Editor's classification: Model-based. Environment. Multinational
operations.

The Glow Coat Paint Factory

Management situation: Manufacture and sale of three types of paint
from four raw materials.
Suitable for: Junior managers; middle managers; senior managers.
Subjects: Sales planning; sales promotion; purchasing; management
accounting; stockholding; pricing.
Description: A game concerned with the way in which product mix and
raw material supply can effect marketing decisions.
Decisions: Plant; purchase of raw material (forward and spot); promotion expense; production; price.
Data available initially: Opening balance sheet; income statement for
previous period; opening data sheet; raw materials ordered for Period 1:
raw material prices (forward and spot); sales last period; production
scheduled for Period 1: opening stock of raw materials.
Feedback: Raw material prices (forward and spot); sales last period;
new plant capacity available, with cost; overhead costs for the period.
Interactive or noninteractive: Interactive.
Number of players: 6–15.
Number of teams: 3 (2–5 per team).
Duration: 4½–7½ hours.
Umpiring device: Micro-computer.
Breaks for umpiring: 15–20 minutes.
Form: Presentation by consultant.
Terms: By negotiation.
Available from: A. I. S. Debenham, 9 Roland Way, London SW7 3RF.
Editor's classification: Model-based. Business. Paint manufacture.

Going Into Business On Your Own

Management situation: The purchase and management of a village stores.
Suitable for: Foremen/supervisors; junior managers; middle managers; those potentially self-employed.
Subjects: Buying and running a small business.
Description: Individual players, or teams, represent a person with a capital sum available who wants to own and run a small business. One such business is described as being for sale. The players must seek out information about it and then, as owners of the business, make decisions in response to questions put to them by the computer. At intervals the computer provides data about income, costs, and profit or loss, and these figures are influenced by the decisions that the players have made.
Decisions: (Examples) Selling price of present house; buying price of store and contents; extent of cash trading to be carried on; employment of staff; development of trade; purchase of new equipment; introduction of new ideas; negotiation with inland revenue.
Data available initially: Past history of store as advertised.
Feedback: Computer print-out on costs, income and profit or loss.
Interactive or noninteractive: Noninteractive.
Number of players: 4–21.
Number of teams: 4–7 (1–3 per team).
Duration: ½–1 day.
Umpiring device: Computer.
Form: Presentation by consultant.
Terms: By negotiation.
Available from: M. A. P. Willmer, Manchester Business School, Booth Street West, Manchester M15 6PB.
Editor's classification: Encounter Game (Computer-based). Company. Village stores.

The Green Revolution Game

Management situation: Rural development, agricultural specialist staff in extension.
Suitable for: Professionals in development studies; international agencies, government and supporting services (e.g. rural banking); students in development studies.
Subjects: Peasant farming under uncertainty; technological change;

social and economic group structures; credit.

Description: Participants act in teams to run a farm and family within a third-world village, with unequal resources, potential natural calamities, external trading possibilities, but with freedom to create a responsive social structure.

Decisions: Negotiation with neighbours and officials, farming investment decisions, any other legal or illegal side activities.

Data available initially: Individual farm and family assets, production functions, environmental probabilities.

Feedback: Extensive de-briefing; aggregate village parameters to contrast with individual parameters.

Interactive or noninteractive: Interactive.

Number of players: 12–24 in one playing group.

Duration: 6 hours.

Form: Self-contained kits.

Terms: in UK £195.00, abroad US $395.00 (air freight).

Available from: The Green Revolution Game, Department of Human Nutrition, London School of Hygiene and Tropical Medicine, Keppel Street, London WC1E 7HT.

Editor's classification: Encounter game. Business. Farming.

Grindtown Plant Project

Management situation: Revitalising a manufacturing plant that is scheduled for closure.

Suitable for: Undergraduates; postgraduates; DMS students; foremen/supervisors; junior managers; middle managers; senior managers; administrators.

Subjects: Production organisation; company organisation; workgroup organisation; personnel policies; industrial relations; motivation; communication; delegation.

Description: Teams are given details of a plant manufacturing calculators, which is beset by various problems and will close down in eighteen months if these are not solved. First as individuals and later as teams, they make policy decisions intended to reverse the downward trend.

Decisions: Identification of possible methods of solving the problems, followed by group evaluation of the alternatives and a consensus conclusion about what to recommend.

Data available initially: A description of the factory circumstances, and the problems.

Feedback: For individuals, the comparison of their preferred solutions with those presented by other members of the group. For the groups, comparison of their solutions with those of other groups, and with the umpires judgement.

Interactive or noninteractive: Noninteractive.

Number of players: 4 upwards.

Number of teams: 1 upwards (4–8 per team).

Umpiring Device: Umpire's assessment.

Form: Self-contained kit.

Terms: By negotiation.

Available from: Verax, 60 High Street, Odiham, Hampshire RG25 1LN.

Editor's classification: Encounter game. Functional – company organisation. Electronics industry.

Join

Management situation: Group problem-solving.

Suitable for: Adult education courses.

Subjects: Interpersonal relationships; problem identification and problem solving techniques.

Description: A game that uses commercially available materials to create a problem situation where both goal and method need further definition.

Decisions: For each individual, how to present his views in discussion and whether or not to modify them as a consequence of what he learns from colleagues.

Data available initially: The rules of the game and the ideas suggested by the physical materials offered.

Feedback: Experience of the way in which objectives can be differently defined without the parties being aware of it. Realisation of the way in which different objectives reflect back into methods, and attitudes and interpersonal communication.

Interactive or noninteractive: Interactive.

Number of players: 5 Upwards.

Number of teams: 1 Upwards. (5–10 per team).

Umpiring device: Primarily, peer group assessment.

Form: Instructor's Manual. Game materials commercially available.

Terms: Instructor's Manual, £15.00.

Available from: Cedric Green, Department of Architecture, University of Sheffield S10 2TN.
Editor's classification: Structural experience. Functional – group effectiveness. General.

JO (QS) Business Management Game

Management situation: The management of a quantity surveying practice.
Suitable for: Undergraduates; postgraduates; junior managers.
Subjects: Economic environment; financing a business; management accounting.
Description: A game that concentrates on the implications of changes in the economy for a quantity surveying partnership, and on the flexibility in staffing, turnover etc. necessary to cope with these changes. Roles are allocated to players with specific areas of responsibility. The practice operates through eight yearly playing periods in each of which it must execute commissions, complete accounts and prepare for the future.
Decisions: Staffing levels; amount of office space; extent of indemnity insurance; turnover sought; number of contracts for which to bid.
Data available initially: Starting capital; details of an initial commission; cost of staff; staff ratios; starting economic climate.
Feedback: Commissions won; changes in economic climate; random chances.
Interactive or noninteractive: Noninteractive.
Number of players and teams: Any number, governed only by size of room.
Duration: 4 hours.
Umpiring device: Guidelines for instructor regarding award of commissions in different economic circumstances.
Breaks for umpiring: 10 minutes between sessions.
Form: Self-contained kit.
Terms: Gratis, by special agreement. The game is not freely available outside the auspices of the competition run by the Institution.
Available from: JO (QS) Divisional Committee, Royal Institution of Chartered Surveyors, 12 Great George Street, London SW1P 3AD.
Editor's classification: Model-based. Company. Quantity surveying.

Lawn Trimmers

Management situation: Managing a company that manufactures and sells lawn trimmers.
Suitable for: Undergraduates; postgraduates; DMS students; foremen/supervisors; junior managers; middle managers.
Subjects: Financing a business; corporate planning; domestic marketing; sales promotion; production organisation; management accounting; pricing.
Description: The exercise is based on a market segmented by price, with customer behaviour being different in each segment. Choosing a segment to enter gives clues about the appropriate size of factory to set up and the appropriate quality of product to offer. The game rewards a balanced corporate plan and penalises one that is ill-prepared.
Decisions: Initially, scale of production; quality. Monthly, production quantity; price; advertising; retailers margin; length of guarantee.
Data available initially: Costs of production; price brackets defining the market segments; previous sales volume in each segment and number of existing suppliers; cost of working capital.
Feedback: Sales demand; cost of repairs made under guarantee.
Interactive or noninteractive: Interactive.
Number of players: 6–50.
Number of teams: 2–10 (3–5 per team).
Duration: 3–5 hours.
Umpiring device: Manual calculation or micro-computer.
Form: Self-contained kit.
Terms: £90.00 per set.
Available from: Chris Elgood Associates Limited, The Studio, Cranbrook Road, Hawkhurst, Kent TN18 4AR.
Editor's classification: Model-based. Business. Consumer durable.

The Light Fingered Storeman

Management situation: Disciplinary problem (industrial environment).
Suitable for: DMS students; foremen/supervisors; junior managers; middle managers.
Subjects: Industrial relations.
Description: A maze exercise in which players work through a text, taking decisions one after another as the problem develops. Players experience consequences appropriate to their choices.

Decisions: Which of certain given options to choose when dealing with a case of minor theft at work.

Data available initially: Current situation on employee concerned and on company policy.

Feedback: Experience of the consequences attached to the choice made (predetermined but previously unknown to the players).

Interactive or noninteractive: Noninteractive.

Number of players: 6–20 as individuals or small groups.

Duration: 15–20 minutes and discussion time.

Form: Self-contained kit in the form of a reproducible master.

Terms: £45.00 per kit.

Available from: Supervisory Management Training Limited, Peak House, 66 Croydon Road, Beckenham, Kent BR3 4AA.

Editor's classification: Maze. Functional – industrial relations. Stores.

The Liteblock Company

Management situation: Manufacture, sale and distribution of a product.

Suitable for: Junior managers; middle managers; senior managers.

Subjects: Financing a business; sales planning; purchasing; pricing; domestic marketing; production methods; stockholding; company organisation; management accounting; distribution.

Description: A game in which teams choose between different possible options in several functional areas. Having chosen, they experience the consequent effects upon their organisation as they handle the business won.

Decisions: Purchasing (choosing from spot and two forward rates); production methods (batch, small process and large process options); transport methods (routes; agency or own sales force distribution); sales areas; promotion expense.

Data available initially: Options available and costs. All teams start from scratch.

Feedback: Units sold.

Interactive or noninteractive: Noninteractive.

Number of players: 4–16.

Number of teams: 2–4 (2–4 per team).

Duration: 10–15 hours.

Umpiring device: Micro-computer.

Breaks for umpiring: 15 minutes.

Form: Presentation by consultant.

Terms: By negotiation.
Available from: A. I. S. Debenham, 9 Roland Way, London SW7 3RF.
Editor's classification: Model-based. Company. Manufacturing industry.

Long Time No See

Management situation: Problem of sickness absence and performance (office environment).
Suitable for: DMS students; foremen/supervisors; junior managers; middle managers.
Subjects: Industrial relations.
Description: A maze exercise in which players work through a text, taking decisions one after another as the problem develops. Players experience consequences appropriate to their choices.
Decisions: Which of certain given options to choose when dealing with a case of sickness absence and poor performance.
Data available initially: Current situation on employee concerned and data on recent action.
Feedback: Experience of the consequences attached to the choice made (predetermined but previously unknown to the players).
Interactive or noninteractive: Noninteractive.
Number of players: 6–20 as individuals or small groups.
Duration: 15–20 minutes and discussion time.
Form: Self-contained kit in the form of a reproducible master.
Terms: £45.00 per kit.
Available from: Supervisory Management Training Limited, Peak House, 66 Croydon Road, Beckenham, Kent BR3 4AA.
Editor's classification: Maze. Functional – industrial relations. Office work.

LUGS (Land Use Gaming – Simulation)

Management situation: Land use, development and management.
Suitable for: Undergraduates; junior managers; land administrators.
Subjects: Economic environment; communication; land use.
Description: Players make decisions about the administration, management and development of land areas, plotting these on a visual display and seeking to maximise the benefits derived from land use.

Decisions: What to do with different areas of land.
Data available initially: Descriptive scenario and details of resources.
Feedback: Extent and condition of land held. Financial balances.
Interactive or noninteractive: Interactive.
Number of players: 3–36.
Number of teams: 3–6 (1–6 per team).
Duration: 1½–4 hours.
Umpiring device: Rules administered by the tutor.
Form: Fully described in "Instructional Planning Systems". (J. C. Taylor, 1971. Cambridge University Press).
Terms: Book priced at £12.00.
Available from: Bookshops. Cambridge University Press.
Editor's classification: Model-based. Business. Land use.

The Hoppermute

Management situation: Pricing and manufacturing in the capital-equipment industry.
Suitable for: Undergraduates; postgraduates; junior managers; DMS students; middle managers.
Subjects: Domestic marketing; export marketing; industrial marketing; production; management accounting; pricing.
Description: Players are given detailed rules about the cost of operating a factory and the manner in which this will vary with the workload imposed upon it. They are then asked to quote for various different orders, which, if their tender is accepted, will place constraints on the capacity available in the following three months and the economy with which it will operate. In this new situation they are asked to tender for further contracts. The game thus simulates the on-going nature of a business, with current commitments modifying future plans.
Decisions: What price to quote for particular contracts offered.
Data available initially: The manner in which factory costs will behave. Information about likely customers, in terms of their commercial potential.
Feedback: Experience of profit/loss and favourable/adverse cash-flow depending on the skill shown in foreseeing, and calculating correctly, the effect of contracts tendered for.
Interactive or noninteractive: Noninteractive.
Number of players: 3–36.
Number of teams: 1–6 (3–6 per team).

Duration: 3–6 hours.
Umpiring device: The instructor is required to accept or reject quotations, basing his judgement on knowledge of the game.
Form: Self-contained package.
Terms: £70.00 per set.
Available from: Chris Elgood Associates Limited, The Studio, Cranbrook Road, Hawkhurst, Kent TN18 4AR.
Editor's classification: Encounter game. Company. Manufacturing industry.

Hospitex

Management situation: Management of a hospital ward.
Suitable for: Nurses and nursing students.
Subjects: Hospital ward management (Six wards in all available).
Description: After being given full details of the existing situation in a hospital ward, students receive 'event slips' at approximately 15-minute intervals. These describe events happening in the ward at the moment stated. Students are required to decide upon, and record, their action in relation to each event, and these are reviewed in the final session of the game.
Decisions: Action to be taken on each incident reported.
Data available initially: Patients list, and detailed report on the situation at the start of the exercise. Staff rota list. Time sheet.
Feedback: Experience of the implications of each decision as subsequent problems develop. Comparison of the actions taken with those taken by other groups.
Interactive or noninteractive: Noninteractive.
Number of players: 2–30.
Number of teams: 2–15 (1 or 2 per team).
Duration: 2½–3½ hours.
Additional resources: Instructor requires a degree of medical knowledge.
Form: Self-contained kit.
Terms: £250.00 per ward.
Available from: Management Games Limited, 2 Woburn Street, Ampthill, Bedford MK45 2HP.
Editor's classification: Encounter game. Functional – ward management. Hospital service.

Human Synergistics Consensus Experiences – desert survival

Management situation: A group seeking to reach a good decision by optimal use of the personal skills and resources of its members.

Suitable for: Undergraduates; postgraduates; DMS students; foremen/ supervisors; junior managers; middle managers; senior managers; administrators.

Subjects: Workgroup organisation; motivation; communication; desert survival.

Description: Individuals and teams are asked to rank fifteen items according to their importance to the team's survival after a crash landing in the desert. The simulation demonstrates that when team members work well together their final decision will be better than any individual could have produced alone.

Decisions: Individually, how to rate the importance of the fifteen items. In discussion, how hard to press one's own arguments and to what extent to accept the arguments of others. How to conduct oneself generally during the group deliberations. For the group as a whole, when to accept an existing ranking list as the group's firm solution.

Data available initially: A description of the circumstances leading up to the crash and details of the fifteen items to be ranked.

Feedback: For individuals, the response of others to one's arguments and attitudes. For the groups, comparison of their ratings with the model answer held by the umpire.

Interactive or noninteractive: Noninteractive.

Number of players: 4 upwards.

Number of teams: 1 upwards.

Duration: 3–4 hours.

Umpiring device: Model answer held by the umpire.

Form: Self-contained kit.

Terms: Approximately £3.00 per player.

Available from: Verax, 60 High Street, Odiham, Hampshire RG25 1LN.

Editor's classification: Encounter game. Functional – group effectiveness. Desert survival.

Human Synergistics Consensus Experiences – project planning

Management situation: Planning the implementation of a new project emanating from the R & D function.

Suitable for: Undergraduates; postgraduates; DMS students; foremen/ supervisors; junior managers; middle managers; senior managers; administrators.

Subjects: Workgroup organisation; motivation; communication; project analysis; recruitment; training; budgeting.

Description: The teams are asked to sequence twenty management activities in the order they believe to be correct. This is done first by individual team members, and then by the team as a whole. The team's sequence is usually more accurate than the efforts of any one individual.

Decisions: Individually, how to sequence the twenty activities. In discussion, how hard to press one's own arguments and to what extent to accept the arguments of others. How to conduct oneself generally during the group deliberations. For the group as a whole, when to accept an existing sequence as the group's firm solution.

Data available initially: A description of the project and of the twenty management activities.

Feedback: For individuals, the response of others to one's arguments and attitudes. For the groups, comparison of their sequence with the model answers held by the umpire.

Interactive or noninteractive: Noninteractive.

Number of players: 1 upwards.

Number of teams: 1 upwards.

Duration: 3–4 hours.

Form: Self-contained kit.

Terms: Approximately £3.00 per player.

Available from: Verax, 60 High Street, Odiham, Hampshire RG25 1LN.

Editor's classification: Encounter game. Functional – group effectiveness. General.

Human Synergistics Consensus Experiences – Sub-arctic survival

Management situation: A group seeking to reach a good decision by optimal use of the personal skills and resources of its members.

Suitable for: Undergraduates; postgraduates; DMS students; foremen/ supervisors; junior managers; middle managers; senior managers; administrators.

Subjects: Workgroup organisation; motivation; communication; sub-arctic survival.

Description: Individual and teams are asked to rank fifteen items according to their importance to the team's survival after a crash landing in the Canadian subarctic. The simulation demonstrates that when team members work well together their final decision will be better than any individual could have produced alone.

Decisions: Individually, how to rate the importance of the fifteen items. In discussion, how hard to press one's own arguments and to what extent to accept the arguments of others. How to conduct oneself generally during the group deliberations. For the group as a whole, when to accept an existing ranking list as the group's firm solution.

Data available initially: A description of the events leading up to the crash. A map of the area. Details of the fifteen items, the clothing of the survivors, the terrain, the temperatures, the expected snowfall, the light and the windchill factor.

Feedback: For individuals, the response of others to one's arguments and attitudes. For the groups, comparison of their ratings with the model answer held by the umpire.

Interactive or noninteractive: Noninteractive.

Number of players: 1 upwards.

Number of teams: 1 upwards.

Duration: 3–4 hours.

Umpiring device: Model answer held by the umpire.

Form: Self-contained kit.

Terms: Approximately £3.00 per player.

Available from: Verax, 60 High Street, Odiham, Hampshire RG25 1LN.

Editor's classification: Encounter game. Functional – group effectiveness. Subarctic survival.

Industry Simulation

Management situation: Management/trade union relationships.

Suitable for: Middle managers; senior managers; trade union members.

Subjects: Economic environment; corporate planning; domestic marketing; industrial marketing; pricing; personnel policies; industrial-relations; management services; negotiation.

Description: Participants manage manufacturing companies and unions, for five quarters.

Decisions: Companies: production; marketing; finance; industrial relations. Trade unions: industrial action; recruitment.

Data available initially: Company report; departmental reports; trade

union briefing.
Feedback: Sales; staff movements; industrial action; financial reports.
Interactive or noninteractive: Interactive.
Number of players: 18–70.
Number of teams: 3–10 (6–7 per team).
Duration: 2–2½ days.
Umpiring device: Computer.
Form: Presentation by consultant.
Terms: By negotiation.
Available from: B. R. Aston, Henley, The Management College, Henley-on-Thames, Oxfordshire RG9 3AU.
Editor's classification: Model-based. Business. General.

INHABS – instructional housing and building simulation

Management situation: Managing the development of housing.
Suitable for: Undergraduates; sixth form schoolchildren.
Subjects: Economic environment; inter-group relations; planning and urban design at local level.
Description: A simulation that examines the problems concerned with the growth of housing, paying special attention to economics and to forms of building. Players adopt the roles of different parties to the housing development process and debate the problem using representative symbols and visual aids.
Decisions: For each member, how best to promote the viewpoint he is representing and how to reach sensible compromises with others. For the group, what final solution to adopt.
Data available initially: The instructions describing the context of the game and the roles. Ideas drawn from the materials, plans and visual aids provided.
Feedback: For individuals, the response of colleagues to their ideas. For the group, critical assessment of the agreed plan by themselves and by the umpire.
Interactive or noninteractive: Interactive.
Number of players: 10–40 depending on the number collectively assigned to a role.
Duration: 8 hours.
Umpiring device: Principally, peer group assessment.
Form: Presentation by consultant, or handbook from which a kit can be prepared.

Terms: Presentation, by negotiation. Handbook, £15.00.
Available from: Cedric Green, Department of Architecture, University of Sheffield S10 2TN.
Editor's classification: Structured experience. Functional – planning. Housing development.

The Institute of Clay Technology Executive Game

Management situation: Production and marketing of three products from the brick and cladding industry.
Suitable for: Undergraduates; postgraduates; DMS students; junior managers; middle managers; senior managers.
Subjects: Economic environment; corporate planning; domestic marketing; sales planning; production organisation; stockholding; management accounting; pricing; company organisation; workgroup organisation; delegation.
Description: A flexible game based on the heavy clay industry and using realistic data. The environmental scenario may be changed to suit the circumstances in which it is being used. The three-product situation allows for division of responsibility within the playing teams.
Decisions: Strategy and product mix; capital expenditure; operating decisions; stockholding policy.
Data available initially: Economic forecast; product descriptions; market research reports; capital equipment options; costs.
Feedback: Production and stock levels; market performance; financial performance.
Interactive or noninteractive: Interactive.
Number of players: 3 upwards.
Number of teams: 3–12.
Duration: 5 hours.
Umpiring device: Computer.
Form: Self-contained kit. Presentation by consultant. Component of training course.
Terms: By negotiation.
Available from: Dr. M. R. Harrison, Department of Management Studies, North Staffordshire Polytechnic, College Road, Stoke-on-Trent.
Editor's classification: Model-based. Business. Heavy clay industry.

Interbank

Management situation: Management of a large bank in a competitive environment.
Suitable for: Undergraduates; postgraduates; DMS students; junior managers; middle managers; senior managers.
Subjects: Economic environment; financing a bank; corporate planning; domestic marketing of banking services; management accounting; pricing of loans and deposits; management of major decision areas in a bank such as loan portfolio, deposit base, branch network, liquidity and investment, capital base and dividend policy.
Description: The game provides players with a close approximation to the experience of managing all the main operations of a large bank in a realistic economic environment. After a detailed briefing, teams arrange their organisational structure and prepare a three-year corporate plan plus operational decisions for the first period. The cycle of decisions – results – analysis – decisions continues, with teams submitting their decisions, receiving their results and analysing them in preparation for the next round. The game administrator provides guidance and advice while the game is in progress. After every four periods there is a 'progress evaluation exercise' aided by a computer graphics presentation which displays and analyses team's progress. After 9–12 periods there is a presentation of results and a de-briefing session.
Decisions: Lending (marketing, interest rate, lending limits); deposits (interest rates, current account charges waived, use of money markets); investment decisions; corporate strategy (base rate, branch network, new capital, dividends).
Data available initially: Statement of previous policies on lending and deposits. Key statistics; balance sheet; cash-flow; investment portfolio; branch network; economic forecast; regulatory guidelines.
Feedback: Loans made; deposits raised; results of changes in investment portfolio; changes in statutory reserves; balance sheet; profit/loss; cash-flow; share price.
Interactive or noninteractive: Interactive.
Number of players: 9–60.
Number of teams: 3–12 (3–5 per team).
Duration: 3½–5 days.
Umpiring device: Computer.
Form: Presentation by consultant.
Terms: By negotiation.
Available from: L. C. Galitz, Institute of European Finance, University

College of North Wales, Bangor, Gwynedd LL57 2DG.
Editor's classification: Model-based. Business. Banking.

Interface

Management situation: Selling consumer goods to supermarket chains.
Suitable for: Undergraduates; postgraduates; DMS students; junior managers; middle managers.
Subjects: Corporate planning; domestic marketing.
Description: A consumer item is sold to the central buying department of various supermarket chains. The game deals only with special promotions and focuses upon successive negotiations with 'the buyer' which are independent of each other but can involve very large sales volumes. Teams take supply side decisions and then make proposals to the different buyers at specified times, the proposals varying with the level of success a team has so far achieved and its keenness to win the extra sales. The 'buyers' are programmed to respond according to commercial criteria of their own, which are only hinted at in the information given to the teams.
Decisions: Quantity to be produced; price to be quoted in each proposal.
Data available initially: Costs of producing the item; general policy of each supermarket chain; size of each supermarket chain.
Feedback: After each proposal the 'buyer' reveals his estimate of the sales volume he would expect to achieve, and the total margin, if he were to accept it. Teams are thus able to build up a picture of the criteria which each buyer uses.
Interactive or noninteractive: Noninteractive.
Number of players: 8–36.
Number of teams: 2–6 (4–6 per team).
Duration: 3–6 hours.
Umpiring device: Micro-computer.
Form: Presentation by consultant.
Terms: By negotiation.
Available from: Chris Elgood Associates Limited, The Studio, Cranbrook Road, Hawkhurst, Kent TN18 4AR.
Editor's classification: Encounter game. Functional – marketing. Consumer goods.

International Corporate Simulation

Management situation: International trade between a multinational and host governments.
Suitable for: Senior managers; government officials.
Subjects: Financing a business; corporate planning; international marketing; pricing; economic management of a developing country.
Description: The international company, consisting of a parent company and two subsidiary companies, markets process control systems to two host governments consisting of a Finance Ministry, a National Fertiliser Corporation and a National Bean Company.
Decisions: Finance; corporate management; economic management.
Data available initially: Report for previous year. Consultants' report.
Feedback: Financial reports.
Interactive or noninteractive: Interactive.
Number of players: 15–35.
Number of teams: 5 (3–7 per team).
Duration: 1½–2 days.
Umpiring device: Micro-computer.
Form: Presentation by consultant.
Terms: By negotiation.
Available from: B. R. Aston, Henley – The Management College, Henley-on-Thames, Oxfordshire RG9 3AU.
Editor's classification: Model-based. Environment. Multinational operations.

Irrigation Management Game

Management situation: Operation and maintenance of a gravity-fed irrigation network for agriculture.
Suitable for: Undergraduates; postgraduates; middle managers; senior managers.
Subjects: Water distribution; communication.
Description: Players assume the roles of Farmers (16) and Officials (2). The farmers make choices about what crops they will grow and then negotiate with the officials for the supply of water at timely moments and in the right quantity. The officials make choices about water allocation, so that each farmer gets a certain total quantity in each time period (not always as much as he asked for) which he must then allocate amongst his crops. There are also a sequence of 'events' (controlled by

the umpire) which influence the overall progress of the game.

Decisions: For the farmers, what crops to choose at the beginning; what water allocation to seek; how to allocate each supply, taking into account the state and the needs of each crop. For the officials; how to allocate the available water. For both, how to cope with the 'events' introduced by the umpire.

Data available initially: Crop price range; crop water requirements (at various stages of growth); potential crop yields; crop costs; previous years water supply.

Feedback: The experience of crop growth allowed under the rules of the game (with the associated financial consequences) following from the supply of water obtained and the way it was allocated.

Interactive or noninteractive: Interactive.

Number of players: 9–18.

Number of teams: Usually two teams of 9.

Duration: 4–6 hours.

Umpiring device: The decisions are recorded on maps, from which allocations can be traced and costs and crop growth calculated.

Form: Presentation by consultant, exercise thereafter available to client by agreement.

Terms: By negotiation.

Available from: J. I. M. Dempster, Sir M. MacDonald and Partners Limited, Demeter House, Station Road, Cambridge CB1 2RS or Dr. I. Carruthers, Agrarian Development Unit, Wye College (University of London), Nr. Ashford, Kent TN25 5AH.

Editor's classification: Encounter game. Functional – planning. Agriculture.

It's A Deal

Management situation: Bargaining.

Suitable for: Undergraduates; postgraduates; DMS students; foremen/ supervisors; junior managers; middle managers; senior managers; administrators.

Subjects: Purchasing; pricing; communication; bargaining and negotiation.

Description: The exercise sets up a succession of different encounters between 'buyers' and 'sellers' and for every transaction a score is recorded. The experience provides data for a study of the negotiating and bargaining processes.

Decisions: For each bargaining team, decisions about what to ask and what to offer, and to what extent to compromise.

Data available initially: The details of each potential transaction are different, only being made known to the designated buying and selling teams when they meet. Buyer and seller get separate briefs, but about the same subject.

Feedback: The experience of success or failure in reaching agreement. Satisfaction or otherwise with one's own performance when discovering the extent to which the other party has modified his original objectives in the light of one's declared position. Comparison of one's performance with that of others.

Interactive or noninteractive: Interactive.

Number of players: 12 upwards.

Number of teams: 2. The division into teams is only for the purpose of allowing a convenient rotation of buyers and sellers.

Duration: 2–3 hours.

Form: Self-contained kit. Presentation by consultant.

Terms: By negotiation.

Available from: D. V. Marshall, Department of Law, North Staffordshire Polytechnic, Brindley Building, Leek Road, Stoke-on-Trent, Staffordshire ST4 2DF.

Editor's classification: Structured experience. Functional – bargaining. General.

It's Your Job Now

Management situation: Delegation of work within a company.

Suitable for: DMS students; office supervisors; junior managers; middle managers.

Subjects: Delegation.

Description: A maze exercise in which players work through a text, taking one decision after another as the problem develops. Players experience consequences appropriate to their choices.

Decisions: Which of certain options to choose when dealing with problems arising over the delegation of work.

Data available initially: Details about the company concerned, the staff situation, and the circumstances surrounding the delegation problem.

Feedback: Experience of the consequences attached to the choice made (predetermined but previously unknown to the players).

Interactive or noninteractive: Noninteractive.

Number of players: Flexible. The exercise is used by individuals or small groups and larger numbers only require additional copying of material.
Duration: 25–50 minutes plus discussion time.
Form: Self-contained kit in the form of a reproducible master.
Terms: £45.00 per kit.
Available from: Supervisory Management Training Limited, Peak House, 66 Croydon Road, Beckenham, Kent BR3 4AA.
Editor's classification: Maze. Functional – delegation. Office management.

Machiavellian Dynamics

Management situation: A negotiating situation.
Suitable for: Undergraduates; postgraduates; DMS students; foremen/ supervisors; junior managers; middle managers.
Subjects: Bargaining.
Description: A bargaining game in which teams must reach agreement with one or more other teams in order to tender for contracts that are beyond the capability of one team on its own. The rules are so framed that the game reproduces the uncertainty and distortion of information that often exist in real life.
Decisions: What terms to settle for in negotiation with other teams.
Data available initially: Details of contract outlines for the teams to bargain over.
Feedback: Terms of accepted contracts. Performance of contract partners in comparison with each other's perception of the agreement.
Interactive or noninteractive: Interactive.
Number of players: 8–21.
Number of teams: 4–7 (2–3 per team).
Duration: ½–1 day.
Form: Presentation by consultant.
Terms: By negotiation.
Available from: M. A. P. Willmer, Manchester Business School, Booth Street West, Manchester M15 6PB.
Editor's classification: Organisation game. Functional – negotiating. General.

Managed Croquet

Management situation: The training, development and management of specialists.
Suitable for: Undergraduates; postgraduates; DMS students; foremen/ supervisors; junior managers; middle managers; senior managers; administrators.
Subjects: Workgroup organisation; personnel policies; training; motivation; communication; delegation; policy/strategy.
Description: Two teams plan for and conduct a game of croquet, but the normal 'player' role is split into the roles of 'plain hitter', 'hoop runner', 'croquet stroker', 'croquet trainer' and 'croquet manager'. The exercise explores the relationships that develop around specialist functions, and their effect upon an organisation.
Decisions: Who is to assume which role; how relationships between them are to be handled; training of operators. Subsequently, conduct of the game (including strategic and tactical decision-making) in the manner previously agreed.
Data available initially: Conditions applying to team organisation and the research aspects of the exercise. The normal rules of croquet.
Feedback: Evident from the physical progress of the game.
Interactive or noninteractive: Interactive.
Number of players: 8–36.
Number of teams: 2–4 (4–9 per team including optional roles).
Form: Full descriptive manual.
Terms: By negotiation.
Available from: John R. Cooper, 7, St. George's Avenue, Rugby, Warwickshire CV22 5PN.
Editor's classification: Organisation game. Functional – use of authority. General.

Managing Time

Management situation: The use of a managers own time in two weeks of the expected future.
Suitable for: Undergraduates; postgraduates; DMS students; foremen/ supervisors; junior managers; middle managers.
Subjects: The management of time.
Description: Teams receive a brief describing the role they are to assume, and must plan the use of their time for a two week period.

Subsequently, an audio cassette tests their forward planning by presenting problems that might arise.

Decisions: To what activities managerial time shall be assigned and in what measure.

Data available initially: A brief describing the role to be assumed.

Feedback: Realisation by the teams of inadequacies in their planning as the tape presents problems that they might not be able to deal with.

Interactive or noninteractive: Noninteractive.

Number of players: 1–12 in small groups.

Umpiring device: Subjective self-assessment by players as they listen to the tape.

Form: Self-contained kit.

Terms: £75 per set plus postage and packing.

Available from: M. Lynch, Northgate House, Perrymead, Bath, Avon BA2 5AX.

Editor's classification: Encounter game. Functional – planning. General.

Manco

Management situation: Theoretical analysis of management concepts.

Suitable for: Undergraduates; postgraduates; DMS students; junior managers; middle managers; senior managers.

Subjects: Activities, skills, behaviour and qualities commonly seen as integral parts of 'management'.

Description: Players are dealt cards that carry the name of a management concept (e.g. delegation, information handling) and have also a stock of arrow cards which denote relationships. Players, in turn, place cards beside those already set out, the objective being to construct a conceptual diagram expressing their view of management, and the interdependence of its sub-concepts.

Decisions: Where to place a concept card or arrow card in relation to those already displayed.

Data available initially: Rules of the game. Cards dealt to an individual.

Feedback: Difference between one's own concept of management and that held by opponent or by the tutor.

Interactive or noninteractive: Interactive.

Number of players: Any number, in pairs.

Duration: 1 hour.

Umpiring device: Tutor's model answer.

Form: Self-contained kit.
Terms: On application.
Available from: G. I. Gibbs, 46, Grange Avenue, Kenilworth, Warwickshire CV8 1DD.
Editor's classification: Exploratory game. Functional – use of authority. General.

Mapperly

Management situation: Management of a manufacturing company in a two company market situation.
Suitable for: Undergraduates; postgraduates; DMS students; junior managers; middle managers; senior managers.
Subjects: Economic environment; corporate planning; domestic marketing; consumer goods marketing; management accounting.
Description: A game in which each team is placed in the role of being one out of two companies in a market. Each competes against the model, seeking to achieve a larger market share and a larger cumulative profit than the other competitors.
Decisions: Selling price; advertising; production levels; manning levels; overtime; market research.
Data available initially: Full history of the company being operated and full history of the other company competing in the market.
Feedback: Sales; stocks; production; manpower; profit.
Interactive or noninteractive: Interactive between tutor and teams.
Number of players: 2 upwards.
Number of teams: 1 upwards (2–6 per team).
Duration: 6 hours.
Umpiring device: Nomograph. Computer if available.
Breaks for umpiring: 20 minutes per decision period, assuming four playing teams.
Form: Self-contained kit or presentation by consultant.
Terms: On application.
Available from: Maxim Consultants Limited, 6 Marlborough Place, Brighton, East Sussex BN1 1UB.
Editor's classification: Model-based. Business. General.

Mark 1

Management situation: Manufacturing and marketing a product in competitive conditions.

Suitable for: Undergraduates; postgraduates; DMS students; junior managers; middle managers.

Subjects: Financing a business; international marketing; domestic marketing; consumer goods marketing; sales planning; stockholding; management accounting; pricing; communication.

Description: The teams compete against each other in several markets. As well as production and marketing decisions, there are additional factors such as strikes, exchange rate fluctuations and accidents to senior executives.

Decisions: Volume of production; stock levels; price in each market; promotional strategy in each market.

Data available initially: Basic data is given on costs, past prices and past market shares.

Feedback: Units produced; sales volume and market share in each market; profit performance; sales of competitors products.

Interactive or noninteractive: Interactive.

Number of players: 9–36.

Number of teams: 3–6 (3–6 per team).

Duration: 3–4 hours.

Umpiring device: Micro-computer.

Form: Self-contained kit, including computer program (disc).

Terms: £100.00 per set.

Available from: R. L. Ritchie, Business Studies Department, North Staffordshire Polytechnic, Brindley Building, Leek Road, Stoke-on-Trent, Staffordshire ST4 2DF.

Editor's classification: Model-based. Business. Manufacturing industry.

The Mark II Vehicle

Management situation: Engineering project management.

Suitable for: Undergraduates; postgraduates; DMS students; junior managers; middle managers; senior managers.

Subjects: All aspects of engineering project management.

Description: A thorough simulation of the management of a large engineering project. It starts with project organisation and then goes through each element of project planning in turn. The teams then complete, physically, the construction that has been planned. The finished item is judged by time, quality and performance against the bid entered. The game is concerned with techniques of organisation and also with the dynamics inside each team.

Decisions: Choice of organisational form; determination of estimates; deployment of team members.

Data available initially: Case description; project specification.

Feedback: Observable success or failure of physical construction compared with the plan. Evaluative comments of tutor.

Interactive or noninteractive: Noninteractive.

Number of players: Up to 15 per team.

Number of teams: Normally 1.

Duration: 6–8 hours.

Form: Presentation by consultant.

Terms: By negotiation.

Available from: C. A. Voss, London Graduate School of Business Studies, Sussex Place, Regent's Park, London NW1 4SA.

Editor's classification: Practical simulation. Functional – engineering project management. Engineering.

Marketit

Management situation: Area sales management.

Suitable for: Postgraduates; junior managers; middle managers; senior salesmen.

Subjects: Domestic marketing; consumer goods marketing; sales planning; sales promotion; stockholding; pricing; forecasting.

Description: The game is primarily concerned with the development of a marketing strategy that will cause wholesalers and stockists to place enquiries with the firm, and of a sales activity that will convert these into firm orders. Efficiency and economy in these two directions are crucial for success.

Decisions: Selling price; advertising; units to be ordered from factory; salesmen; salaries; expenses; training; hiring and firing; sales-force motivation.

Data available initially: Factory capability; production costs; sales-force size and experience; average of salesmen's salary, commission and expenses; cost of training; number of customers and number of units previously sold; cost of market research; distribution costs; stock levels and stockholding charges; past advertising level and pricing policy;

available cash.

Feedback: Enquiries received; customers won and lost, and current total of customers; percentage of customers buying this period; number of units bought by each customer (average).

Interactive or noninteractive: Interactive.

Number of players: 6–30.

Number of teams: 3–6 (2–5 per team).

Duration: 6–8 hours.

Umpiring device: Nomographs and tables.

Breaks for umpiring: 15 minutes between each decision period.

Form: Self-contained kit.

Terms: £500.00 per set.

Available from: Management Games Limited, 2, Woburn Street, Ampthill, Bedford MK45 2HP.

Editor's classification: Model-based. Business. Consumer goods.

Matador

Management situation: Building and civil engineering.

Suitable for: Middle managers; senior managers.

Subjects: Economic environment; financing a business; corporate planning; management accounting; pricing.

Description: Each team runs an identical construction company and is required to achieve a satisfactory rate of growth while maintaining a sound financial position. Every three-month period a certain amount of work at known basic costs comes onto the market. Companies decide levels of markup and submit bids, accompanied by balance sheets and cash statements. Contracts are awarded and then managed. This involves allocating staff resources to contracts, deciding on plant investment, planning and controlling cash-flow and the use of finance, arranging loans, coping with competition and changes in government policy and/or the economic situation, and setting up management controls.

Decisions: Pricing of tenders; hiring or owning plant; type of work to undertake.

Data available initially: Company assets; size and type of market.

Feedback: Contracts awarded; competitors' bids.

Interactive or noninteractive: Interactive.

Number of players: 9–25.

Number of teams: 3–5 (3–5 per team).

Duration: 7 hours.
Umpiring device: Charts and tables.
Additional resources: Two umpires are needed.
Breaks for umpiring: 10–15 minutes after each 45–60 minute decision period.
Form: Presentation by consultant.
Terms: By negotiation.
Available from: Urwick Management Centre, Baylis House, Stoke Poges Lane, Slough, Berkshire. Micro-computer version available from Dr. P. R. Woolliams, Anglian Regional Management Centre, Danbury Park, Chelmsford, Essex.
Editor's classification: Model-based. Business. Construction.

Maximasia

Management situation: Simple manufacturing in a competitive market.
Suitable for: Undergraduates; junior managers.
Subjects: Economic environment; financing a business; sales planning; production organisation; purchasing; stockholding; management accounting; pricing; tendering.
Description: A model-based game that highlights the problems of decision-making under certainty.
Decisions: Selling price; advertising; purchasing price; manning levels.
Data available initially: Brief description of the current situation. Specific details of all costs involved.
Feedback: Market share; sales; revenue; costs; profits.
Interactive or noninteractive: Interactive.
Number of players: 2 upwards.
Number of teams: 1 upwards (2–5 per team).
Duration: 3 hours.
Umpiring device: Nomograph. Computer if available.
Breaks for umpiring: 5 minutes per team per tutor.
Form: Self-contained kit or presentation by consultant.
Terms: On application.
Available from: Maxim Consultants Limited, 6 Marlborough Place, Brighton, East Sussex BN1 1UB.
Editor's classification: Model-based. Business. General.

Melnikoff

Management situation: Setting up and running a company that manufactures and markets instant mashed potato.

Suitable for: Postgraduates; DMS students; foremen/supervisors; junior managers; middle managers; senior managers; administrators.

Subjects: Economic environment; financing a business; corporate planning; domestic marketing; sales planning; sales promotion; production methods; purchasing; stockholding; management accounting; pricing; company organisation; personnel policies; industrial relations; communication; cash-flow.

Description: The playing teams start up the business from scratch, making quarterly decisions about production, marketing, financial and industrial relations matters. The decisions are entered into a computer, and the results for each team obtained.

Decisions: Labour requirement; machinery requirement; material requirement; maintenance spending; production quantity; deployment of salesmen; pricing; promotion; research and development spending; wage and commission rates; methods of raising capital; dividends to be paid.

Data available initially: Description of the start-up environment, the conditions of the game and the basic costs that will apply.

Feedback: Units produced; market share; sales made; financial situation; price of company's shares; labour and industrial relations developments.

Interactive or noninteractive: Interactive.

Number of players: 8–35.

Number of teams: 2–5 (4–7 per team).

Duration: 15–18 hours.

Umpiring device: Computer.

Form: Presentation by consultant. Component part of training course.

Terms: By negotiation.

Available from: Task Management Services, 1, Southby Close, Abingdon OX13 5LE.

Editor's classification: Model-based. Business. Processed food.

The Merger

Management situation: A merger of two companies identified as 'acquirer' and 'acquired'.

Suitable for: Undergraduates; postgraduates; DMS students; senior managers; administrators.

Subjects: Economic environment; financing a business; corporate planning; pricing; committee work; communication.

Description: The company seeking to acquire another makes a valuation of it and puts forward an offer in terms of cash or exchange of shares. The company considered for take-over has a range of possible responses, each of which will influence their share price and make them more or less vulnerable to the take-over. The time periods for decisions are rigidly set, and the share prices of both companies announced at the end of each such period whether they have responded to the latest move or not. The game simulates the relative speed at which decisions of this type are frequently made in practice.

Decisions: For the company seeking to acquire, the total value of the offer to be made and the way in which this value is to be made up. For the company likely to be taken over, a choice of defensive strategies.

Data available initially: An outline of the basic structure and the financial positions of the two companies.

Feedback: Market price of shares of each company; percentage of shareholders of the company likely to be taken over who have accepted the offer.

Interactive or noninteractive: Interactive.

Number of players: 6–12 in two teams.

Duration: 1½–2 hours.

Umpiring device: A nomograph, supplemented by the discretion of the umpire to add new features. Micro-computer version (Apple) available Autumn 1984.

Form: Self-contained kit.

Terms: Manual version, £100.00 per set.

Available from: R. L. Ritchie, Business Studies Department, North Staffordshire Polytechnic, Brindley Building, Leek Road, Stoke-on-Trent, Staffordshire ST4 2DF.

Editor's classification: Model-based. Functional – finance. General.

The Metal Box Business Game

Management situation: Manufacture of central heating boilers for sale in batches to wholesale outlets.

Suitable for: Students on business studies courses; trainee managers; sixth form schoolchildren.

Subjects: Financing a business; industrial marketing; sales planning; sales promotion; production organisation; management accounting; pricing; workgroup organisation; research and development.

Description: Teams decide each time period on their production, their prices and their marketing activity. Batches are sold by a sales person calling on one of twenty-five customers each having a different sales potential. Time lags are involved in building factories, ordering materials, recruiting, training and receiving payment for sales.

Decisions: Level of investment; production quantity; price; marketing strategy.

Data available initially: Full details of opportunities and costs are given in the players' manual.

Feedback: Response of the individuals called on by the company's salespeople, indicating a number ordered, or no order being placed at all, or an order being placed with a competitor.

Interactive or noninteractive: Interactive.

Number of players: 12–36.

Number of teams: 4–6 (3–6 per team).

Duration: Approximately 7 hours in all.

Umpiring device: Calculations carried out by the umpire.

Form: Self-contained kit.

Terms: On application.

Available from: The Careers Research and Advisory Council Limited, Bateman Street, Cambridge CB2 1LZ.

Editor's classification: Model-based. Business. Manufacturing industry.

Meteor

Management situation: Cost saving activities within an organisation.

Suitable for: Undergraduates; postgraduates; DMS students; junior managers; middle managers; senior managers.

Subjects: Economic environment; company organisation; workgroup organisation; committee work; management services; data processing.

Description: A carefully structured role-playing exercise focusing on the services to be provided by a data processing department and the projects that should or should not be continued.

Decisions: The manner in which to present a case; the attitude to be adopted towards other role-players; whether to support or oppose any proposal after assessing the likely impact of either action on the achievement of one's own objectives.

Data available initially: History of the company; the background to its data processing activity; current utilisation of the data processing department; current projects; political situation within the company.

Feedback: Outcome of the simulated board meeting that ends the role-play, seen in relation to the objectives of each role-playing party.

Interactive or noninteractive: Interactive.

Number of players: 5 upwards.

Number of teams: 1 upwards (5–8 per team).

Duration: 3 hours.

Umpiring device: A formal scoring system.

Form: Self-contained kit or presentation by consultant.

Terms: On application.

Available from: Maxim Consultants Limited, 6 Marlborough Place, Brighton, East Sussex BN1 1UB.

Editor's classification: Organisational simulation. Functional – company organisation. Computer services.

The Midshires Health Authority

Management situation: Resource allocation within the context of the National Health Service.

Suitable for: Undergraduates; postgraduates; DMS students; junior managers; middle managers; senior managers; administrators.

Subjects: Financing a business; corporate planning; company organisation; workgroup organisation; personnel policies; industrial relations; distribution; communication.

Description: Two groups are formed, to represent the health authority and the trade union interests of those employed in it. Full details are supplied of the existing commitments of the authority, the staffing requirements, the national policy guidelines, and the capital projects that have to be initiated. Against this background, the two groups must conduct formal negotiations with regard to the allocation of projected resources for the next five years.

Decisions: Group decisions to be taken on each side about attitudes to be adopted, strategies for promoting them, and the extent to which compromise is acceptable. Topical elements are introduced such as privatisation.

Data available initially: A detailed brief giving the breakdown of existing facilities and proposed developments.

Feedback: The response of the other group to attitudes adopted and arguments put forward. The experience of reaching agreement or having to register, and justify, failure to do so.
Interactive or noninteractive: Interactive.
Number of players: 10.
Number of teams: 2 groups of 5. Several games can be played in parallel.
Duration: 6–8 hours.
Form: Self-contained kit. Presentation by consultant.
Terms: By negotiation.
Available from: D. V. Marshall, Department of Law, North Staffordshire Polytechnic, Brindley Building, Leek Road, Stoke-on-Trent, Staffordshire ST4 2DF.
Editor's classification: Organisational simulation. Functional – financial negotiation. Health authority.

Mindmend

Management situation: The economic simulation of resource allocation outside the market place.
Suitable for: Undergraduates; postgraduates; DMS students; foremen/supervisors; junior managers; middle managers; senior managers; local authority employees.
Subjects: Economic environment; workgroup organisation; committee work; charity organisation.
Description: A role-play ending with a committee meeting. It has five stages; preparation, presentation, meeting, decision and review.
Decisions: Degree of support or opposition to be expressed for various projects discussed in committee.
Data available initially: Details of the organisation simulated and the projects under consideration.
Feedback: Response of other parties in the committee. Final committee decision.
Interactive or noninteractive: Interactive.
Number of players: 5 upwards.
Number of teams: 1 upwards (5–10 per team).
Duration: 2 hours.
Form: Self-contained kit or presentation by consultant.
Terms: On application.
Available from: Maxim Consultants Limited, 6 Marlborough Place, Brighton, East Sussex BN1 1UB.

Editor's classification: Organisational simulation. Environment. Social service.

The Mini Co Kit

Management situation: Setting up and running a mini-company.
Suitable for: Undergraduates; YTS employees; schoolchildren.
Subjects: Economic environment; financing a business; domestic marketing; consumer goods marketing; industrial marketing; sales planning; sales promotion; production methods; production organisation; purchasing; stockholding; management accounting; pricing; company organisation; workgroup organisation; personnel policies; industrial relations; management services; distribution; motivation; communication; delegation.
Description: With discreet assistance from an adviser, players set up and run their own trading organisation, making and selling a real product or service. Conventional roles (e.g. director) are assigned to the team members, meetings are held and minutes kept after the manner of the normal commercial world.
Decisions: All necessary decisions for providing and marketing a simple product or service on a small scale.
Data available initially: The collective knowledge of team members. Limited assistance is provided where necessary by the adviser.
Feedback: The experience of success or failure in the chosen endeavour.
Interactive or noninteractive: Noninteractive.
Number of players: Any.
Number of teams: Any.
Duration: 2 weeks to 1 year, depending on the time per day to be assigned to the activity.
Umpiring device: None.
Form: Self-contained kit.
Terms: £18 per set. (Provisional price).
Available from: Longman Resources Unit, 33–35 Tanners Row, York YO1 1JP.
Editor's classification: Practical simulation. Business. General.

Mocon

Management situation: Exploration of sales and production alternatives in unspecified business.

Suitable for: DMS students; middle managers; senior managers.

Subjects: Financing a business; corporate planning; consumer goods marketing; sales planning; production; pricing.

Description: Mocon is a computer program which creates a company model to provide an exercise in strategic decision-making. There are three parts: gathering information to create the model, feeding the information into the computer to produce a possible contribution analysis, and experimenting with different sales and cost levels to improve profitability.

Decisions: Sales volume; stockholding; production costs, etc.

Data available initially: Expected sales, stock, etc.

Feedback: Contribution by product group; liquidity; profit/loss.

Interactive or noninteractive: Noninteractive.

Number of players: 6–25.

Number of teams: 2–5 (3–5 in a team).

Duration: 2½–4 hours.

Umpiring device: Computer program.

Form: Presentation by consultant.

Terms: By negotiation.

Available from: Urwick Management Centre, Baylis House, Stoke Poges Lane, Slough, Berkshire.

Editor's classification: Encounter game. Company. General.

Molliette Limited

Management situation: Running a company that makes diesel engines for the marine industry.

Suitable for: Undergraduates; postgraduates; DMS students; junior managers; middle managers; senior managers; MBA students.

Subjects: Economic environment; financing a business; corporate planning; domestic marketing; consumer goods marketing; industrial marketing; sales planning; purchasing; stockholding; management accounting; pricing; financial success measures.

Description: A game that concentrates on financing a business. Players analyse the current state of the company as shown in the manual, and then have access to a micro-computer on which they can experiment with alternative decisions. As well as altering the decision variables, they have the opportunity to experiment under different future scenarios.

Decisions: Those concerned with alternative sources of finance with which to run the business.

Data available initially: Detailed description of the company and its affairs, with ten-year forecasts.

Feedback: Forecasts of what the financial result would be, according to the model, given each set of decisions entered to the computer and the scenario applying to them. The forecasts include cash-flow statements, profit and loss accounts, balance sheets, and project appraisal reports.

Interactive or noninteractive: Noninteractive.

Number of players: 1 upwards.

Number of teams: 1 upwards.

Duration: 8–16 hours.

Umpiring device: Micro-computer (CP/M) with tutor's marking/assessment scheme.

Form: Presentation by consultants and subsequent use of self-contained kit. (Micro-computer required.)

Terms: £450.00.

Available from: Dr. P. Woolliams and J. Cooper, Anglian Regional Management Centre, Danbury Park, Chelmsford, Essex.

Editor's classification: Encounter game. Functional-financial planning. Engine manufacture.

National Transport Company Limited

Management situation: State intervention in private sector industry.

Suitable for: Undergraduates; postgraduates; DMS students; junior managers; middle managers; senior managers; administrators.

Subjects: Economic environment; financing a business; corporate planning; domestic marketing; management accounting; company organisation; communication; political intervention.

Description: The scenario postulates a national transport company formed by the amalgamation of several motor manufacturers, and now in financial difficulty. The players are divided into four groups which represent The Government, The National Enterprise Board, The NTC and The Unions. They have to negotiate a solution to the crisis which adequately meets their different needs and responsibilities.

Decisions: For each group, how to conduct itself in negotiations; what attitude to adopt and how to present its arguments; to what extent to compromise; in what way to interpret its responsibilities; how to respond to the cases presented by the other parties.

Data available initially: Each party has a detailed brief about its own position. The state of the NTC, the law and the economy is known to all.

Feedback: Experience of the negotiating sessions; the response of other parties to the arguments presented; the achievement of agreement or failure to agree.

Interactive or noninteractive: Interactive.

Number of players: 20–60.

Number of teams: 1 team, comprising the four role-groups.

Duration: 6–8 hours.

Umpiring device: None. The results are provided by the outcome of the negotiations.

Form: Presentation by consultant.

Terms: By negotiation.

Available from: D. V. Marshall, Department of Law, North Staffordshire Polytechnic, Brindley Building, Leek Road, Stoke-on-Trent, Staffordshire ST4 2DF.

Editor's classification: Organisational simulation. Functional – negotiating. Government – industry relationships.

The National Union Of Knocklethrosters

Management situation: Improving recruitment of members to a professional body.

Suitable for: Undergraduates; postgraduates; DMS students; foremen/supervisors; junior managers; middle managers; senior managers.

Subjects: Recruitment to a professional organisation.

Description: Each player assumes the role of recruitment officer of the union and proposes solutions to the problems set. All players then assume, collectively, the role of the council of the union. They use their individual solutions to represent their current opinions. The collective decision forms one assessment of the individual ideas, and the umpire makes an overall assessment at the end.

Decisions: How to handle successive problems in the way that will best improve recruitment.

Data available initially: The current state of affairs in the National Union of Knocklethrosters and various problems related to recruitment.

Feedback: Group evaluation of individual decisions, and evaluation of the group decision by the umpire. Each individual discovers the effect his ideas and attitudes have on others and the degree of influence he can

wield. He also learns about the ideas and attitudes of others.
Interactive or noninteractive: Interactive.
Number of players: 6–20 in a single group.
Duration: 1½–2 hours.
Form: Self-contained kit.
Terms: £10.00 per set.
Available from: J. Snowdon, FCIS, Faculty of Teachers in Commerce Limited, 141 Bedford Road, Sutton Coldfield, West Midlands B75 6DB.
Editor's classification: Exploratory game. Functional – recruitment. Trade union.

Newtown

Management situation: Commercial and political decision-making in regard to the development of a new town.
Suitable for: Undergraduates; postgraduates; DMS students; foremen/supervisors; junior managers; middle managers; senior managers; fifth and sixth form schoolchildren; administrators.
Subjects: Economic environment; financing a business; corporate planning; management accounting; workgroup organisation; committee work; communication; politics.
Description: Players adopt the principal roles appropriate to the development of a new town – social, administrative, commercial and political. The decisions that they take are translated into 'fact' by the growth of a town layout using models and symbols. The umpire has a set of rules which enable him to examine the layout at various stages and calculate a series of ratios. These are a means of measuring the development and allow the different role-players to quantify their own degree of success.
Decisions: The decisions are different for each role-player, always relating to his own special area of responsibility.
Data available initially: Basic data about the development is provided for all parties, and the local authority have a special brief of their own.
Feedback: The series of ratios calculated by the umpire, which allow the role-players to measure their own success.
Interactive or noninteractive: Interactive.
Number of players: 20–100.
Number of teams: It is a game for a single group, but the number of roles is flexible, as is the number of people who can collectively assume a role.

Duration: 6–12 hours.
Umpiring device: Formal rules for calculating ratios.
Form: Descriptive manual, not including materials. Presentation by consultant.
Terms: By negotiation.
Available from: D. V. Marshall, Department of Law, North Staffordshire Polytechnic, Brindley Building, Leek Road, Stoke-on-Trent ST4 2DF.
Editor's classification: Model-based. Environment. Urban development.

Norse Staff Products Limited

Management situation: Maintaining effective industrial relations, within a context that is both local and national.
Suitable for: Undergraduates; postgraduates; DMS students; foremen/supervisors; junior managers; middle managers; senior managers.
Subjects: Company organisation; personnel policies; industrial relations; communication; political environment.
Description: The exercise simulates two levels in the industrial relations structure, assigning players to four groups: a company, a local trade union branch, the national executive of that union (with the TUC) and the CBI (with the government). There are negotiations to be conducted about local matters at one level and policy matters at the other, but as the exercise progresses there is interaction between the two. Policy matters concern immunity from civil action and an industry-wide change in methods of calculating wages.
Decisions: For each party, what negotiating stance to adopt, and how to respond to the activities of others.
Data available initially: All players have a common description of the overall environment, and more detailed briefs about their particular difficulties, seen from their own point of view.
Feedback: Experience of the attitudes taken by other parties, and their arguments. The response of other parties to one's own performance. The nature of the final agreements reached, if any.
Interactive or noninteractive: Interactive.
Number of players: 20–50.
Number of teams: One, comprising the four role-groups.
Duration: 6–10 hours.
Form: Presentation by consultant.

Terms: By negotiation.
Available from: D. V. Marshall, Department of Law, North Stafford-shire Polytechnic, Brindley Building, Leek Road, Stoke-on-Trent, Staffordshire ST4 2DF.
Editor's classification: Organisational simulation. Functional – negotiating. Engineering industry.

North Sea Oil

Management situation: The economic problems of North Sea Oil exploration and exploitation.
Suitable for: Undergraduates; postgraduates; DMS students; junior managers; middle managers; senior managers; administrators.
Subjects: Economic environment; financing a business; corporate planning; management accounting; communication; social policies.
Description: Players are assigned to three different roles, the UK government, an oil company, and the country physically affected by a proposed offshore drilling operation. The company must appraise and cost the project while conducting negotiations with the other groups to secure licensing approval and the development of shore-based facilities. The other parties must use the negotiations, and their own powers, to ensure that their legitimate interests are safeguarded.
Decisions: For each party, what negotiating stance to adopt and what arguments to put forward; how to use its bargaining power; how to respond to the tactics of the other parties.
Data available initially: Each of the three groups has full details of the situation, and the requirements of its role.
Feedback: Experiencing the result of the negotiations; matching the achievement against the original objectives; comparing the outcome with similar real-life situations.
Interactive or noninteractive: Interactive.
Number of players: 20–50.
Number of teams: A single team, comprising the three role-groups.
Duration: 6–8 hours.
Form: Presentation by consultant.
Terms: By negotiation.
Available from: D. V. Marshall, Department of Law, North Stafford-shire Polytechnic, Brindley Building, Leek Road, Stoke-on-Trent, Staffordshire ST4 2DF.

Editor's classification: Organisational simulation. Functional – negotiation. North Sea exploration.

North–South

Management situation: Relations between transnational corporations and host governments.
Suitable for: Undergraduates; postgraduates; middle managers; administrators.
Subjects: Financing a business; corporate planning; international marketing; communications; north-south trade.
Description: Participants simulate the relationship between developing countries and transnational corporations over a three-year period, preceded by a planning period. Finance is obtained from the World Bank and from UK investors.
Decisions: Buying and selling decisions about capital goods and commodities. Decisions take the form of contracts agreed and tokens exchanged.
Data available initially: Full description of the playing conditions.
Feedback: Assessment of one's own success; changes observed in the attitudes of one's trading partners.
Interactive or noninteractive: Interactive.
Number of players: 7–48.
Number of teams: 7–16 (1–3 per team).
Duration: 4–5 hours.
Umpiring device: Trading activities and environmental conditions are governed by rules.
Form: Presentation by consultant.
Terms: £550.00
Available from: B. R. Aston, Henley – The Management College, Greenlands, Henley-on-Thames, Oxon. RG9 3AU.
Editor's classification: Organisation game. Functional – negotiating. International commerce and industry.

Now Is The Hour

Management situation: Administration in an office environment.
Suitable for: DMS students; office supervisors; junior managers; middle managers.

Subjects: Workgroup organisation; personnel policies; time management.

Description: Players are given background data to read. During the game they are given in-tray documents and have one hour to decide on priorities and to recommend action.

Decisions: Personnel; accounting; safety; customer relations.

Data available initially: Background data on company and current personal circumstances; contents of in-tray.

Feedback: Discovery, in the discussion after the exercise, of how each individual's decisions compared with those of others.

Interactive or noninteractive: Noninteractive.

Number of players: 6–20 (individual exercise).

Duration: 1 hour and discussion time.

Form: Self-contained kit for 10 players. Additional kit available for a further 10 players.

Terms: £55.00 plus VAT for basic kit. £20.00 plus VAT for additional kit.

Available from: Supervisory Management Training Limited, Peak House, 66 Croydon Road, Beckenham, Kent BR3 4AA.

Editor's classification: In-basket. Company. Office work.

Odsim

Management situation: Organisation behaviour in a production or service industry.

Suitable for: Undergraduates; postgraduates; DMS students; junior managers; middle managers; senior managers; social work team leaders.

Subjects: Production organisation; company organisation; workgroup organisation; time management and priorities.

Description: Players constitute themselves as an organisation and the tutor presents this organisation with a succession of tasks. These can vary in type and complexity and are chosen to meet the needs of the training situation. Performance of the tasks is linked to a quantified measure reflecting quality, importance and urgency. The effectiveness of the organisation can thus be observed.

Decisions: Organisation structure within group; allocation of tasks; determination of priorities; operational decisions on specific tasks.

Data available initially: General statements about the organisation that would be appropriate. Otherwise only details of tasks as they are introduced by the tutor.

Feedback: Degree of success achieved in terms of tasks completed and revenue earned; quality of the internal operation of the group.

Interactive or noninteractive: Noninteractive.

Number of players: 8 upwards.

Number of teams: 3 upwards (2 or more per team).

Duration: 3–12 hours.

Form: Presentation by consultant.

Terms: On application.

Available from: Denys J. Page, 'Orbit', 15 Ashurst Road, Seaford, East Sussex BN25 1AH.

Editor's classification: Organisation game. Company. General.

The Old Soldier

Management situation: Problem of sickness absence and poor performance (industrial environment).

Suitable for: DMS students; foremen/supervisors; junior managers; middle managers.

Subjects: Industrial relations.

Description: A maze exercise in which players work through a text, taking one decision after another as the problem develops. Players experience consequences appropriate to their choices.

Decisions: Which of certain options to choose when dealing with a case of sickness absence and poor performance.

Data available initially: Current situation on employee concerned and data on recent action.

Feedback: Experience of the consequences attached to the choice made (predetermined but previously unknown to the players).

Interactive or noninteractive: Noninteractive.

Number of players: 6–20 as individuals or small groups.

Duration: 15–20 minutes and discussion time.

Form: Self-contained kit in the form of a reproducible master.

Terms: £45.00 per kit.

Available from: Supervisory Management Training Limited, Peak House, 66 Croydon Road, Beckenham, Kent BR3 4AA.

Editor's classification: Maze. Functional – industrial relations. General.

Oligopoly

Management situation: Management of a packaging company marketing a luxury product.
Suitable for: Undergraduates; postgraduates; DMS students; foremen/supervisors; junior managers; middle managers; senior managers; sixth form schoolchildren; MBA students.
Subjects: Domestic marketing; consumer goods marketing; sales planning; sales promotion.
Description: A game that puts a dominant emphasis on marketing. Players analyse a case study and prepare a marketing plan. This is followed by game-playing periods in which decisions made by the players are umpired by a computer model.
Decisions: Price; advertising; promotion; production capacity.
Data available initially: A case study describing the company operations and including recent accounts.
Feedback: Market share; market growth.
Interactive or noninteractive: Interactive.
Number of players: 12–48.
Number of teams: 4 (3–12 per team).
Duration: 1–2 days.
Umpiring device: Micro-computer using BASIC program.
Form: Self-contained kit of computer program and instructions (all common micro-computers). Presentation by consultant. Also in 'The Management of the Business' (D. J. Moul and P. R. Woolliams. Wiley 1984).
Terms: Kit, on application. Presentation by consultant, £200.00 per day.
Available from: D. J. Management Consultants, 87 Beehive Lane, Ilford, Essex.
Editor's classification: Model-based. Functional – marketing. Packaging.

Outlet

Management situation: A retail store.
Suitable for: DMS students; junior managers; middle managers.
Subjects: Purchasing; stockholding; personnel policies; forecasting; merchandise display.
Description: Players assume the role of manager of a retail store that is a branch of a larger organisation. They are required to choose what items

they will stock from the 'head office' range, and where they will display them. The umpiring device gives credit for both the general aspects of shop management and for special 'additional sales' generated by sensible positioning of merchandise.

Decisions: What to stock; where to display it; staffing; training; advertising.

Data available initially: Details of the range of goods available from head office, with their size, the space needed to display them, the margin earned by the sale of one unit of each, and the number that would be sold if any one of five different sales levels was to be achieved. Details of the size of the store and its physical arrangement.

Feedback: General sales level achieved (one of five possible levels); additional sales achieved for each product stocked.

Interactive or noninteractive: Noninteractive.

Number of players: 3–24.

Number of teams: 1–6 (3 or 4 per team).

Duration: 3–4 hours.

Umpiring device: Manual computation, using tables and a transparent overlay.

Breaks for umpiring: 5 minutes per team after each decision period. (Teams can be handled in the order in which they are ready, without waiting for all to be in step.)

Form: Self-contained kit.

Terms: £75.00 per set.

Available from: Chris Elgood Associates Limited, The Studio, Cranbrook Road, Hawkhurst, Kent TN18 4AR.

Editor's classification: Model-based. Company. Retail trading.

Pantheon

Management situation: Running a small retail outlet and trying to maximise profit while coping with the paperwork.

Suitable for: Undergraduates; BEC students; ONC/OND students; 'O' level commerce students.

Subjects: Purchasing; stockholding; pricing; paperwork.

Description: Each team consists of a manager, a buyer, an accountant and a clerk (though in reality the business could not support such a team). The game calls for weekly decisions on ordering, pricing and promotion and also places an emphasis on paperwork. This includes a weekly cash account, order record and PAYE/VAT records. At the end of a quarter there are bank reconciliation, profit/loss account and balance sheet to be done. Success depends on marrying prices to the stocks available and operating in the most profitable section of the price/demand curve.

Decisions: Order quantities; selling price; wages; number of staff; promotion budget; insurance to be carried.

Data available initially: The teams take over an existing concern five weeks into a quarter and full trading records of that period are available to them.

Feedback: Units sold (of five products); deliveries; changes in conditions; market events.

Interactive or noninteractive: Noninteractive.

Number of players: 2–30.

Number of teams: 1–6 (2–5 per team).

Duration: 15–20 hours.

Umpiring device: Price/demand curves administered by the umpire.

Form: Self-contained kit. Presentation by consultant.

Terms: Kit, £80.00. Presentation, by negotiation.

Available from: Tony Pope, Buckinghamshire College of Higher Education, Gorelands Lane, Chalfont St. Giles, Buckinghamshire.

Editor's classification: Model-based. Business. Retail trading.

The Paraffin File

Management situation: Marketing paraffin in the UK.

Suitable for: Undergraduates; postgraduates; DMS students; junior managers; middle managers; fifth and sixth form schoolchildren.

Subjects: Economic environment; financing a business; corporate planning; consumer goods marketing; management accounting; pricing.

Description: Three teams represent different companies competing for a share of a declining market.

Decisions: Price; advertising; number of sales staff.

Data available initially: A briefing sheet that describes the current company position. It gives the state of other groups, past pricing strategy, the economic situation, material costs, allowable actions and objectives.

Feedback: Sales; market share; profit.

Interactive or noninteractive: Interactive.

Number of players: 3–21.

Number of teams: 3 (1–7 per team).
Duration: ½–3 hours.
Umpiring device: Micro-computer. (Apple; BBC; 38OZ).
Form: Self-contained kit.
Terms: £18.00 per set, but £11.95 to UK schools. (Includes discs).
Available from: BP Educational Service, Britannic House, Moor Lane, London EC2Y 9BU.
Editor's classification: Model-based. Functional – marketing. Oil industry.

Peterduck Limited

Management situation: Managing a small manufacturing company that produces family cruisers.
Suitable for: Undergraduates; postgraduates; DMS students; junior managers; middle managers; senior managers; MBA students.
Subjects: Economic environment; financing a business; domestic marketing; sales planning; production methods; purchasing; stockholding; management accounting; pricing.
Description: Players analyse a case study and then have access to a micro-computer on which they can try out alternative policies to see what the results, according to the model, will be. In so doing they gain an understanding of the effect of the decision variables, singly or in combination.
Decisions: Prices; marketing strategy; capacity; credit control.
Data available initially: Case study manual describing the company and the conditions.
Feedback: A prediction of the financial performance for the year, if the decisions entered to the computer were to be made. This includes full financial accounts, monthly cash-flow statement, year end profit and loss account, and balance sheet.
Interactive or noninteractive: Noninteractive.
Number of players: 1–3 per keyboard.
Number of teams: As many as the available keyboards.
Duration: 3–6 hours.
Umpiring device: Micro-computer.
Form: Presentation by consultant and subsequent use of self-contained kit. (Micro-computer required.)
Terms: £250.00.

Available from: Dr P. Woolliams and J. Cooper, Anglian Regional Management Centre, Danbury Park, Chelmsford, Essex.
Editor's classification: Encounter game. Business. Boatbuilding.

The Petty Cashier

Management situation: A disciplinary problem (office environment).
Suitable for: DMS students; foremen/supervisors; junior managers; middle managers.
Subjects: Industrial relations.
Description: A maze exercise in which players work through a text, taking one decision after another as the problem develops. Players experience consequences appropriate to their choices.
Decisions: Which of certain given options to choose when dealing with problems involving discipline.
Data available initially: Current situation on employee concerned and on company policy.
Feedback: Experience of the consequences attached to the choice made (predetermined but previously unknown to the players).
Interactive or noninteractive: Noninteractive.
Number of players: 6–20 as individuals or small groups.
Duration: 15–20 minutes and discussion time.
Form: Self-contained kit in the form of a reproducible master.
Terms: £45.00 per kit. Also in CBT form at £150 plus VAT.
Available from: Supervisory Management Training Limited, Peak House, 66 Croydon Road, Beckenham, Kent BR3 4AA.
Editor's classification: Maze. Functional – industrial relations. Office work.

Pieceparts Limited

Management situation: Manufacturing industry.
Suitable for: Undergraduates; postgraduates; DMS students; foremen/ supervisors; junior managers; middle managers.
Subjects: Production: stockholding; finance and cash-flow; domestic marketing.
Description: Players are required to determine (daily) which of eight different products shall be manufactured on each of the three machines in a small factory. The value of each product is known, and the speed of

operation of each machine. Orders for the products are presented, giving the identity of the customer, and a problem arises over the priority of manufacture, the machine to be used, its length of run, and so on. Different choices are made by each team, and their policies are compared in a review session. Every possible criterion for allocating work has some corresponding disadvantage, and it becomes obvious that a policy must be subject to regular scrutiny.

Decisions: Criteria to be used when allocating work to machines.

Data available initially: Value of each product; setup time for each machine; production rate of each machine.

Feedback: Experience of the disadvantages that arise from the constant pursuit of one policy, in terms of other desirable ends that are never achieved.

Interactive or noninteractive: Noninteractive.

Number of players: 3–30.

Number of teams: 1–10 (about 3 per team).

Duration: 1½–3 hours.

Form: Self-contained kit.

Terms: £70.00 per set.

Available from: Chris Elgood Associates Limited, The Studio, Cranbrook Road, Hawkhurst, Kent TN18 4AR.

Editor's classification: Encounter game. Functional – production scheduling. Manufacturing industry.

The Planning Game

Management situation: Production scheduling in response to predicted market demand.

Suitable for: Sixth formers; undergraduates; foremen/supervisors; junior managers.

Subjects: Economic environment; financing a business; production organisation; purchasing; stockholding; cash-flow.

Description: A planning game based on probabilities. The progress of work through a factory is shown by symbols displayed on a board. At each stage there is a known probability about the movement of goods and decisions must be made on this evidence. Once they are made, the actual outcome is determined by a statistically controlled chance mechanism. The symbols are then moved to show the new situation. The game demonstrates the build-ups and shortages that can arise and their effect upon sales and upon cash.

Decisions: What materials to order; whether to schedule overtime or short-time at any production stage.

Data available initially: Costs of materials and production activities; fixed sales price; probabilities attaching to different sections of the production facility.

Feedback: Observable distribution of goods throughout the factory; sales in relation to demand; sales revenue; costs.

Interactive or noninteractive: Noninteractive.

Number of players: 3–20.

Number of teams: 1–5 (3–4 per team).

Duration: 1½ hours.

Form: Self-contained kit.

Terms: £80.00 per set.

Available from: Chris Elgood Associates Limited, The Studio, Cranbrook Road, Hawkhurst, Kent TN18 4AR.

Editor's classification: Encounter game. Functional – planning. Manufacturing industry.

Planning, Organising and Controlling

Management situation: Area management of a company that manufactures and sells a revolutionary micro-computer of human appearance.

Suitable for: Undergraduates; postgraduates; DMS students; junior managers; middle managers; senior managers.

Subjects: Setting objectives and targets; preparing and coordinating a plan; time management; delegation; organisational structure; reporting mechanisms; planning evaluation; control techniques; controlling a project.

Description: Twelve interrelated programmed simulations that achieve detailed coverage of the subject.

Decisions: In each simulation, choices between different courses of action offered by the text as the exercise moves through consecutive stages.

Data available initially: Written description of the situation at the moment the first choice is required.

Feedback: Discovery of the author's assessment of the answer given. (Predetermined but not known to the players beforehand).

Interactive or noninteractive: Noninteractive.

Number of players: 3–20 participants as individuals or teams.

Duration: 6–9 hours or equivalent in separate sessions.

Umpiring device: Programmed simulation.
Form: Self-contained kit.
Terms: £400.00 per set.
Available from: Management Games Limited, 2, Woburn Street, Ampthill, Bedford MK45 2HP.
Editor's classification: Programmed simulation. Functional – company organisation. Electronics.

Plasticity Plight

Management situation: Managing the machine parts division of a large conglomerate organisation.
Suitable for: Undergraduates; postgraduates; DMS students; employees of banks; sixth form schoolchildren; MBA students.
Subjects: Economic environment; financing a business; purchasing; stockholding; management accounting; pricing.
Description: Players receive a case study describing the division they are to manage, and have access to a computer model that allows them to test out alternative strategies. This allows them to see the predicted effect of changing any or all of the decision variables.
Decisions: Price; credit; production targets.
Data available initially: A detailed case study manual.
Feedback: Full financial accounts, including a cash-flow statement, showing the effect that any decision entered into the computer is expected to have, according to the model.
Interactive or noninteractive: Noninteractive.
Number of players: 1–3 keyboard.
Number of teams: As many as the available keyboards.
Duration: 3–6 hours.
Umpiring device: Micro-computer using BASIC program.
Form: Presentation by consultants and subsequent use of self-contained kit. (Micro-computer required).
Terms: £350.00 per day including training of client's staff.
Available from: D. J. Management Consultants, 87 Beehive Lane, Ilford, Essex.
Editor's classification: Encounter game. Functional – management/business accounting. Machine parts.

The Policy Game

Management situation: Departments/divisions within an organisation having different perceptions of the overall task. Circumstances in which individuals wish to explore potential futures.
Suitable for: Middle managers; senior managers; administrators.
Subjects: Economic environment; corporate planning; company organisation; workgroup organisation; communication; delegation; specific subject areas dependent upon current needs.
Description: The exercise is a framework for modelling the component parts of an organisation and examining the problems of policy formation and execution. It requires research by the consultants before it can be mounted. Each part of the organisation is modelled to reflect its real ethos and culture, and to include its relationship with the whole.
Decisions: For each department modelled, what proposals to lay before interdepartmental meetings and what data to use to support them. How to behave in response to alternative and perhaps competing views expressed by other departments.
Data available initially: Research data from the real-life situation, prepared and presented by the consultant.
Feedback: The response of other departments encountered at negotiating/planning sessions. The experience of encountering novel ideas and considering unforeseen possibilities.
Interactive or noninteractive: Interactive.
Number of players: Dependent on the company situation being modelled.
Number of teams: 1. This is usually an exercise undertaken by a single group who are regularly associated.
Duration: 1–5 days.
Umpiring device: Dependent on the situation being modelled. Computer desirable as a data source but not usually essential for umpiring.
Form: Presentation by consultant.
Terms: By negotiation.
Available from: Maxim Consultants Limited, 6 Marlborough Place, Brighton BN1 1UB.
Editor's classification: Organisational simulation. Business. General.

Posser

Management situation: Making and selling washing machines in a peroid of 'stop and go' economics.

Suitable for: Undergraduates; postgraduates; DMS students; middle managers.

Subjects: Economic environment; financing a business; international marketing; domestic marketing; consumer goods marketing; sales planning; management accounting; pricing; industrial relations; negotiation.

Description: An exercise which simulates the difficulties of the white goods market by using dramatic shifts in the economic climate and corresponding changes in demand. The office-bearers in the company have separate briefs, and a wide range of actions are allowed. This makes reaching a team decision a realistic and testing process.

Decisions: Sales price; advertising; number and salaries of sales staff; research and development budget; wages and personnel policy; recruitment policy; overtime; machine replacement; use of financial resources.

Data available initially: Opening balance sheet; history of the market over the past three years; necessary data to construct an approximate profit/loss account.

Feedback: Sales; labour turnover; service calls; technical breakthroughs. All these require further evaluation by the teams.

Interactive or noninteractive: Interactive.

Number of players: 12–36.

Number of teams: 3–6 (4–6 per team).

Duration: 4–5 days.

Umpiring device: Tables and matrices administered by tutor. Computer version (Apple) imminent.

Breaks for umpiring: 30 minutes after each decision period.

Form: Self-contained kit. Presentation by consultant.

Terms: Kit, £100.00. Presentation, by negotiation.

Available from: Tony Pope, Buckinghamshire College of Higher Education, Gorelands Lane, Chalfont St. Giles, Buckinghamshire.

Editor's classification: Model-based. Business. White goods industry.

Problem Analysis

Management situation: Groups attempting to solve an open-ended problem.

Suitable for: Undergraduates; postgraduates; DMS students; foremen/

supervisors; junior managers; middle managers; senior managers.

Subjects: Communication; situation analysis; deduction.

Description: Players are faced with a problem on which they have inadequate data for good decision-making. They ask questions, and receive small cards carrying additional data. The cards received depend on the questions asked. The umpire uses a card log to locate the required cards and to record what data each group has obtained.

Decisions: What information is necessary; how to frame a suitable question; what priority to give to the various enquiries.

Data available initially: A brief that gives carefully limited data, from which players can deduce what questions they ought to ask.

Feedback: For each enquiry, the data contained on the card received. Generally, discovering the quality of the questions asked through the degree of usefulness of the cards received.

Interactive or noninteractive: Noninteractive.

Number of players: 1 upwards.

Number of teams: 1 upwards.

Duration: 1–1½ hours.

Umpiring device: Umpire's judgement on cards to be given in response to questions.

Form: Self-contained kit.

Terms: £35.00 per set plus postage and packing.

Available from: M. Lynch, Northgate House, Perrymead, Bath, Avon BA2 5AX.

Editor's classification: Enquiry study. Functional – group effectiveness. General.

Production Management – The Bradford Game

Management situation: Production management.

Suitable for: Fifth and sixth form schoolchildren; undergraduates; postgraduates.

Subjects: Production methods; production organisation; purchasing; management accounting.

Description: Teams of 6–12 participants set up a production facility to make a range of paper booklets. They receive orders from the controlling tutor and experience realistic problems in scheduling and manufacturing them.

Decisions: Production layout; methods of operation; sequence of manufacture of orders received.

Data available initially: Outline of product range; production activities; equipment; material.

Feedback: The experience of success or failure in producing the goods ordered at the right time and to the right standard.

Interactive or noninteractive: Noninteractive.

Number of players: 6–12 per team. Number of teams depends on available space and tutor support.

Duration: 2–2½ hours.

Form: Self-contained kit.

Terms: On application.

Available from: The Careers Research and Advisory Centre, The Publications Department, Bateman Street, Cambridge CB2 1LZ.

Editor's classification: Practical simulation. Functional – production. Manufacturing industry.

Production Marketing Game 1

Management situation: Production and sale of dishwashers.

Suitable for: Undergraduates; postgraduates; DMS students; junior managers; middle managers; senior managers.

Subjects: Financing a business; corporate planning; domestic marketing; consumer goods marketing; sales planning; production methods; production organisation; stockholding; management accounting; pricing; workgroup organisation; machine replacement.

Description: The game simulates companies producing and marketing dishwashers in a dynamic, competitive environment. The dishwashers pass through a three-stage production process and are marketed in twenty-four different sales areas, which have different characteristics. The teams first formulate their strategies and then, in successive periods, make decisions on pricing, production levels, manpower levels, location of salesmen and similar subjects. Decisions are made on forms or on pre-purchased computer cards, and are umpired by computer. The results are provided as a computer print out. There are contracts available for tender at the discretion of the umpire and there is an option that features the injection of new capital.

Decisions: Buying and scrapping machines; ordering raw materials; scheduling production; hiring and firing workmen and salesmen; pricing; advertising; research and development; location of salesmen; factory space; purchase of information.

Data available initially: Capital resources available to project; indication of the costs of each activity; factory sizes; space requirement and nominal capacity of machines; characteristics of sales areas; taxation rules.

Feedback: Goods and labour on strength; units produced by each machine; sales achieved by area and model; cash account and statement of assets; taxation information; competitors' price and product quality; purchased information (e.g. forecasts).

Interactive or noninteractive: Interactive.

Number of players: 9–30.

Duration: 4–8 hours.

Number of teams: 3–6 (3–5 per team).

Umpiring device: Computer (Manual version also available).

Breaks for umpiring: Limited breaks are needed between decision periods.

Form: Self-contained kit. (Computer version contains manuals and listings plus program on cards or magnetic tape. Equipment required is computer with Fortran IV compiler, 24 K of CPU and disk for back-up storage.)

Terms: By negotiation.

Available from: Department of Management Science, Imperial College, London SW7 2BX. (C. D. T. Watson-Gandy.)

Editor's classification: Model-based. Business. Consumer durables.

Production Marketing Game 2

Management situation: Production and sale of a consumer durable.

Suitable for: Undergraduates; postgraduates; DMS students; junior managers.

Subjects: Financing a business; corporate planning; international marketing; domestic marketing; consumer goods marketing; sales planning; sales promotion; production organisation; stockholding; management accounting; pricing; appreciation of long-term versus short-term objectives.

Description: Playing teams compete in the production and sale of a consumer durable into two markets – home and export. After studying the information provided, they formulate a strategy and then, in successive periods, make decisions about pricing, production levels, advertising expenditure and similar matters. The decisions are recorded on a form and umpired by computer. The results are made known through a computer print out. After sufficient rounds have been played there is a feedback session which terminates the exercise.

Decisions: Buying and selling machines; scheduling production; purchase of raw material; quantity to export; pricing; investment in development or applied research and development; advertising (newspaper or TV); purchase of information (e.g. forecasts).

Data available initially: Details of amount of raw material and finished goods on hand, and cash balance; costs of different activities; details of accounting procedures.

Feedback: Machines available and their ages; production record; stock record; orders and sales made in home and export markets; prices charged by competitors; purchased information, if any; balance sheet.

Interactive or noninteractive: Interactive.

Number of players: 9–160.

Number of teams: 3–20 (3–8 per team).

Duration: 2–5 hours.

Umpiring device: Computer.

Breaks for umpiring: Limited breaks between decision periods.

Form: Self-contained kit. (Contains manuals and listings and program on cards or magnetic tape. Equipment required is computer with Fortran IV compiler, 24K of CPU and storage for sequential files).

Terms: £150.00.

Available from: Department of Management Science, Imperial College, London SW7 2BX. (C. D. T. Watson-Gandy.)

Editor's classification: Model-based. Business. Consumer durables.

Profile (The Manager Game)

Management situation: An examination of management skills.

Suitable for: Undergraduates; postgraduates; DMS students; foremen/ supervisors; junior managers; middle managers; senior managers.

Subjects: Skills abilities and characteristics relevant to the work of managers.

Description: Players are given a pack of cards. Each card names a skill/ability/characteristic that might be thought important for a manager. Players must sort the cards into groups, showing by their choices the degree of importance that they attach to each and so suggesting their own managerial 'profile'.

Decisions: Into which group each card should be placed.

Data available initially: The words on the cards and the individual

player's interpretation of them.
Feedback: Comparison of an individual's choice with the collective decision of his team, and with a model held by the umpire.
Interactive or noninteractive: Noninteractive.
Number of players: 1–24.
Number of teams: 1–4 (1–6 per team).
Duration: 1–1½ hours.
Umpiring device: A model classification held by the umpire, with which the classifications made by the teams are compared.
Form: Self-contained kit.
Terms: £30.00 per set plus postage and packing.
Available from: M. Lynch, Northgate House, Perrymead, Bath, Avon BA2 5AX.
Editor's classification: Exploratory game. Functional – use of authority. General.

Project Cost Model

Management situation: Engineering and construction projects.
Suitable for: Postgraduates; junior managers; middle managers; senior managers.
Subjects: Production methods; production organisation; pricing; project management; planning; estimating; client/contractor relationships.
Description: Teams prepare a tender for building a dam. Each team then commits itself to specific construction activities by choosing between alternatives offered. At intervals they encounter predetermined interferences and changes, in response to which they must decide on a strategy.
Decisions: Resources to be used; sequence of work; negotiating strategy.
Data available initially: Full details of the construction project.
Feedback: Experience of an advantageous or disadvantageous position consequent upon a choice made or negotiating attitude adopted. Experience of cash-flow position. At completion of the game, profit won, time taken for completion, return on investment.
Interactive or noninteractive: Interactive or noninteractive.
Number of players: 9–48.
Number of teams: 3–8 (3–6 per team).
Duration: 6–9 hours.
Form: Presentation by consultant.

Terms: By negotiation.
Available from: Project Software Limited, Foden Lane, Woodford, Stockport, Cheshire SK7 1PT.
Editor's classification: Encounter game. Functional – project construction. Civil engineering.

Project Management, Phase One – Design Management

Management situation: Preparing a design for a building to satisfy a client's requirements.
Suitable for: Postgraduates; DMS students; foremen/supervisors; middle managers; senior managers.
Subjects: Economic environment; financing a business; production methods; production organisation; purchasing; industrial relations; motivation; communication; delegation.
Description: Players are assigned different professional roles, and given access to models showing the basic conception of the building. The model seen by each member only gives details of his own speciality. By communicating with each other and with the client, coordinated by their project managers, the team must prepare an acceptable final design.
Decisions: For each player, the ideal solution to each design problem from his own point of view: then what degree of compromise to accept when negotiating with his colleagues.
Data available initially: The preliminary design; the personnel in the design team; the physical, financial and time constraints within which the design must be prepared.
Feedback: The experience of working through the problem; the apparent quality of the final design; tutor assessment.
Interactive or noninteractive: Noninteractive.
Number of players: 5–24.
Number of teams: 1–4 (5–6 per team).
Duration: 4–5 hours.
Umpiring device: Comparison of the finished design with the constraints imposed and with other designs.
Form: Presentation by consultant.
Terms: By negotiation.
Available from: D. Langford, Department of Building Technology, Brunel University, Uxbridge, Middlesex.
Editor's classification: Practical simulation. Functional – design. Construction industry.

Project Management, Phase Two – The Building Process

Management situation: The construction of a building in accordance with an agreed design.

Suitable for: Postgraduates; DMS students; foremen/supervisors; middle managers; senior managers.

Subjects: Financing a business; sales promotion; production methods; production organisation; purchasing; stockholding; workgroup organisation; committee work; industrial relations; motivation; communication; delegation.

Description: The team members are assigned roles as project manager, architect, contractor, contractor's buyer, contractors' quantity surveyor and contractor's site agent. The architect is allowed access to a master model of the building and has to communicate the requirements to the other team members through working drawings. Materials are available through the tutor for the construction of a replica of the model. The team members have to carry out their responsibilities by estimating, ordering, scheduling and building – all under cost and time constraints.

Decisions: For each role-player, the same decisions that would be required of him in real life.

Data available initially: For the architect, sight of the master model. For all team members, drawings as produced by the architect; cost of materials; lead times for obtaining materials; time penalties attaching to the contract; expected times of progress payments and construction necessary to win them.

Feedback: Observable progress of the building; progress payments made or withheld; likeness of the final structure to the master model.

Interactive or noninteractive: Noninteractive.

Number of players: 5–6 per umpire.

Number of teams: 1 per umpire.

Duration: 4–5 hours.

Form: Presentation by consultant.

Terms: By negotiation.

Available from: D. Langford, Department of Building Technology, Brunel University, Uxbridge, Middlesex.

Editor's classification: Practical simulation. Functional – project management. Construction industry.

The Property Investment Company

Management situation: Investment in residential property.

Suitable for: Undergraduates; postgraduates; DMS students; foremen/
supervisors; junior managers; middle managers; senior managers;
accountants.

Subjects: Financing a business.

Description: Players make decisions about buying, selling and renting
out flats based on their estimate of how market prices will alter. The
tutor releases these prices as the game moves forward in time.

Decisions: Sale, purchase, and letting of flats.

Data available initially: Procedure to be followed; current costs of
purchase and construction (with lead times); revenue from letting; cost
of borrowing and limits.

Feedback: Number and value of flats owned; net worth from balance
sheet.

Interactive or noninteractive: Noninteractive.

Number of players: 1–21.

Number of teams: 1–7 (1–3 per team).

Duration: 45 minutes to 1½ hours.

Umpiring device: Instructor's assessment based on table supplied.

Form: Self-contained kit.

Terms: On application.

Available from: A. I. S. Debenham, 9 Roland Way, London SW7 3RF.

Editor's classification: Encounter game. Company. Property investment.

Reaction

Management situation: Decision-making at supervisory level in a
generalised environment.

Suitable for: Foremen/supervisors; junior managers.

Subjects: Company organisation; personnel policies; industrial relations; production; management services; technical aspects of supervision.

Description: By throwing a dice, each team is brought into contact with
questions on supervisory skills related to principles and practice of
supervision, communications, technical aspects of supervision,
economics and finance, production and industrial relations. Written
answers are required from the teams and while the game continues the

adjudicator examines and scores these and feeds the information back to the team. By means of an in-built scoring mechanism the team marks up its own score. When a time limit has expired the scores of the teams are compared. There is an appeal mechanism and a means of doubling the stake on an answer believed to be a good one.

Decisions: How to tackle each new problem encountered.

Feedback: Effectiveness of decisions as shown by the score awarded.

Interactive or noninteractive: Noninteractive.

Number of players: 6–10.

Duration: 30 minutes.

Umpiring device: Evaluation of solutions by the umpire and assignment of a score.

Form: Self-contained kit of two sets.

Terms: £32.00 (including p. & p.) + V.A.T.

Available from: Guardian Business Services Limited, 119 Farringdon Road, London EC1R 3DA.

Editor's classification: Encounter game. Functional – use of authority. General.

The Redundancy

Management situation: Redundancy within a department of a business.

Suitable for: Postgraduates; DMS students; foremen/supervisors; junior managers; middle managers.

Subjects: Industrial relations.

Description: Each participant is provided with a copy of the initial brief and a record sheet on which to write his decisions. Copies of the remaining 51 briefing/decision sheets are placed, in numbered folders, on a large table or on the floor in the centre of the room. As each participant takes a decision on the situation described in the initial briefing sheet, he records the number of his decision on the record sheet and takes his next sheet from the folder bearing the number of his decision. As he makes subsequent decisions he follows the same procedure until he recognises himself as having solved the problem or having gone as far as he can go. At one stage there is the opportunity for players to write out their own preferred solution instead of being forced to choose an option provided.

Decisions: Which action, out of a number of alternatives set out, to take.

Data available initially: A simple description of the situation in which the manager has to take a decision.

Feedback: The outcome of the decision taken, as revealed by the next decision sheet.

Interactive or noninteractive: Noninteractive.

Number of players: 4–20.

Duration: 1 hour.

Umpiring device: A 'result' for every decision possible in the game. This is prepared as part of the package and written into all sheets other than the first.

Form: Self-contained kit.

Terms: £60.00 per set.

Available from: J. Snaith, Management Learning Systems, 14, Glencree Park, Newtownabbey, Co. Antrim BT37 0QS.

Editor's classification: Maze. Functional – industrial relations. General.

Road Construction – a training game for site managers

Management situation: Planning and control of road construction.

Suitable for: Undergraduates; postgraduates; foremen/supervisors; junior managers; middle managers.

Subjects: Production methods; production organisation; management accounting; workgroup organisation.

Description: The game simulates the construction of a length of road pavement. The road is represented by a sequence of activities from subgrade trim to finishes, which are carried out by gangs of subcontract workmen and machines. The progress of each process is influenced by factors causing variations in weekly production and interference between gangs and resources used, to which each player must react in order to control construction time and cost.

Decisions: Obtaining subcontract workgroups and machines; assigning them to appropriate tasks at appropriate times so as to maximise progress and minimise costs; adapting plans to meet novel situations arising.

Data available initially: Tender plan and estimate; details of resources planned and production targets.

Feedback: Production achieved; cost to date; value of work done; amount of work remaining.

Interactive or noninteractive: Noninteractive.

Number of players: 1–100 as individuals or groups.

Number of teams: Unrestricted.

Duration: 15–20 hours.

Umpiring device: A computer prints out, or presents on a visual display unit, the progress implied by a team's decisions when they have been subjected to the rules of the game.

Form: Self-contained kit of computer program and instructions. Also published in *Modern Construction Management* by Harris F.C. and McCaffer R. (Granada, St. Albans, Herts 1983).

Terms: £300.00.

Available from: F. C. Harris, Department of Civil Engineering, Loughborough University of Technology, Leicestershire.

Editor's classification: Encounter game. Functional – production scheduling. Civil engineering.

Route Planning Project for Salesmen

Management situation: Planning the calls to be made daily.

Suitable for: Salesmen.

Subjects: Sales planning.

Description: Players complete a planning sheet showing their intended use of a day. The quality of their plan for one day is judged by the umpire (and sales allocated) while their plan for the next day is being made. As successive days are completed, planning should approach more nearly the umpire's model of a 'good' method.

Decisions: Who to visit; route to be followed; time allowed for travel and call.

Data available initially: Map of the area; customer addresses and status; normal monthly order book.

Feedback: Sales made.

Interactive or noninteractive: Noninteractive.

Number of players: 4–20.

Number of teams: 2–4 (2–5 per team).

Duration: 1½ to 3 hours.

Umpiring device: Micro-computer.

Form: Presentation by consultant.

Terms: By negotiation.

Available from: A. I. S. Debenham, 9 Roland Way, London SW7 3RF.

Editor's classification: Enquiry Game, Functional – sales route planning. General.

Safe and Sound

Management situation: Conflict between safety and production targets.
Suitable for: DMS students; foremen/supervisors; junior managers; middle managers.
Subjects: Safety.
Description: A maze exercise in which players work through a text, taking one decision after another as the problem develops. Players experience consequences appropriate to their choices.
Decisions: Which of certain given options to choose when confronted with problems involving safety and production targets.
Data available initially: Current situation; production objectives; recent events.
Feedback: Experience of the consequences attached to the choice made (predetermined but previously unknown to the players).
Interactive or noninteractive: Noninteractive.
Number of players: 6–20 as individuals or small groups.
Duration: 15–20 minutes and discussion time.
Form: Self-contained kit in the form of a reproducible master.
Terms: £35.00 per kit.
Available from: Supervisory Management Training Limited, Peak House, 66 Croydon Road, Beckenham, Kent BR3 4AA.
Editor's classification: Maze. Functional – safety. Manufacturing industry.

A Safe Conduct

Management situation: Conflict between safety and output targets in an office environment.
Suitable for: DMS students; foremen/supervisors; junior managers; middle managers.
Subjects: Safety.
Description: A maze exercise in which players work through a text, taking one decision after another as the problem develops. Players experience consequences appropriate to their choices.
Decisions: Which of certain given options to choose when confronted with problems involving safety and output targets.
Data available initially: Current situation; work objectives; recent events.

Feedback: Experience of the consequences attached to the choice made (predetermined but previously unknown to the players).
Interactive or noninteractive: Noninteractive.
Number of players: 6–20 as individuals or small groups.
Duration: 15–20 minutes and discussion time.
Form: Self-contained kit in the form of a reproducible master.
Terms: £35.00 per kit.
Available from: Supervisory Management Training Limited, Peak House, 66 Croydon Road, Beckenham, Kent BR3 4AA.
Editor's classification: Maze. Functional – safety. Manufacturing industry.

Sellem

Management situation: Regional marketing for a company manufacturing a consumer durable.
Suitable for: Undergraduates; junior managers; middle managers; sales representatives.
Subjects: Domestic marketing; consumer goods marketing; sales planning; sales promotion; pricing.
Description: A game that emphasises the creative aspects of marketing. It models the situation facing an area or regional manager in an organisation selling through wholesalers and the larger retail chains.
Decisions: Production to be called for; price; size of salesforce; advertising; market research; trade discounts; salesforce remuneration; sales training; calling rate; market coverage.
Data available initially: Description of the product and its market. Playing conditions of the game.
Feedback: Sales data.
Interactive or noninteractive: Interactive.
Number of players: 4–24.
Number of teams: 2–6 (2–4 per team).
Duration: 4–9 hours.
Umpiring device: Circular slide rule.
Form: Self-contained kit, comprising Instructor's Manual, 20 sets of participants' notes, slide rule and all necessary forms.
Terms: £500.00 per set plus VAT.
Available from: Management Games Limited, 2 Woburn Street, Ampthill, Bedford MK45 2HP.
Editor's classification: Model-based. Functional – marketing. Consumer goods.

Service Industry Management Game

Management situation: Competition for business in a new service industry.

Suitable for: Postgraduates; DMS students; junior managers; middle managers; senior managers; bankers; accountants; other professionals.

Subjects: Financing a business; corporate planning; domestic marketing; sales planning; sales promotion; stockholding; management accounting; pricing; workgroup organisation; communication.

Description: After briefing by the umpires, the teams formulate objectives and policies for their business. They have to prepare forecasts and make basic decisions such as what level of capacity to create. These are followed by operating decisions for successive time periods. The exercise can be combined with functional inputs from the umpires.

Decisions: Price of service; service centres to be created; staff to be employed; raw materials to be ordered; advertising and quality decisions.

Data available initially: Full information on objectives with which the business might be set up, the variables to be manipulated, and the costs attaching to them.

Feedback: Demand for services generated and satisfied; profit/loss statement; material flows; cash-flow; statement of assets.

Interactive or noninteractive: Interactive.

Number of players: 9–28.

Number of teams: 3 or 4 (3–7 per team).

Duration: 15–30 hours.

Umpiring device: Computer.

Form: Presentation by consultant.

Terms: By negotiation.

Available from: Midland Management Exercises, 349 Clarence Road, Sutton Coldfield, West Midlands B74 4LX.

Editor's classification: Model-based. Business. Service Industry.

Shtaffel

Management situation: Administration of a management team in an unspecified industry.

Suitable for: Undergraduates; postgraduates; DMS students; junior managers; middle managers; senior managers.

Subjects: Company organisation; personnel policies; management style.

Description: Players are required to make typical 'year-end' decisions about the treatment of a team of 18 management employees. This means choosing between a number of realistic options such as training, promotion, job rotation, etc. The umpiring device determines the efficiency with which each member will operate during the following year, and this is multiplied by the degree of responsibility which the player has allocated to him, to give 'usefulness'. The 'total usefulness' of the management team is used to determine profit or loss.

Decisions: Which action, out of a number of possibilities, to take in relation to each member of the management team. What degree of responsibility to give him.

Data available initially: Age, length of service, responsibility and efficiency of each member of the management team.

Feedback: Improvement or deterioration in the overall efficiency of the management team and, hence, in profit and loss.

Interactive or noninteractive: Noninteractive.

Number of players: 4–40.

Number of teams: 2–8 (2–5 per team).

Duration: 3–5 hours.

Umpiring device: Tables.

Breaks for umpiring: 5 minutes per team after each decision period (assuming one umpire).

Form: Self-contained kit.

Terms: £70.00 per set.

Available from: Chris Elgood Associates Limited, The Studio, Cranbrook Road, Hawkhurst, Kent TN18 4AR.

Editor's classification: Model-based. Functional – organisation development. General.

Sickness Absences

Management situation: Making a decision about a specific case of sickness.

Suitable for: Foremen/supervisors; junior managers; personnel managers.

Subjects: Industrial relations with specific reference to sickness absenteeism.

Description: The scenario describes a particular case of sickness absence and players choose one action to take out of three described. The outcome of the choice is made known and choices of action offered for the new situation. The exercise moves through several steps in this way. The presentation is in the form of a board, with twenty-four items of text each covered by a numbered shutter or tile. The arrangement makes for an instant and dramatic feedback cycle.

Decisions: At each stage, which of the permitted actions to choose.

Data available initially: Single page scenario describing the case.

Feedback: Discovery of the consequence of each choice by lifting the appropriate numbered shutter.

Interactive or noninteractive: Noninteractive.

Number of players: 2–3 per playing board.

Number of teams: Up to 5 per instructor.

Duration: Including discussion, a maximum of 1 hour.

Form: Self-contained kit: board, scenario and Tutor's Manual.

Terms: £70.00 per set of 5 boards and materials. Singles £15.00.

Available from: Sigma Consultants, c/o Chris Elgood Associates Limited, The Studio, Cranbrook Road, Hawkhurst, Kent TN18 4AR.

Editor's classification: Programmed simulation. Functional – industrial relations. General.

Simet – 1 (Company Simulation by Computer)

Management situation: Control of production and finance in a manufacturing company.

Suitable for: Undergraduates; postgraduates; DMS students; junior managers; middle managers; senior managers.

Subjects: Economic environment; management accounting; pricing.

Description: A game that concentrates on the production side of a business, emphasising the need for decisions that are financially sensible in relation to market demand. The game leads on to Simet–2 and Simet–3.

Decisions: Production levels; re-order quantities; pricing; marketing expenditure.

Data available initially: The operating situation of the company, with profit/loss account and balance sheet. Physical and financial data for decision-making.

Feedback: Outcome of operating decisions; new profit/loss account; new balance sheet.

Interactive or noninteractive: Interactive.

Number of players: 6–100.

Number of teams: 2–20 (3–5 per team).

Duration: 3–5 hours.
Umpiring device: Computer.
Form: Presentation by consultants.
Terms: By negotiation.
Available from: Metis Management Services, 25 Farrar Lane, Adel, Leeds LS16 6AD.
Editor's classification: Model-based. Functional – production. Manufacturing industry.

Simet – 2 (Marketing Simulation by Computer)

Management situation: Marketing decision-making.
Suitable for: Undergraduates; postgraduates; DMS students; junior managers; middle managers; senior managers.
Subjects: Sales planning; sales promotion; pricing.
Description: A game that supplements Simet–1 by concentrating on the marketing side of a business and the need to win sales of satisfactory volume at a satisfactory price.
Decisions: Pricing; marketing strategy.
Data available initially: The operating situation of the company, with profit/loss account and balance sheet. Description of the options available to players and the financial implications.
Feedback: Results of the marketing and pricing strategy chosen; new profit/loss account; new balance sheet.
Interactive or noninteractive: Interactive.
Number of players: 6–100.
Number of teams: 2–20 (3–5 per team).
Duration: 3–12 hours.
Umpiring device: Computer.
Form: Presentation by consultants.
Terms: By negotiation.
Available from: Metis Management Services, 25 Farrar Lane, Adel, Leeds LS16 6AD.
Editor's classification: Model-based. Functional – marketing. General.

Simet–3 (Corporate Strategy Simulation by Computer)

Management situation: Corporate decision-making.
Suitable for: Undergraduates; postgraduates; middle managers; senior

managers; administrators.

Subjects: Economic environment; financing a business; corporate planning.

Description: An exercise that supplements Simet–1 and Simet–2 by placing the player in the position of a decision maker at corporate level in a group of companies. Planning relates to the future welfare of the group as a whole.

Decisions: Matters of concern to the group head office of a corporate organisation. Specifically, working capital, loan finance and the valuation of member companies.

Data available initially: Financial and operational data about the member companies of a group.

Feedback: An up-date of the situation of each company, consequent upon the decisions taken at group level.

Interactive or noninteractive: Interactive.

Number of players: 6–100.

Number of teams: 2–20 (3–5 per team).

Duration: 3–12 hours.

Umpiring device: Computer.

Form: Presentation by consultants.

Terms: By negotiation.

Available from: Metis Management Services, 25 Farrar Lane, Adel, Leeds LS16 6AD.

Editor's classification: Model-based. Functional – corporate planning. General.

Simstrat

Management situation: General management of a company.

Suitable for: Middle managers; senior managers.

Subjects: Economic environment; financing a business; corporate planning; international marketing; domestic marketing; consumer goods marketing; industrial marketing; sales planning; sales promotion; production organisation; purchasing; pricing.

Description: A generalised simulation that allows adjustments to the model so that it can reflect different products, different market areas, different distribution methods and different production options.

Decisions: Typical production, marketing and financial decisions of the business for which the adaptation has been made.

Data available initially: Handbook; historical data; cost tables; sample

runs.
Feedback: Trading results; cash-flow position; balance sheet.
Interactive or noninteractive: Either.
Number of players: 3–30.
Number of teams: 1–6 (3–5 per team).
Duration: 1–2 days.
Umpiring device: Computer.
Form: A basic simulation intended for adaptation to the requirements of specific customers.
Terms: Development of a custom-built version, £3,000.00 to £5,000.00.
Available from: Doug Wood, Manchester Business School, Booth Street West, Manchester M15 6PB.
Editor's classification: Model-based. Business. General.

Simulex

Management situation: Management of a company in a semi-durable consumer product market.
Suitable for: Middle managers; senior managers; postgraduates.
Subjects: Economic environment; financing a business; corporate planning; domestic, consumer goods marketing; sales promotion; production planning; company organisation; distribution.
Description: A computer-based game in which teams manage their own company, and set and implement a strategy for it. Decisions are involved on finance, production, marketing, labour relations, purchasing and inventory control, in relation to the needs of shareholders, management, customers and workforce. Companies compete for finance and markets.
Data available initially: Briefing booklet containing necessary information; first-period decisions.
Feedback: Production, distribution, sales figures; profit/loss and cash-flow statements; share prices of all companies; economic data.
Interactive or noninteractive: Either.
Number of players: 8 upwards.
Number of teams: 2 upwards (4–8 per team).
Duration: 1½–2½ days (including umpiring time).
Umpiring device: Micro-computer (supplied).
Breaks for umpiring: 15 minutes after each decision period of 75 minutes.
Form: As self-contained programme, including services of consultants

or by leasing.

Terms: By negotiation, approximately £15.00 – £30.00 per participant per day.

Available from: Doug Wood, Manchester Business School, Booth Street West, Manchester M15 6PB.

Editor's classification: Model-based. Business. Consumer durables.

Sixgam

Management situation: Selling word-processors to up to six countries in Europe.

Suitable for: Undergraduates; DMS students; junior managers; school-children aged 14 and above.

Subjects: Economic environment; pricing.

Description: A game about business economics that centres on the concepts of fixed and variable costs, demand curves, and cost and profit based pricing. Up to six teams compete in the market for a maximum of ten years. A result sheet facilitates the review of the exercise by the umpire.

Decisions: Price; wages; advertising strategy; allocation of product.

Data available initially: Present scale of operations; material costs; limits of allowable actions.

Feedback: Sales made; cash-flow.

Interactive or noninteractive: Interactive, when played by more than one team.

Number of players: 2–30.

Number of teams: 1–6 (2–5 per team).

Duration: 1½–3 hours. (½ hour per 'year'.)

Umpiring device: Micro-computer.

Form: Self-contained kit. (Includes disc for Apple II, BBC Model B, or RML 38OZ)

Terms: £28.75 including VAT.

Available from: Pitmansoft, Pitman Publishing, Southport PR9 9YF.

Editor's classification: Model-based. Functional – marketing. High Technology.

The Slough Soap Company

Management situation: Establishing and running a company manufacturing a consumer product.

Suitable for: Postgraduates; DMS students; middle managers; senior managers.

Subjects: Economic environment; financing a business; corporate planning; domestic marketing; consumer goods marketing; sales planning; sales promotion; production methods; purchasing; stockholding; management accounting; pricing; company organisation; workgroup organisation.

Description: The players plan and set up their own company, starting only with a capital sum. The game is concerned with manufacturing and marketing a consumer product by breaking into an existing market.

Decisions: Conventional production and marketing subjects.

Data available initially: Present state of the market; cost of resources; finance with which to undertake the project.

Feedback: Sales.

Interactive or noninteractive: Noninteractive.

Number of players: 3–20.

Number of teams: 1–5 (3–4 per team).

Duration: 10–12 hours.

Umpiring device: Charts, graphs, tables.

Form: Presentation by consultant.

Terms: By negotiation.

Available from: Nicholas Rints and Derek Hayes, The Management Centre, Slough College of Higher Education, Wellington Street, Slough, Berkshire.

Editor's classification: Model-based. Business. Consumer goods.

Small Business Management Exercise

Management situation: Manufacture and sale of a single product in a single market.

Suitable for: Undergraduates; postgraduates; DMS students; junior managers; middle managers.

Subjects: Economic environment; domestic marketing; industrial or consumer goods marketing; production; sales promotion; stockholding; management accounting; pricing; company organisation; personnel policies.

Description: A game that includes most of the significant factors experienced in a general manufacturing and selling business. Decision periods simulate quarters.

Decisions: Selling price; quality; advertising; production quantity; research and development; stockholding.

Data available initially: Economic situation, current and forecast; past pricing; past production cost; stocks available.

Feedback: Market share; sales (units); precise cost of production.

Interactive or noninteractive: Interactive.

Number of players: 6–24.

Number of teams: 3–6 (2–4 per team).

Duration: 3½–4½ hours.

Umpiring device: Nomograph.

Breaks for umpiring: 10 minutes between decision periods.

Form: Self-contained kit.

Terms: £500.00 per set.

Available from: Management Games Limited, 2 Woburn Street, Ampthill, Bedford MK45 2HP.

Editor's classification: Model-based. Business. General.

So You Think You Would Make a Managing Director

Management situation: The superior-subordinate interface in a production environment.

Suitable for: Undergraduates; postgraduates; DMS students; foremen/supervisors; junior managers; middle managers; senior managers.

Subjects: Superior-subordinate relations.

Description: A game that explores the establishment, implementation and interpretation of formal criteria by which a subordinate is to be judged. It highlights the distortions that arise through imperfect understanding or lack of trust, and demonstrates that a managing director can easily be ignorant of what is actually going on. The game can accommodate a third level in the hierarchy and can simulate many of the characteristics of information flow in an organisation.

Decisions: (By one party or the other or by agreement between the two). What the 'rules' should be; what the production target should be; what should actually be achieved and to what extent the 'rules' should be broken; what the superior should be told after the event.

Data available initially: Technical data about the production facility. Observable facts about the other party.

Feedback: To subordinate, performance data about the production facility. To the superior, less complete data plus information supplied to him by the subordinate.

Interactive or noninteractive: Noninteractive.
Number of players: 4–21.
Number of teams: 4–7 (1–3 per team).
Duration: 1 day.
Umpiring device: Computer.
Form: Presentation by consultant.
Terms: By negotiation.
Available from: M. A. P. Willmer, Manchester Business School, Booth Street West, Manchester M15 6PB.
Editor's classification: Organisational simulation. Functional – use of authority. Manufacturing industry.

SPASM (Simulation of Programming and Systems Management)

Management situation: Planning and controlling the work of programmers and systems analysts.
Suitable for: DMS students; middle managers; senior managers; project leaders.
Subjects: Management services; resource scheduling.
Description: Each syndicate takes on the task of a data processing manager who has to get three new projects operational as soon as possible. Resources consist of three systems analysts and six programmers. There is a chief systems analyst and a chief programmer (additional) and these have already estimated how much work will be required. Each syndicate must plan how the work is to be done, give firm completion dates, budget and control costs, and allocate the work to the available resources for at least the month ahead. Periods in the game represent one calendar month and at the end of each a report is produced showing how much work has been carried out and which stages have been completed. This may mean revision of the plan made at the start.
Decisions: Allocation of available staff to project tasks.
Data available initially: Duration and interrelationship of tasks within projects; staff experience and availability.
Feedback: Detailed report of work done by each analyst and programmer during the past month.
Interactive or noninteractive: Noninteractive.
Number of players: 4–25.
Number of teams: 2–5 (2–5 per team).
Duration: 1–1½ days.

Umpiring device: Computer.
Form: Self-contained kit, or presentation by a consultant.
Terms: By negotiation.
Available from: Urwick Management Centre, Baylis House, Stoke Poges Lane, Slough, Berkshire.
Editor's classification: Encounter game. Functional – planning and scheduling. Computer services.

Splosh Major

Management situation: Test marketing and national launch of an operation funded by NEDC.
Suitable for: Adaptable to different levels.
Subjects: Financing a business; corporate planning; domestic marketing; consumer goods marketing; sales planning; sales promotion; management accounting; company organisation; workgroup organisation; committee work; industrial relations; relationship with a funding body; conception and planning of a test-market operation; utilisation of test-market data for a larger operation.
Description: A development of Splosh Minor using similar data and similar variables but introducing additional relationships, requirements and restrictions. NEDC participation lapses after test-market operation.
Decisions: As for Splosh Minor, plus agreements to be reached with NEDC and policy to be adopted as a result of test-market operation.
Data available initially: As for Splosh Minor plus financial conditions of relationship with NEDC and policies demanded by NEDC.
Feedback: As for Splosh Minor.
Interactive or noninteractive: Interactive.
Number of players: 15–30.
Number of teams: 3–6 (5 per team).
Duration: 4 days.
Umpiring device: Computer.
Form: Presentation by consultant.
Terms: By negotiation.
Available from: Ian MacHorton, TSL (Training Services), 235 High Holborn, London WC1V 7DN.
Editor's classification: Model-based. Business. Consumer goods.

Splosh Minor

Management situation: Setting up and running a medium-sized manufacturing and sales company.
Suitable for: Adaptable to different levels.
Subjects: Financing a business; corporate planning; domestic marketing; consumer goods marketing; sales planning; sales promotion; management accounting; company organisation; workgroup organisation; committee work; industrial relations.
Description: The game is concerned with setting up and running a business to make and market a consumer product. It starts with considerations of finance and factory construction, moving on to production and marketing. Costs are known to the players and detailed forecasts must be made. Sales are made known on completion of the umpiring procedure. The game is flexible, with an emphasis on its use as a learning experience.
Decisions: Borrowing; credit policy towards government buyer; production level; R & D; deployment of sales force; advertising; tendering; purchase of information.
Data available initially: Nature and state of the market to be entered; details of cash in hand; bank facilities; production possibilities and costs; R & D costs; selling prices; costs of salesmen; market information.
Feedback: Market shares; sales achieved.
Interactive or noninteractive: Interactive.
Number of players: 15–30.
Number of teams: 3–6 (5 per team).
Duration: 4 days.
Umpiring device: Computer.
Form: Presentation by consultant.
Terms: By negotiation.
Available from: Ian MacHorton, TSL (Training Services), 235 High Holborn, London WC1V 7DN.
Editor's classification: Model-based. Business. Consumer goods.

Spriggs

Management situation: Running a four-process, two-product production unit and pricing the products.
Suitable for: Undergraduates; DMS students; foremen/supervisors; junior managers; middle managers.

Subjects: Production organisation; stockholding; pricing; workgroup organisation; industrial relations; communication; delegation.

Description: Teams are composed of works manager, production manager, production superintendents (four) and a stock controller. They all contribute by examining the data related to their subject areas and making decisions that affect unit cost. Collectively, they integrate their decisions and choose production quantities so that unit cost is known to them and is acceptable. They then fix prices.

Decisions: What level of production to fix and what price to charge.

Data available initially: The capabilities, costs and availability of staff, machines and materials. A rough forecast of market size.

Feedback: Sales; deliveries; personnel problems role-played by the umpire.

Interaction or noninteractive: Noninteractive.

Number of players: 5–42.

Number of teams: 1–7 (5–6 per team).

Duration: 2½–3 days.

Umpiring device: Tables used by the umpire to determine sales volume.

Form: Self-contained kit. Presentation by consultant.

Terms: Kit, £80.00 per set. Presentation, by negotiation.

Available from: Tony Pope, Buckinghamshire College of Higher Education, Gorelands Lane, Chalfont St. Giles, Buckinghamshire.

Editor's classification: Model-based. Functional – production. Manufacturing industry.

Sprods

Management situation: Running a small engineering works.

Suitable for: Undergraduates; postgraduates; DMS students; foremen/ supervisors; junior managers.

Subjects: Financing a business; production; purchasing; stockholding; pricing; personnel policies; industrial relations.

Description: The game is played in a series of decision periods, each set of decisions being evaluated by the umpire and the results (in terms of Sprods sold and raw material delivered) given back to the players. The final period is followed by a review session.

Decisions: Purchasing of raw materials; machine programming; sales price; purchase of equipment; wage rates; overtime.

Data available initially: Starting stocks (raw materials, partly finished goods, finished goods); cost of steel bars in various lengths; stockholding charges; cutting patterns; time required to manufacture; wage rates; overhead costs.

Feedback: Number of Sprods (of different sizes) sold; deliveries of different lengths of steel bar.

Interactive or noninteractive: Noninteractive.

Number of players: 6–36.

Number of teams: 2–6 (3–6 per team).

Duration: 5–9 hours.

Umpiring device: Charts.

Breaks for umpiring: 5 minutes after each decision period.

Form: Self-contained kit.

Terms: £500.00 per set.

Available from: Management Games Limited, 2 Woburn Street, Ampthill, Bedford MK45 2HP.

Editor's classification: Model-based. Company. Manufacturing industry.

Squabble

Management situation: Relationships between designer, employer, planner and user.

Suitable for: Undergraduates; postgraduates; sixth form schoolchildren; adult education courses.

Subjects: Relationships between people with interests in the same matter, but a need to cooperate.

Description: A board game that examines the interpersonal process when there is a divergence of goals and rewards for the actors.

Decisions: For each player, how to act in a specific situation so that personal rewards will be maximised but relationships with others will not break down.

Data available initially: The formal, highly structured rules of the game.

Feedback: The observed success of each player relative to the others as judged by the win/lose criterion of the game.

Interactive or noninteractive: Interactive.

Number of players: 4.

Number of teams: 1 (Commercial game, requiring more sets for more teams).

Duration: 1–2 hours.

*Umpiring device:*The rules of the game.

Form: Instructor's manual. Game is commercially available.

Terms: Instructor's manual, £15.00.
Available from: Cedric Green, Department of Architecture, University of Sheffield S10 2TN.
Editor's classification: Encounter Game. Functional – group effectiveness. General.

Statistics Workshop

Management situation: Application of statistical techniques to industrial problems.
Suitable for: Undergraduates; postgraduates; DMS students; junior managers; middle managers; senior managers.
Subjects: Statistical analysis; quality control; engineering management.
Description: A short book on statistical techniques, accompanied by a set of 1050 numbered counters. These can be used for constructing 20 different simulations of conditions known to appear in real life. By using the counters in different ways it is possible to give practice in the recognition of different conditions, in forecasting and the assignment of probabilities.
Decisions: Typically, what prediction to make on the basis of incomplete evidence and what degree of confidence to place in such a prediction.
Data available initially: Explanation of statistical theory presented in the text.
Feedback: Discovery of the accuracy of the prediction made when full data are revealed.
Interactive or noninteractive: Noninteractive.
Number of players: 1 or more.
Number of teams: 1 or more (1–5 per team).
Duration: 1–3 hours (excluding time required to read the book).
Form: Self-contained kit.
Terms: £5.00 per set.
Available from: David J. Smith, 26 Orchard Drive, Tonbridge, Kent.
Editor's classification: Encounter game. Functional – quality control, engineering, management services. General.

Stella Limited

Management situation: Managing a manufacturing company that produces a basic outboard motor for the marine markets.

Suitable for: Undergraduates; postgraduates; DMS students; junior managers; middle managers; senior managers; MBA students.

Subjects: Economic environment; financing a business; corporate planning; international marketing; domestic marketing; consumer goods marketing; sales planning; sales promotion; stockholding; management accounting; pricing; company organisation; business financing.

Description: The game concentrates on planning and controlling financial resources, with particular reference to the use of medium and long term capital, leasing arrangements, tax rates and capital allowances. Players have access to a computer model and make experiments with the decision variables in a number of different scenarios.

Decisions: How to obtain financial resources; whether to obtain equipment by capital purchase or leasing; pricing; asset planning.

Data available initially: A detailed manual describing the company and the environment and including a ten year forecast.

Feedback: A projection of the expected results over a ten-year period if the decisions of the current experiment were to be made, in the scenario stated. The projection includes cash-flow statement, profit and loss account, and balance sheet.

Interactive or noninteractive: Noninteractive.

Number of players: 1 upwards.

Number of teams: 1 upwards.

Duration: 8–16 hours.

Umpiring device: Micro-computer (CP/M) and tutor's marking/assessment scheme.

Form: Presentation by consultants and subsequent use of self-contained kit. (Micro-computer required.)

Terms: £450.00.

Available from: Dr. P. Woolliams and J. Cooper, Anglian Regional Management Centre, Danbury Park, Chelmsford, Essex.

Editor's classification: Encounter game. Functional – financial planning. Manufacturing industry.

The Symbol Game

Management situation: Achieving a common understanding within a group about action to be taken.
Suitable for: Undergraduates; postgraduates; DMS students; junior managers; middle managers; senior managers.
Subjects: Communication; logic.
Description: A single group of players is confronted with an investigatory task – in a generalised form – for which it is appropriate to lay down a questioning procedure. They have to understand the nature of the task, and agree on a procedure that all members believe they can follow successfully. The tutor then sets up a particular case and chooses one member of the group to handle it. If he fails, the entire group is deemed to have failed.
Decisions: For the group, what procedure to agree; how to ensure that all members understand it. For the chosen individual, how to operate the procedure.
Data available initially: The generalised description of the task.
Feedback: Experience of success or failure in the investigation.
Interactive or noninteractive: Noninteractive.
Number of players: 5–12.
Number of teams: 1.
Duration: 30 minutes plus discussion time.
Form: Self-contained kit.
Terms: £30.00 per set.
Available from: Chris Elgood Associates Limited, The Studio, Cranbrook Road, Hawkhurst, Kent TN18 4AR.
Editor's classification: Structured experience. Functional – communication. General.

Teamwork

Management situation: Management of a team of employees in an unspecified industry.
Suitable for: Postgraduates; DMS students; middle managers; senior managers.
Subjects: Company organisation; personnel policies; management style.
Description: Players are required to manage a team of employees who all have individual needs. Certain rewards, are available with which

these employees can be motivated, but understanding of the needs of each employee, and the rewards he values, can only be obtained by devoting time to becoming acquainted with him. Company efficiency is affected by the personal work achievement of the player (which is reduced each time he stops working to conduct an interview) and by the efficiency shown by the employees. Players must therefore balance the value of their own time against the improvement that may result from more understanding of, and better motivation of their workforce.

Decisions: How much time to devote to the affairs of each employee. What rewards to offer each employee.

Data available initially: Statement of the six basic types of reward which employees can be offered in the game.

Feedback: Performance of each employee as indicated by the umpire.

Interactive or noninteractive: Noninteractive.

Number of players: 2–24.

Number of teams: 1–6 (1–4 per team).

Duration: 3 hours.

Umpiring device: Tables.

Breaks for umpiring: 2 minutes per team after each decision period (assuming one umpire).

Form: Self-contained kit.

Terms: £90.00 per set.

Available from: Chris Elgood Associates Limited, The Studio, Cranbrook Road, Hawkhurst, Kent TN18 4AR.

Editor's classification: Model-based. Functional – group effectiveness. General.

Temple

Management situation: Decision making and personal interaction within a group facing physical danger.

Suitable for: DMS students; foremen/supervisors; junior managers; middle managers.

Subjects: Utilisation of human resources of the playing group; utilisation of data provided within the game.

Description: The players are assigned identities within a story. This can have various different outcomes, dependent on the choices that they make. The tutor describes the situations that confront them, they decide upon an appropriate action (within the rules of the game) and the tutor reveals the outcome before they move on down the story line. There are six characters trying to escape from a temple. Varying numbers succeed, or die, or are abandoned along the route.

Decisions: The story assigns skills, abilities and resources to each character. The decisions are about which of these to deploy, and in what manner, when danger threatens. Decisions are made known to the tutor verbally.

Data available initially: Full data about the capabilities of the characters. Data about the fictional situation of comparable detail to that available in an ordinary adventure story.

Feedback: Information from the tutor about what has happened as a result of the decisions made. (e.g. victory, escape, wounds, loss of weapons, death, etc.)

Interactive or noninteractive: Interactive.

Number of players: 6, plus 3 observers.

Number of teams: 1.

Form: Self-contained kit or presentation by consultant.

Terms: By negotiation.

Available from: Oldfield Payne Management Associates, Oldfield House, Coniston Close, Daventry, Northants. NN11 5EE.

Editor's classification: Adult role-playing game. Functional – group effectiveness. General.

Tensim

Management situation: Obtaining business by competitive tender.

Suitable for: Undergraduates; postgraduates; junior managers; middle managers; senior managers.

Subjects: Industrial marketing; pricing; tendering; estimating.

Description: Teams compete with each other to obtain contracts by tender. All teams work from the same estimated cost and add a percentage to give a profit margin. The umpire applies the percentages to an actual cost figure for each team and awards the contract to the lowest tender resulting. The cost attributed to each team is produced by a computer program and varies within prescribed statistical limits from the estimated cost. Teams are, therefore, entering quotes in the situation without knowing quite how accurate their estimates are. Profits are assumed to be the tender amount minus a fixed figure.

Decisions: What profit margin to be added to an estimated cost figure when submitting a tender.

Data available initially: Conditions of game. No further data needed.

Feedback: The identity of the successful tenderer for each contract.
Interactive or noninteractive: Interactive.
Number of players: 4–32.
Number of teams: 4–8 (1–4 per team).
Duration: 1½–2 hours.
Form: Presentation by consultant.
Terms: On application.
Available from: Martin Barnes and Partners, Foden Lane, Woodford, Stockport, Cheshire SK7 1PT.
Editor's classification: Encounter game. Functional – tendering. General.

Theta

Management situation: Producing, selling and delivering a consumer product.
Suitable for: Postgraduates; DMS students; middle managers; senior managers.
Subjects: Economic environment; financing a business; corporate planning; domestic marketing; consumer goods marketing; management accounting; pricing; company organisation; workgroup organisation; distribution; delegation.
Description: A complex game that simulates four companies making a common product. Each has a 'home' market and competes with the others in a 'common' market. There are also contract sales. Besides manufacturing and selling, they must deliver the product, using their own transport or hired transport or public transport. Additionally, the financial side of the business includes borrowing and plant investment decisions.
Decisions: Price in each market; production quantity; marketing expenditure in each area; research and development expenditure; plant and vehicle investment; hire of vehicles; borrowing and repaying; purchase of information; purchase of consultancy; sales of surplus plant.
Data available initially: Full details of the operations of the company for the past two years.
Feedback: Overall market statistics; company's own marketing performance; production performance; stock analysis; transport costs, according to methods used; profit and loss account; balance sheet; contracts available in coming year.
Number of players: 12 upwards.

Number of teams: 4 upwards. (Not more than 6 per team)
Duration: 6–8 hours.
Umpiring device: Mainframe computer.
Form: Presentation by consultant.
Terms: £150.00 plus expenses.
Available from: B. D. Najak, Durham University Business School, Mill Hill Lane, Durham DH1 3LB.
Editor's classification: Model-based. Business. Consumer products.

Tiecard

Management situation: Manufacture and sale of a simple consumer product.
Suitable for: Postgraduates; DMS students; foremen/supervisors; junior managers; middle managers; senior managers.
Subjects: Domestic marketing; consumer goods marketing; production; quality control; pricing; company organisation; industrial relations.
Description: Given details of a type of product that they have to manufacture, teams spend four hours planning the manner in which they would make it. This planning is done in the knowledge that they will at a later stage have to employ one of the other groups as 'workers' and put their plans to the test by physically making the product. After the planning stage, the first team selected to act as 'managers' is given three one-hour periods for production, separated by three half-hour sales and accounting periods. In the latter they are required to sell what they have made and to complete accounts. Teams act as 'managers' in turn.
Decisions: Wage and salary levels, methods of production, and design of product.
Data available initially: Price of materials and equipment; materials and product specification; timetable indicating duration of each phase.
Feedback: Experience of success or failure in making and selling goods profitably.
Interactive or noninteractive: Noninteractive.
Number of players: 6–20.
Number of teams: 2–4 (3–5 per team).
Duration: 2 full days.
Form: Presentation by consultant, or the operating instructions and briefing sheets can be purchased.
Terms: £300.00 for rights to duplicate and use in client's organisation.

Available from: J. Snaith, Management Learning Systems, 14, Glencree Park, Newtonabbey, Co. Antrim BT37 0QS.
Editor's classification: Practical simulation. Company. General.

Tourism Business Game

Management situation: Operation of a small coach tour business running weekend trips from London to the Lake District.
Suitable for: Undergraduates; postgraduates; DMS students; junior managers; middle managers; senior managers.
Subjects: Sales planning; pricing; workgroup organisation; forecasting; interpreting statistics; using cash-flow statements.
Description: A game that requires players to estimate demand for a coach tour and commit themselves to plans while still uncertain about the accuracy of their estimate. The game allows players the facility to simulate the future – at a cost – and so increase the probability of making a good estimate.
Decisions: Price per coach trip; advertising expenditure; accommodation to reserve in advance; repayment of bank loans.
Data available initially: Participant's instructions, including statistical information and cost information.
Feedback: Customer demand; actual customer trips; cash-flow statement.
Interactive or noninteractive: Noninteractive.
Number of players: 4–36.
Number of teams: 2–6 (2–6 per team).
Duration: 5–6 hours.
Umpiring device: Micro-computer.
Form: Self-contained kit including program for North Star microprocessor. Presentation by consultant.
Terms: Kit £60. Presentation by negotiation.
Available from: Ray Garnett, Ealing College of Higher Education, St. Mary's Road, Ealing, London W5 5RF.
Editor's classification: Model-based. Functional – planning and forecasting. Tourism.

Tricopoly – The Synergy Game

Management situation: Understanding conditions and effects when members of a society or an organisation feel poverty or powerlessness.
Suitable for: Undergraduates; postgraduates; junior managers; middle managers; sixth form schoolchildren; students on courses in Third World Studies.
Subjects: Human responses to adverse conditions.
Description: A simulation that immerses participants in an organisation where issues of freedom, control, identity, survival and respect become very real indeed. The game promotes a personal and emotional understanding of what such a state is like.
Decisions: Personal decisions on how to conduct oneself when apparently possessing little or no power.
Data available initially: Description of the situation, the conditions, and the possibilities for action.
Feedback: The responses of other players and groups to one's actions and attitudes.
Interactive or noninteractive: Interactive.
Number of players: Flexible.
Number of teams: Flexible.
Duration: 1–3 hours.
Umpiring device: The function is performed by the rules of the game and the reactions of the players.
Form: Self-contained kit.
Terms: £5.50 per set. (Royalties to charities for the relief of third world poverty).
Available from: Pavic Productions, Sheffield City Polytechnic, Department of Education Services, 36 Collegiate Crescent, Sheffield S10 2BP.
Editor's classification: Structured Experience. Functional – employee relations. General.

Trouble

Management situation: Handling a series of problems connected with employment law.
Suitable for: DMS Students; foremen/supervisors; junior managers.
Subjects: Employment legislation; industrial relations.
Description: A board game, in which the throw of a dice determines the type of problem which a player must tackle. The problems are presented

on packs of cards.

Decisions: What answer to give to each specific problem, as it is encountered.

Data available initially: None, beyond the players existing knowledge of employment legislation and industrial relations.

Feedback: There is an answer for each of the cards, which is revealed by the tutor after the player has committed himself.

Interactive or noninteractive: Noninteractive.

Number of players: 1–20.

Number of teams: 1–5 (1–4 per team).

Duration: 1–2 hours.

Umpiring device: Predetermined model answers.

Form: Self-contained kit.

Terms: On application.

Available from: Hotel and Catering Industry Training Board, P.O. Box 18, Ramsey House, Central Square, Wembley, Middlesex HA9 7AP.

Editor's classification: Encounter game. Functional – industrial relations. Hotels and catering.

Tycoon

Management situation: The manufacture of a single consumer product and its sale in a single competitive market place. Several versions are available of different levels of complexity.

Suitable for: In appropriate versions, school pupils; undergraduates; postgraduates; foremen/supervisors; DMS students; junior managers; middle managers; senior managers.

Subjects: Economic environment; financing a business; corporate planning; domestic marketing; consumer goods marketing; sales promotion; purchasing; stockholding; management accounting; pricing; personnel policies; industrial relations.

Description: The title covers four versions of a generalised model-based game concerned with establishing a factory and then making and selling a single product. Each successive version has greater sophistication than its predecessor, introducing new aspects of reality and making it harder to operate the company profitably.

Decisions: Material purchasing; manufacturing level; borrowing; pricing; advertising; number of salesmen; research and development; engineering investment; distribution.

Data available initially: Description of the market to be entered and the expected costs of all items necessary for establishing and running the company.

Feedback: An operating statement that records all the decisions made and presents consequential data such as sales achieved, revenue, costs and shock.

Interactive or noninteractive: Interactive.

Number of players: 6–36.

Number of teams: 2–6 (3 to 6 per team).

Duration: 3–8 hours.

Umpiring device: Proprietary 'market share calculator'.

Breaks for umpiring: Not significant.

Form: Self-contained kit.

Price: £500.00 per set plus VAT.

Available from: Management Games Limited, 2 Woburn Street, Ampthill, Bedford MK45 2HP.

Editor's classification: Model-based. Business. Consumer goods.

Urbism

Management situation: The control of urban growth.

Suitable for: Undergraduates; postgraduates; professionals concerned with development; local groups.

Subjects: Economic environment; intergroup relations; planning and urban design.

Description: A role-play concerned with applying theoretical ideas about urban development to a real site. Players adopt the roles of the parties properly involved in such developments.

Decisions: Each player must decide how the concepts operating in his own area should be applied on the real site and argue his case with his colleagues. As an entity, the group must choose a preferred solution.

Data available initially: Current beliefs in the contributory disciplines; the physical realities of the site.

Feedback: For individuals, the response of colleagues to their ideas. For the group, critical assessment of the agreed plan by themselves and by the umpire.

Interactive or noninteractive: Interactive.

Number of players: 18–50 depending on the number collectively assigned to a role.

Duration: A minimum of 12 hours.

Umpiring device: Principally, peer group assessment.

Form: Presentation by consultant, or handbook from which a kit can be prepared.

Terms: Presentation, by negotiation; Handbook, £15.00.

Available from: Cedric Green, Department of Architecture, University of Sheffield S10 2TN.

Editor's classification: Organisation game. Functional – planning. Urban development.

Urmandex

Management situation: Manufacture and marketing of an unspecified product under competitive conditions.

Suitable for: DMS students; middle managers; senior managers; systems analysts.

Subjects: Economic environment; financing a business; corporate planning; domestic marketing; consumer goods marketing; sales planning; sales promotion; production; purchasing; stockholding; pricing; cashflow.

Description: The exercise represents a situation where a number of companies, each managed by a team of students, are the competing suppliers of the same product to a single market. The objective for each team is to regulate its use of company cash, plant, material and other resources so as to accumulate the greatest possible net profit. This is done by decisions, made to cover periods of three months, which are handed to the umpire. The decisions are processed by a computer which provides each company with a printed statement showing its results.

Decisions: Price; marketing; research; machine capacity; production; stocks.

Data available initially: Full operating statement and balance sheet.

Feedback: Full operating statement and balance sheet after each decision. Additional data after every fourth decision.

Interactive or noninteractive: Interactive.

Number of players: 9–25.

Number of teams: 3–5 (3–5 per team).

Duration: 1–2 days.

Umpiring device: Computer.

Additional resources: Photocopier.

Breaks for umpiring: 20 minutes after each decision period.

Form: Presentation by consultant.

Terms: By negotiation.

Available from: Urwick Management Centre, Baylis House, Stoke Poges Lane, Slough, Berkshire.
Editor's classification: Model-based. Business. General.

The Value of T

Management situation: A leader in charge of a group task.
Suitable for: Undergraduates; postgraduates; junior managers; middle managers; senior managers.
Subjects: Workgroup organisation; managerial style of behaviour; communication; criteria of success.
Description: A newly appointed leader takes over a group in which the knowledge necessary to do the task is scattered amongst the members but none of them know what the task is or whether their particular items of knowledge are relevant. The leader has a description of the task, but this is quite meaningless unless he becomes familiar with the knowledge of the group members. Communication takes place or does not take place depending on the style of leadership adopted.
Decisions: For the leader, in what manner to approach his group members. For group members, in what way to respond to the leader.
Data available initially: Various small cards whose meaning is unclear.
Feedback: The experience of success or failure in finding the value of T.
Interactive or noninteractive: Noninteractive.
Number of players: 8–15 in a single group.
Duration: 1 hour.
Form: Self-contained kit.
Terms: £25.00 per set.
Available from: Chris Elgood Associates Limited, The Studio, Cranbrook Road, Hawkhurst, Kent TN18 4AR.
Editor's classification: Behavioural. Functional – leadership. General.

Vinewood Limited

Management situation: Competition between manufacturers in inflationary conditions.
Suitable for: Undergraduates; postgraduates; DMS students; junior managers; middle managers; senior managers.
Subjects: Economic environment; financing a business; corporate planning; international marketing; domestic marketing; consumer goods

marketing; sales planning; sales promotion; production organisation; purchasing; stockholding; management accounting; pricing; distribution.

Description: A game that concentrates on the problems of managing a company in inflationary times, highlighting their causes and effects.

Decisions: Conventional production and marketing decisions.

Data available initially: Selling price; distribution arrangements; purchasing arrangements; labour deployment; personnel policies; advertising practice; financial state.

Feedback: Actual distribution; stockholding; labour turnover; revenue generation; costs; profit.

Interactive or noninteractive: Interactive between teams and tutors.

Number of players: 2 upwards.

Number of teams: 1 upwards (2–6 per team).

Duration: 6 hours.

Umpiring device: Nomograph. Computer if available.

Breaks for umpiring: 10 minutes per team per instructor.

Form: Self-contained kit or presentation by consultant.

Terms: On application.

Available from: Maxim Consultants Limited, 6 Marlborough Place, Brighton, East Sussex BN1 1UB.

Editor's classification: Model-based. Business. General.

VISA

Management situation: Any situation in which operations are performed by people and/or machines, and there are various possible causes of delay.

Suitable for: DMS students; foremen/supervisors; junior managers; middle managers; senior managers.

Subjects: Production; work study.

Description: VISA (Variable Incident Simulation Apparatus) is a device for indicating visually whether work is or is not going on at a number of different stations. It also indicates how much work has been done and, if there is a stoppage, for what cause this has taken place. The device is used as the basis of a work-scheduling exercise, first attempting this without detailed study of the conditions, and then after a close examination of them, which can include activity sampling.

Decisions: Job priorities; production plan; work allocation; resource utilisation.

Data available initially: Resources available; components to be produced; operations required; setup and process times expected.

Feedback: Output (in standard minutes); machine utilisation; departmental effectiveness.

Interactive or noninteractive: Noninteractive.

Number of players: 11–16.

Number of teams: At instructor's discretion.

Duration: 8 hours–1½ days.

Umpiring device: Variable Incident Simulation Apparatus (an analogue device).

Additional resources: Centrallograph recorder (adapted).

Breaks for umpiring: 10 minutes at the end of each simulated day.

Form: As a self-contained package or as part of a training course.

Terms: By negotiation.

Available from: Urwick Management Centre, Baylis House, Stoke Poges Lane, Slough, Berkshire.

Editor's classification: Encounter game. Functional – work scheduling. General.

Wakefield Weavers

Management situation: The personnel function in a medium-sized textile company.

Suitable for: Undergraduates; postgraduates; DMS students; foremen/supervisors; junior managers; middle managers.

Subjects: Company organisation; personnel policies; industrial relations.

Description: A detailed enquiry study/role-play which requires students to: (a) investigate a company (be seeking information) so as to identify its personnel needs; (b) form themselves into a personnel department along the lines they believe to be necessary; (c) handle a series of problems put to them in their assumed role.

Decisions: What information to seek; what personnel organisation to establish; what action to recommend in regard to a series of problems presented.

Data available initially: A 'background sheet' giving data about the company, and an indication of the other sources of knowledge available.

Feedback: The usefulness or otherwise of the information obtained; the competence or otherwise of the personnel department when faced with problems – both as perceived by themselves and as discussed in

evaluation sessions.
Interactive or noninteractive: Either.
Number of players: 4–24 (larger numbers are possible with more than one tutor).
Number of teams: 2–4 (larger numbers are possible with more than one tutor).
Duration: 6–10 hours.
Form: Self-contained kit.
Terms: £20.00 per set.
Available from: Pavic Productions, Department of Education Services, Sheffield City Polytechnic, 36 Collegiate Crescent, Sheffield S10 2BP.
Editor's classification: Enquiry study. Functional – personnel. Clothing/textiles.

War and Peace

Management situation: International peace negotiations.
Suitable for: Undergraduates; postgraduates; DMS students; foremen/supervisors; junior managers; middle managers; senior managers.
Subjects: Industrial relations; international negotiations.
Description: By drawing upon the most dramatic available subject, War and Peace shows the reasons for the attitudes adopted by negotiators and the skills required to reach a mutually acceptable solution.
Decisions: Selection of team members; assignment of roles to team members; arguments and attitudes to be taken in negotiation; responses to make to arguments and attitudes of others; when to concede, compromise, stand firm, etc.
Data available initially: Detailed background data about the international situation.
Feedback: Response shown by the other parties to negotiation; comments by tutor and/or colleagues; viewing videotape recording.
Interactive or noninteractive: Interactive.
Number of players: 8–48.
Number of teams: 4–6 (2–8 per team).
Duration: 3–5 hours.
Additional resources: Closed-circuit television is useful.
Form: Self-contained kit.
Terms: £20.00 per set.
Available from: Pavic Publications, Department of Educational Services, Sheffield City Polytechnic, 36 Collegiate Crescent, Sheffield S10

2BP.
Editor's classification: Organisational simulation. Functional – negotiation. International negotiation.

Whitewash

Management situation: Management of a paint manufacturing company.
Suitable for: Undergraduates; postgraduates; DMS students; foremen/supervisors; junior managers; middle managers; senior managers; sixth form schoolchildren; MBA students.
Subjects: Industrial marketing; sales planning; production methods; workgroup organisation; motivation; communication.
Description: A computer based interactive business game used as a group task for helping managers to work together as a team, and to develop decision-making skills.
Decisions: Price; number of employees; plant capacity.
Data immediately available: A case study, describing the operation of the company and including the most recent set of accounts.
Feedback: Commercial measures of each team's performance, and observer comment on each team's effectiveness as a working group.
Interactive or noninteractive: Interactive.
Number of players: 12–50.
Number of teams: 3–10 (4–5 per team).
Duration: 1–2 days.
Umpiring device: Micro-computer using BASIC program.
Form: Self-contained kit of computer program and instructions (all common micro-computers). Presentation by consultant. Also in *'The Management of the Business'* (D. J. Moul and P. R. Woolliams. Wiley 1984).
Terms: Kit, on application. Presentation by consultant, £200.00 per day.
Available from: D. J. Management Consultants, 87 Beehive Lane, Ilford, Essex.
Editor's classification: Model-based. Business. Paint manufacturing.

Whurps

Management situation: Manufacture and sale of an unspecified product.
Suitable for: Undergraduates; postgraduates; DMS students; foremen/supervisors; junior managers; middle managers; school sixth forms.

Subjects: Domestic marketing; sales promotion; production; stock-holding; management accounting; pricing; company organisation.

Description: A game that highlights the importance of making forward estimates, despite uncertain conditions, and adopting the plan that gives the greatest probability of success. Since the position in which a company finds itself changes from one period to another, 'success' has to be continually redefined and new plans laid accordingly. The outcome of each possible combination of production and marketing policies is simulated by the throwing of dice in accordance with sophisticated rules. It is possible for one company to take over another.

Decisions: Production: advertising; sales price.

Data available initially: Explanation of the rules governing the dice throw that will determine production achieved and orders won. From this it is possible to form an estimate of the likely outcome of any course of action.

Feedback: Production achieved; direct orders won by price policy; extra orders won by advertising.

Interactive or noninteractive: Part interactive; part noninteractive.

Number of players: 3–36.

Number of teams: 3–12 (1–3 per team).

Duration: 1–3 hours.

Umpiring device: Specially manufactured dice.

Form: Self-contained package.

Terms: £70.00 per set.

Available from: Chris Elgood Associates Limited, The Studio, Cranbrook Road, Hawkhurst, Kent TN18 4AR.

Editor's classification: Encounter game. Company. General.

Wildcat

Management situation: Developing North Sea oil and gas fields under competitive conditions.

Suitable for: Undergraduates; postgraduates; DMS students; junior managers; middle managers; senior managers.

Subjects: Corporate planning; purchasing; pricing; entrepreneurial behaviour; strategic decision-making.

Description: Competing entrepreneurs bid for possibly lucrative roles in connection with the exploitation of North Sea oil and gas fields. The roles have to be fulfilled by trading between the parties in conditions that are predictable in terms of overall long-term probability but uncertain in the short term.

Decisions: The price of each oil and gas field; the value of a drilling company; how to develop an oil field; when to borrow cash.

Data available initially: Expected income streams from oil and gas fields under different stages of development; costs of development; North Sea hazards.

Feedback: Experience of success or failure as policies adopted encounter the hazards of operating conditions.

Interactive or noninteractive: Interactive.

Number of players: 3–13 as individuals.

Duration: 1 day.

Form: Self-contained kit.

Terms: £45.50 including post and packing and VAT.

Available from: Guardian Business Services Limited, 119 Farringdon Road, London EC1R 3DA.

Editor's classification: Encounter game. Business. Oil industry.

Would You Credit It?

Management situation: Handling credit control problems.

Suitable for: DMS students; office supervisors; junior managers; middle managers; credit control staff; administration staff.

Subjects: Credit control.

Description: A maze exercise in which players work through a text, taking one decision after another as the problem develops. Players experience consequences appropriate to their choices.

Decisions: Which of certain options to choose when confronting problems in the general area of credit control.

Data available initially: Background data about the company and its credit control procedures; description of the current circumstances.

Feedback: Experience of the consequences attached to the choice made (predetermined but previously unknown to the players).

Interactive or noninteractive: Noninteractive.

Number of players: Not limited. Large numbers only mean additional copying from the original papers provided. The exercise can be used individually or by small groups.

Duration: 30–45 minutes plus discussion time.

Form: Self-contained kit in the form of a reproducible master.

Terms: £45.00 per kit.

Available from: Supervisory Management Training Limited, Peak

House, 66 Croydon Road, Beckenham, Kent BR3 4AA.
Editor's classification: Maze. Functional – credit control. General.

Wroperson Case Study

Management situation: A business in decline.
Suitable for: Middle managers; senior managers.
Subjects: Corporate planning; industrial marketing; production; company organisation; personnel policies.
Description: A very detailed role-playing exercise in which staff members act as the existing management of a company and a syndicate of trainees represent the newly appointed 'general manager designate' who is charged with making a thorough examination of the company before getting involved in any executive duties. The quality of the information obtained, and therefore of the solution suggested, depends on the questions put to the staff representatives.
Decisions: What questions to put to the existing management.
Data available initially: Detailed write-up of the Wroperson Company.
Feedback: Value of the information obtained from questions put to the existing management.
Interactive or noninteractive: Noninteractive.
Number of players: 4 upwards.
Number of teams: 1 upwards (4–6 per team).
Duration: 3–4 days (intermittently).
Additional resources: 5 well briefed tutors to simulate the 'existing management'.
Form: Presentation by consultant or component of training course.
Terms: By negotiation.
Available from: Urwick Management Centre, Baylis House, Stoke Poges Lane, Slough, Berkshire.
Editor's classification: Enquiry study. Company. General.

Wyefarm Management Game

Management situation: Managing a farm in South-East England.
Suitable for: Undergraduates; postgraduates; DMS students; junior managers; middle managers; senior managers.
Subjects: Economic environment; financing a business; production organisation; management accounting.

Description: Each team takes over a family farm and makes annual decisions about financial matters for the year just ending (depreciation rates and stock valuation), and about farm management in the year to come. The plans are umpired by computer and the results made known in the form of economic and technical reports.

Decisions: Depreciation rate; stock valuation; what to produce, in what quantity, and by what method.

Data available initially: The participants manual gives full details of the options available and their costs. These cover crops and livestock, labour, machinery, contract ploughing and loan availability. There are also financial and physical details of the state of the farm at the start of the game.

Feedback: Physical production schedules; yields and price achieved; accounts.

Interactive or noninteractive: Noninteractive.

Number of players: Unrestricted.

Number of teams: Unrestricted (Usually 2–6 per team).

Duration: 5–16 hours. (5–8 cycles taking 1–2 hours each).

Umpiring device: Computer.

Form: Self-contained kit with program. The game is the basis of the 'Farmscan' competition.

Terms: By negotiation.

Available from: Enquiries to 'Farmscan', P. Mills, ADAS, National Agricultural Centre, Stoneleigh, Kenilworth, Warwickshire.

Editor's classification: Model-based. Business. Farming.

Yardarm

Management situation: The effect of the attitudes of managers as perceived by their staff.

Suitable for: Foremen/supervisors; junior managers; middle managers; senior managers.

Subjects: Management behaviour; organisational culture; communication.

Description: Players are split into five groups, each group being asked to consider the best attitude for a manager to adopt in one particular situation. From a limited list provided, they have to choose an adjective that describes their choice of behaviour and display a symbol to identify it. Other groups interpret the symbol by relating it to a key and finding the attitude it signals. They must then indicate how they would respond to a manager showing this attitude. Unknown to the players, the keys given to the groups are different so that signals get misinterpreted. (e.g. 'positive' becomes 'dogmatic').

Decisions: Which attitude, out of a range listed, to assume in a given situation.

Data available initially: A few words identifying the situation. Players are asked to think in general terms.

Feedback: Initially, an unsatisfactory response to the displayed attitude. After discussion, an understanding of the misinterpretation that has taken place.

Interactive or noninteractive: Interactive.

Number of players: 15–25.

Number of teams: 5 (3–5 per team).

Duration: About 1 hour.

Form: Self-contained kit.

Terms: £20.00 per set.

Available from: Chris Elgood Associates Limited, The Studio, Cranbrook Road, Hawkhurst, Kent TN18 4AR.

Editor's classification: Structured experience. Functional – use of authority. General.

The York Exercise

Management situation: Distribution of consumer goods.

Suitable for: Junior managers; middle managers.

Subjects: Financing a business; corporate planning; consumer goods marketing; sales planning; stockholding; management accounting; pricing; workgroup organisation; distribution.

Description: Teams are left to organise their own group structure to simulate a head office and three divisions. Corporate policy is agreed although decisions have to be made at both head office and divisional level. Decisions cover three months in the life of the simulated company.

Decisions: Price; advertising; promotion; salesmen; outlets; warranty periods; discount policy; stockholding; transfer pricing.

Data available initially: Previous year's sales figures and forecasts; current balance sheet.

Feedback: Market share; decisions of other teams; financial results.

Interactive or noninteractive: Interactive.

Number of players: 8–80.

Number of teams: 2–8 (4–10 per team).
Duration: 6–9 hours.
Umpiring device: Manual calculation.
Form: Presentation by consultant.
Terms: By negotiation.
Available from: Management Training Services, 14, Claytons Meadow, Bourne End, Buckinghamshire.
Editor's classification: Model-based. Business. Consumer goods.

Index of suppliers of games

Alameda Software (Micro-computers in Business Education),
Friern Lodge, The Avenue, Ampthill, Bedford, MK45 2NR.

B. R. Aston,
Henley – The Management College, Henley on Thames, Oxfordshire,
RG9 3AU.

Simon Baddeley,
Institute of Local Government Studies, University of Birmingham, P.O.
Box 363, Birmingham, B15 2TT.

Martin Barnes and Partners,
Foden Lane, Woodford, Stockport, Cheshire, SK7 1PT.

H. V. Beck,
6 Manland Way, Harpenden, Hertfordshire, AL5 4QS.

BL Systems Limited,
Grosvenor House, Prospect Hill, Redditch, Worcestershire.

BP Educational Services,
Britannic House, Moor Lane, London, EC2Y 9BU.

Building Research Establishment,
Garston, Watford, Hertfordshire, WD2 7JR.

Careers Research and Advisory Centre,
The Publications Department, Bateman Street, Cambridge, CB2 1LZ.

Dr I. Carruthers,
Agrarian Development Unit, Wye College (University of London), Nr.
Ashford, Kent, TN25 5AH.

The Chartered Building Societies Institute,
Fanhams Hall, Ware, Hertfordshire, SG12 2PZ.

John R. Cooper,
7 St George's Avenue, Rugby, Warwickshire, CV22 5PN.

B. E. Cox,
21 Shrewsbury Road, Edgmond, Newport, Shropshire.

A. I. S. Debenham,
9 Roland Way, London, SW7 3RF.

J. I. M. Dempster,
Sir M. MacDonald and Partners Limited, Demeter House, Station
Road, Cambridge, CB1 2RS.

D. J. Management Consultants,
87 Beehive Lane, Ilford, Essex.

Chris Elgood Associates Limited,
The Studio, Cranbrook Road, Hawkhurst, Kent, TN18 4AR.

FM Insurance Company Limited,
Southside, 105 Victoria Street, London, SW1E 6QT.

L. C. Galitz,
Institute of European Finance, University College of North Wales,
Bangor, Gwynedd, LL57 2DG.

Ray Garnett,
Ealing College of Higher Education, St Mary's Road, Ealing, London,
W5 5RF.

T. R. Garrison, MA(OXON) MA(BRUNEL),
10 Tunmers End, Chalfont St Peter, Buckinghamshire, SL9 9LW.

G. I. Gibbs,
46 Grange Avenue, Kenilworth, Warwickshire, CV8 1DD.

Cedric Green,
Department of Architecture, University of Sheffield, Sheffield, S10 2TN.

Department of Human Nutrition,
London School of Hygiene and Tropical Medicine, Keppel Street, London, WC1E 7HT.

Guardian Business Services,
119 Farringdon Road, London, EC1R 3DA.

The Manager,
Management Resources, Guest Keen and Nettlefolds Limited, Group Head Office, Smethwick, Warley, West Midlands, B66 2RZ.

F. C. Harris,
Department of Civil Engineering, Loughborough University of Technology, Leicestershire.

Dr M. R. Harrison,
Department of Management Studies, North Staffordshire Polytechnic, College Road, Stoke-on-Trent.

Dr Margaret Hobson,
15 Malmesbury Park, Hawthorne Road, Edgbaston, Birmingham, B15 3TV.

Hotel and Catering Industry Training Board,
P.O. Box 18, Ramsey House, Central Square, Wembley, Middlesex, HA9 7AP.

IRIC (Institute for Research on Intercultural Cooperation),
Velperweg, 95 6824 HH Arnhem, The Netherlands.

Instructional Technology Unit,
Department of Education Services, Sheffield City Polytechnic, 36 Collegiate Crescent, Sheffield, S10 2BP.

JO(QS) Divisional Committee,
Royal Institute of Chartered Surveyors, 12 Great George Street, London, SW1P 3AD.

D. Langford,
c/o Department of Building Technology, Brunel University, Uxbridge, Middlesex.

Longman Resources Unit,
33/35 Tanners Row, York, YO1 1JP.

S. T. Lunt,
Birklands Management Centre, The Hatfield Centre for Management Studies, 330 London Road, St Albans, Hertfordshire, AL1 1ED.

Michael Lynch,
Northgate House, Perrymead, Bath, Avon, BA2 5AX.

Ian MacHorton,
TSL (Training Services), 235 High Holborn, London, WC1V 7DN.

Management Games Limited,
2 Woburn Street, Ampthill, Bedford, MK45 2HP.

Management Training Services,
14 Claytons Meadow, Bourne End, Buckinghamshire.

D. V. Marshall,
Department of Law, North Staffordshire Polytechnic, Brindley Building, Leek Road, Stoke-on-Trent, Staffordshire, ST4 2DF.

Maxim Consultants Limited,
6 Marlborough Place, Brighton, East Sussex, BN1 1UB.

Metis Management Services,
25 Farrar Lane, Adel, Leeds, LS16 6AD.

Midland Management Exercises,
349 Clarence Road, Sutton Coldfield, West Midlands, B74 4LY.

P. Mills,
ADAS, National Agricultural Centre, Stoneleigh, Kenilworth, Warwickshire.

D. J. Moul and P. R. Woolliams,
Anglian Regional Management Centre, Duncan House, High Street, Stratford, London, E15.

B. D. Najak,
Durham University Business School, Mill Hill Lane, Durham, DH1 3LB.

Oldfield Payne Management Associates,
Oldfield House, Coniston Close, Daventry, Northamptonshire, NN11 5EE.

Denys J. Page,
'Orbit', 15 Ashurst Road, Seaford, East Sussex, BN25 1AH.

Pavic Productions,
Sheffield City Polytechnic, Department of Education Services, 36 Collegiate Crescent, Sheffield, S10 2BP.

Pitmansoft,
Pitman Publishing, Southport, PR9 9YF.

Tony Pope,
Buckinghamshire College of Higher Education, Gorelands Lane, Chalfont St Giles, Bucks.

Project Software Limited,
Foden Lane, Woodford, Stockport, Cheshire, SK7 1PT.

N. Rints and D. Hayes,
The Management Centre, Slough College of Higher Education, Wellington Street, Slough, Berkshire.

R. L. Ritchie,
Business Studies Department, North Staffordshire Polytechnic, Brindley Building, Leek Road, Stoke-on-Trent, Staffordshire, ST4 2DF.

Science Research Associates Limited,
Newtown Road, Henley-on-Thames, Oxfordshire, RG9 1EW.

Sigma Consultants,
25A Market Square, Bicester, Oxfordshire.

David J. Smith,
26 Orchard Drive, Tonbridge, Kent.

J. Snaith,
Management Learning Systems, 14 Glencree Park, Newtownabbey,
County Antrim, BT37 0QS.

J. Snowdon, BA FCIS,
Faculty of Teachers in Commerce Limited, 141 Bedford Road, Sutton
Coldfield, West Midlands, B75 6DB.

Supervisory Management Training Limited,
Peak House, 66 Croydon Road, Beckenham, Kent, BR3 4AA.

Swarmhurst Limited,
36 St Andrews Road, Cambridge, CB4 1DL.

Task Management Services,
1 Southby Close, Abingdon, Berkshire, OX13 5LE.

Professor Bernard Taylor,
Henley – The Management College, Greenlands, Henley-on-Thames,
Oxfordshire, RG9 3AU.

Urwick Management Centre,
Baylis House, Stoke Poges Lane, Slough, Berkshire.

Verax,
60 High Street, Odiham, Hampshire, RG25 1LN.

C. A. Voss,
London Graduate School of Business Studies, Sussex Place, Regent's
Park, London, NW1.

C. D. T. Watson-Gandy,
12 Thorney Hedge Road, Chiswick, London, W4 5SD.

F. Wedgwood-Oppenheim,
Institute of Local Government Studies, Birmingham University,
Birmingham, B15 2TT.

M. A. P. Willmer,
Manchester Business School, Booth Street West, Manchester, M15
6PB.

Dr P. Woolliams and J. Cooper,
Anglian Regional Management Centre, Danbury Park, Chelmsford,
Essex.

Doug Wood,
Manchester Business School, Booth Street West, Manchester, M15
6PB.

Index of background to games

The index shows the background against which each game is set in those cases where it is sufficiently clearly defined to appear relevant. The classifications generally refer to an industry (e.g. construction) or an activity within it (e.g. storekeeping).

Agriculture

Exaction
The Green Revolution Game
Irrigation Management Game
Wyefarm Management Game

Airline operations

The Airways Challenge

Banking

Interbank

Boatbuilding

Peterduck Limited

Brewery operation

C & D Breweries

Building society

The Building Societies
  Management Game

Capital equipment

Alpha
The Hoppermute

Chemicals

Devex Chemical Company
  Limited

Index of functional areas

This index covers only those games that have been classified as 'functional' on pp. 13–14. It does *not* mean that these particular functional areas are necessarily absent from other games – just that in such other games as include them they are considered alongside other functions. The classifications are such as to define a particular area of interest within a business, both traditional ones (e.g. marketing) and contemporary ones (e.g. group effectiveness).

AD
30.26
E41
1984

DATE DUE

11394			
NOV 2 6 2001			